FIELDWORK IN FAMILIAR PLACES

FIELDWORK IN FAMILIAR PLACES

MORALITY, CULTURE, AND PHILOSOPHY

MICHELE M. MOODY-ADAMS

HARVARD UNIVERSITY PRESS
CAMBRIDGE, MASSACHUSETTS
LONDON, ENGLAND
1997

Library of Congress Cataloging-in-Publication Data

Moody-Adams, Michele M.
Fieldwork in familiar places : morality, culture, and philosophy /
Michele M. Moody-Adams.
p.   cm.
Includes bibliographical references and index.
ISBN 0-674-29953-1 (cloth : alk. paper)
1. Ethics.   2. Anthropology—Moral and ethical aspects.
3. Ethical relativism—Controversial works.   I. Title.
BJ52.M66   1997
170'.42—dc21   97-12694

For Harold and Shirley Moody and
James Eli Adams

CONTENTS

Acknowledgments   *ix*

Introduction   *1*

1   **Taking Disagreement Seriously**   *13*

Mapping the Relativist Domain   *13*
Relativism, Ethnocentrism, and the Decline of
    Moral Confidence   *22*
The Empirical Underdetermination of Descriptive
    Cultural Relativism   *29*
Cultural Authority, Cultural Complexity, and the Doctrine
    of Cultural Integration   *43*
The Perspicuous "Other": Relativism "Grown Tame
    and Sleek"   *56*

2   **The Use and Abuse of History**   *61*

History, Ethnography, and the Blurring of Cultural
    Boundaries   *61*
Relativism as a "Kind of Historiography"?   *71*
Moral Debate, Conceptual Space, and the Relativism of
    Distance   *85*
Plus ça change . . . : The Myths of Moral Invention and
    Discovery   *103*

3   **Morality and Its Discontents**   *107*

On the Supposed Inevitability of Rationally Irresolvable
    Moral Conflict   *107*
Pluralism, Conflict, and Choice   *121*
On the Alleged Methodological Infirmity of Moral Inquiry   *130*
Does Pessimism about Moral Conflict Rest on a Mistake?   *142*

4   Moral Inquiry and the Moral Life   *146*

Moral Inquiry as an Interpretive Enterprise   *146*
The Interpretive Turn and the Challenge of "Anti-
    Theory"   *160*
A Pyrrhic Victory?   *169*
Objectivity and the Aspirations of Moral Inquiry   *177*

5   Morality and Culture through Thick and Thin   *187*

The Need for Thick Descriptions of Moral Inquiry   *187*
Moral Conflict, Moral Confidence, and Moral Openness
    toward the Future   *194*
Critical Pluralism, Cultural Difference, and the Boundaries
    of Cross-Cultural Respect   *204*
The Strange Career of "Culture"   *214*

Epilogue   *222*

Notes   *225*

Works Cited   *240*

Index   *255*

ACKNOWLEDGMENTS

I am grateful for research support from the National Endowment for the Humanities and from Indiana University. At a critical juncture in my intellectual life, John Rawls and Hilary Putnam patiently encouraged my decision to put aside my earlier work in the history of philosophy in order to pursue an unexpected inquiry into the foundations of moral objectivity. I can only hope that the results of that inquiry go some way toward repaying their confidence in my plans. Several long-time friends and colleagues in philosophy read and commented on earlier incarnations of the ideas in this book. Kenneth Winkler and Owen Flanagan provided helpful comments, as well as important lessons about the value of friendship. I am especially grateful to Ruth Anna Putnam, who first convinced me that I could find a place in philosophy, and who has consistently offered encouragement and support as a teacher, colleague, and friend. Portions of the arguments in this book grew out of talks delivered at Syracuse University, Wayne State University, Michigan State University, and the University of Illinois at Champaign-Urbana. Audiences at each institution provided lively comments and questions which yielded important opportunities for critical reflection. I am particularly grateful to Marcia Baron, Martin Benjamin, and Michael Stocker for their encouragement at various stages in this project. For other forms of advice and encouragement, many thanks to Claudia Card, Grace Harris, Adrian Piper, Terence Moore, Anita Allen, and Laurence Thomas.

Colleagues in disciplines outside my own have had a profound influence on the conception of moral philosophy defended in this book. The late Christopher Lasch generously included me in the rich intellectual life of the University of Rochester History Department and encouraged me to consider the philosophical implications of debates in the historiography of slavery. Jean Bethke Elshtain—carrying on the tradition of the public intellectual embodied in Lasch's work—continues to teach the value of a practical philosophy attentive to the concerns of real human beings. Derek Phillips kindly encouraged my contributions to social reflection and helped convince me of just how widely the boundaries of intellectual community extend. Lindsay Waters has been a patient and encouraging editor, and his enthusiasm for philosophy has often helped to rekindle my own.

I could not have completed this book without the support and encouragement of my family. My parents, Harold and Shirley Moody, helped lay the groundwork for this project by teaching me to reject facile identifications of culture and race. Their continuing interest in the development of my views has proved personally and professionally invaluable. Although my daughter Katherine cannot yet appreciate her contributions to my work, at a crucial stage in this project her imminent arrival helped—to paraphrase Dr. Johnson—to concentrate my mind wonderfully. The joy and excitement she has added to our lives has already enlarged my understanding of the life worth living. But my greatest debt is to my husband, James Eli Adams, who lovingly and graciously combines exacting criticism with enthusiastic support. His devotion throughout the completion of this book has been "an ever-fixed mark / That looks on tempests and is never shaken."

Portions of Chapter 3 appeared in an earlier version as "On the Alleged Methodological Infirmity of Ethics," *American Philosophical Quarterly* 27 (1990): 225–236; and a portion of Chapter 2 appears in "Culture, Responsibility, and Affected Ignorance," *Ethics* 104 (1994): 291–309.

INTRODUCTION

We all help to determine the content of ethical philosophy so far as we contribute to the race's moral life. In other words, there can be no final truth in ethics any more than in physics, until the last man has had his experience and said his say . . . [H]owever, the hypotheses which we make now while waiting, and the acts to which they prompt us, are among the indispensable conditions which determine what that "say" shall be.

William James, "The Moral Philosopher
and the Moral Life"

This book seeks to provide a plausible conception of moral objectivity and to defend a cautious optimism that moral philosophy can be an aid in serious, everyday moral inquiry.[1] It thus sets itself against two important and mutually reinforcing developments in twentieth-century thought that have seemed to render such efforts quixotic. The first is a pervasive deference to natural science as the arbiter of all rationality. This stance leads many to denigrate moral inquiry because its concerns cannot fit into the "naturalistic" worldview defined by science. As articulated by philosophers such as A. J. Ayer, C. L. Stevenson, and more recently W. V. O. Quine, the authority of science allegedly calls into question the objectivity of morality and the possibility of rational moral inquiry, especially of meaningful philosophical inquiry that might do more than analyze moral language (Ayer 1946; 1984; Stevenson 1944; Quine 1981). This linking of skepticism about moral objectivity and skepticism about substantive moral philosophy is most pointed in the logical positivist beginnings of twentieth-century Anglo-American philosophy, and in the work of positivism's contemporary heirs. But even those who reject positivist skepticism about the rationality of moral inquiry may be concerned by the apparent failure of philosophical moral theories to function like theories in natural science. On this approach, it is possible to know what morality requires without the benefit of philosophical moral inquiry; indeed, such inquiry is often deemed superfluous to, or dangerously disengaged from, the real demands of the moral life.

These skepticisms have been reinforced by the rise of moral relativism, a skepticism about moral objectivity based on claims about the diversity of moral practices. In its most persuasive forms, relativist challenges to moral objectivity are grounded in allegedly "neutral" observations of cultural diversity in moral practices—observations most fully discussed by social and cultural anthropologists. Relativism did not begin with Evans-Pritchard's *Witchcraft, Oracles, and Magic among the Azande*, or with Ruth Benedict's *Patterns of Culture*; it is at least as old as Herodotus and some of the Sophists. Yet moral relativism has taken on renewed vigor from developments in twentieth-century social science. It is widely accepted, in both academic and broader public discourse, that the ethnographic findings of cultural and social anthropology conclusively "show" that morality is not objective, and that there is no hope of finding a standpoint from which to assess objectively the validity of culturally diverse or conflicting moral claims. Even philosophers who claim to be suspicious of most relativist conclusions—Richard Rorty and Bernard Williams are notable examples—may accept relativist characterizations of the implications of moral diversity and disagreement. Many of these thinkers go on to question whether there is any point to moral philosophy, which is believed to rest on the hope of finding, or sometimes "constructing," just such a point of view. Alongside the skepticism derived from the model of contemporary natural science, then, a relativism rooted in the claims of empirical social science has also raised powerful doubts about the point and the possibility of philosophical moral inquiry.

These skeptical positions, moreover, share a powerful discontent about the persistence of serious moral disagreement. In this volume I show that this discontent rests on misconceptions of the nature of moral inquiry, the requirements of objectivity, and the concept of culture. To that end, I engage in what can be called "fieldwork" in the complex intellectual culture from which all of these misconceptions emerge: a scrutiny of the shared beliefs, assumptions, and methods of argument that underwrite contemporary skepticism about moral objectivity and moral inquiry.[2] I then provide an account of the connections between morality, culture, and philosophical moral inquiry that is rich enough to show why taking moral disagreement seriously does not require skepticism about moral objectivity or about the value of moral philosophy to everyday moral reflection.

For philosophers, much of my argument—for example, my scrutiny of debates between emotivism and critics of emotivism such as Alasdair MacIntyre—involves fieldwork in familiar places. Yet while I explore familiar philosophical territory in this work, sometimes I also seek to make the familiar unfamiliar. In particular, I challenge several claims about morality and moral argument often defended by philosophers as "obvious." Thus, for instance, I argue that familiar claims about the intrinsic "infirmity," in Quine's phrase, of the methods of moral inquiry rest on implausible conceptions of agreement in science and of the relation of moral inquiry to experience. I also take issue with those philosophers who think it self-evident that rationally irresolvable moral disagreements are an unavoidable fact of experience. According to some philosophers, even some non-relativistic moral pluralists such as Isaiah Berlin, it is intellectually "immature" to think otherwise. But the conception of rationality presupposed by this claim, and its underlying understanding of what it means to resolve any disagreement rationally, are deeply problematic. Still another confusion in moral philosophy arises from frequent appeals to what "we" think about morality, and to "our" moral intuitions, that fail to explain why a particular moral concept or intuition should be embraced as "ours," or to clarify how the identity of the relevant "we" might be determined. Ironically, this tendency is sometimes most evident in relativist moral philosophy, which might be expected to be more attentive to the need to explain and clarify such claims about what "we" think. Thus, for instance, Gilbert Harman and David Wong claim that moral relativism best explains "our intuitions" about moral disagreement and diversity without considering that they might be addressing an audience that does not share their intuitions about the implications of serious moral disagreement.[3] More generally, philosophers are often tempted to confuse intuitions shaped by their narrowly philosophical concerns with intuitions shaped by the non-philosophical cultures which most people inhabit.

The foundational assumptions and methods of empirical anthropology are part of the intellectual culture from which moral relativism emerges. I show, in fact, that even some philosophical moral relativisms which purport to transcend assumptions about cultural diversity can be seen to depend on them nonetheless. Yet those who defend conclusions rooted in relativist claims from anthropology—whether knowingly or not—have rarely examined the foundations of their skeptical commitments. I challenge these allegedly empirical foundations by challenging several of the most influential methods and assumptions that have shaped empirical anthropology—in the works of, among others, E. E. Evans-Pritchard, Ruth Benedict, Melville Herskovits, and Margaret Mead. Some moral philosophers may wonder, however, why a philosophical examination of the roots of skepticism about morality and moral philosophy should devote so much attention to a detailed scrutiny of the claims of empirical anthropology regarding cultural difference. My answer to this important question is fourfold.

First, contemporary philosophical discussions of moral diversity and disagreement frequently appeal to conclusions from empirical anthropology that—as I will show—rest on questionable non-empirical assumptions about culture, human agency, and the problems and possibilities of moral language. Contemporary discussions of philosophical relativism continue to rely on these assumptions, yet virtually no philosophical attention has been devoted to questioning the conclusions which derived from them.[4] The failure to scrutinize influential claims drawn from empirical anthropology is especially pointed in the "rationality and relativism" debates that continue to shape philosophical discussion about the nature of social science.[5] Such debates typically begin by rounding up the usual suspects in descriptive anthropology, with no attention to the non-empirical (and sometimes quite implausible) assumptions about cultural difference on which many of the most debated ethnographic claims were based. Many of those claims—for instance, about the nature of particular "primitive" beliefs, or about whether members of "traditional" societies are able to question cultural traditions—are not securely grounded in cultural observation. A host of non-empirical assumptions about the nature of cultural differences will be at work in any seemingly "neutral" ethnographic account, and these assumptions are properly the subject of philosophical scrutiny, which this book undertakes.

Second, it has become a commonplace, both in and outside of philosophy, that taking moral diversity and disagreement seriously requires (perhaps means) taking "culture" seriously—an enterprise most obviously associated with anthropology. Many philosophers assume, moreover, that the empirical claims of influential ethnographies have conclusively established the truth of several forms of relativism. Evans-Pritchard's work on the Azande, largely through the influence of Peter Winch's appeals to his writings, has been especially important in this regard. Moreover, many quite recent defenses of relativism—for instance, David Wong's defense of moral relativism and the arguments of David Bloor for cognitive relativism—contend that Evans-Pritchard has successfully shown that different societies accept radically different conceptions of rationality. But, once again, the empirical claims of the classic ethnographies rest on methodological assumptions that properly invite a philosophical scrutiny that they have not received. Indeed, many foundational methodological assumptions of early twentieth-century anthropology originate in philosophy, from Herder's eighteenth-century arguments about the "genius of a people" to the social philosophy of pragmatists such as John Dewey and G. H. Mead. Anthropological thinking about relativism is thus one of the most important intersections of morality, culture, and philosophy. Only by scrutinizing that intersection can one see that taking moral diversity seriously does not entail relinquishing confidence in the objectivity of moral inquiry and the usefulness of philosophical moral inquiry.

Third, there is a powerful irony—one with special point for moral philosophers—in the fact that anthropology has succeeded in independently reinforcing skepticisms that are so closely linked with confidence in the natural sciences. For the question whether anthropology is properly construed as continuous with the natural sciences—indeed, whether it is a science at all—remains a topic of heated debate. Debate about the status of anthropology continues, moreover, despite the efforts of its early twentieth-century practitioners to defend its claims as a science. Thus, for instance, while Benedict confidently proclaimed in *Patterns of Culture* (1934) to have discovered pristine "laboratories" for the study of social forms, Clifford Geertz's more recent contentions that anthropology is a humanistic, interpretive discipline exemplify ongoing resistance to the scientific pretensions of anthropology.[6] Yet anthropology has nonetheless managed to set many of the terms of twentieth-century debate about moral diversity and disagreement, even in a cultural climate that is increasingly inhospitable to any discipline that cannot unambiguously demonstrate technical success as a "science."

What accounts for the extraordinary influence of anthropology's claims in spite of such challenges to its authority as a science? The main explanation, I think, is that (at least for the first half of the twentieth century) anthropologists managed to keep alive a tradition of general intellectual discourse, whereby at least some of its claims remained accessible and compelling to a larger intellectual audience. It did so, moreover, at a time when philosophy was effectively in retreat from engagement with the concerns of that audience. Ayer's expressions of emotivism have had some impact outside philosophy (owing largely to their intellectual brashness and bravado), yet ironically emotivism ultimately denied that philosophy might have anything meaningful to say about the substantive moral concerns of everyday moral inquirers. Emotivism is not the only culprit in this matter; the professionalization of Anglo-American philosophy had already begun a tradition of philosophical disengagement from everyday moral reflection.[7] In response to that estrangement, some contemporary philosophers have expressed concern that literate, morally engaged non-specialists generally lack interest in contemporary moral philosophy. But if moral philosophy is to reclaim a broader cultural influence, it is necessary to ask why other disciplines—not just anthropology but literature and history as well—have managed to capture the moral imagination of vast numbers of non-specialists, and thereby to help set the terms of popular as well as philosophical debate about central concerns of moral inquiry.

The cultural ascendancy of anthropology leads to the fourth reason for scrutinizing its claims in such detail. Anthropological claims about morality and culture will help determine the future of public moral discourse—and thus ultimately the future of much meaningful philosophical moral inquiry. Anthropological theories propounding the importance of culture have given rise to the notion that cultures have moral standing, and thereby helped shape much contemporary moral and political debate. Arguments about multiculturalism, most notably, defend the collective moral and political claims of groups asserting a collective cultural identity. In addition, arguments about rights of cultural survival and the moral importance of cultural diversity have profoundly altered the moral and political discourse that shapes international relations. Still further, the concept of cultural property underwrites specific claims for the return of cultural treasures—such as the Greeks' demand for the return of the Elgin marbles—and raises questions about the morality of collecting and displaying another culture's artifacts as a way of expressing appreciation for culture in general. But the relativism derived from conventional anthropological assumptions about culture rarely acknowledges that many of these assumptions are incompatible with defenses of the moral claims of cultures. Adequate philosophical understanding of such claims depends crucially on philosophical scrutiny of anthropological assumptions about culture.

Such scrutiny reveals, as I indicate in Chapters 1 and 2, that serious misconceptions and implausible assumptions underwrite relativist claims about the nature of cultural diversity in moral practices. In Chapter 1 I show that a fundamental premise of the most compelling arguments for moral relativism is a seldom discussed doctrine—a doctrine most informatively characterized as descriptive cultural relativism—which asserts that cultural differences in moral beliefs may generate "ultimate" moral disagreements. Descriptive cultural relativism purports to make a neutral empirical observation about the nature of serious cross-cultural moral conflict. But that allegedly empirical claim embodies several implausible non-empirical assumptions about cultures, and these mistakes are primarily a function of inadequate attention to the internal complexity of cultures. I show that this internal complexity consistently thwarts relativist efforts to confine moral judgments to a single culture: cultural boundaries are not morally impenetrable walls. I argue, further, that an unfamiliar judgment or belief can be a moral judgment or belief—and can be recognized as such—only if it fits into a complex set of beliefs and judgments that strongly resembles one's own "familiar" set. Thus I contend that serious cross-cultural moral disagreement is possible only against a background of basic cross-cultural agreement on a substantial number of fundamental moral judgments and beliefs. My arguments ultimately suggest that the most compelling and influential moral relativisms fail to take cross-cultural moral disagreement seriously because they rely on methodological assumptions which mask the conditions that make cross-cultural moral agreement possible.

In Chapter 1 I am concerned primarily with relativism about moral conflict between roughly contemporaneous cultures. In Chapter 2 we see that attempts to treat historical epochs as impenetrable to contemporary moral criticism rest on equally indefensible assumptions about culture and moral disagreement. In a wide array of contemporary intellectual debate, thinkers often extend relativist hypotheses about moral diversity to the understanding of historical reflection, defending a relativism of "historical distance"—in Bernard Williams's phrase— which seeks to shield past practices from contemporary moral reflection and criticism. In a familiar example, some historians have claimed that contemporary readers cannot fault Thomas Jefferson for being a slave-holder—in spite of his defense of equality—because to do so is to judge him according to standards that do not apply to the past (Wilson 1992).[8] But the view that historical boundaries are not morally penetrable is also undermined by the complexity of human cultures. I show in Chapter 2, moreover, that historical relativism—perhaps even more than relativism about contemporaneous cultures—presupposes indefensibly deterministic conceptions of culture and implausible notions of the possibility of radical moral change and invention.

Morally speaking, there is never anything fundamentally "new" in a new historical epoch. Rather, new and different ways of articulating and interpreting fundamental moral ideas can illuminate features of the moral world obscured or disguised by old interpretations. Any human being who learns a natural language, I argue, is capable of reinterpreting the moral ideas revealed by historical reflection so as to become a potentially authoritative moral critic of past practices and beliefs. In examining the assumptions and methods of empirical anthropology and philosophy that inform the contrary view, I also devote attention to important historiographic debates about the application of familiar moral categories to the understanding of New World slavery. These debates are of special interest to philosophers, especially in light of claims by several contemporary moral realists that social change sometimes derives from the sudden perception of previously unnoticed "moral facts" and "moral properties." I show that such claims rest, perhaps unexpectedly, on the misconceptions implicit in the relavitism of historical distance, and that they do not stand up to critical scrutiny. In Chapter 2 I also set down some requirements that any adequate conception of culture must meet, most notably the recognition that cultures are not self-contained, internally consistent wholes. Relativist arguments in philosophy and the social sciences which suppose otherwise simply ignore important facts about the internal complexity of cultures, the historical interconnection of cultures, and the complex conditions of cultural survival.

Relativism remains compelling because of widespread discontent about the persistence of serious moral disagreement. Many philosophers who explicitly reject the meta-ethical claims of relativism nonetheless find some truth in relativism's commitment to the inevitability of rationally irresolvable moral disagreement. This is because discontent about the persistence of moral disagreement also has sources quite independent of the claims of social science. Emotivism and other attempts to denigrate the claims of moral inquiry typically appeal to an idealized model of inquiry and argument in science. In Chapter 3 I argue that these views rest on misconceptions of the nature of rationality in moral inquiry, the nature of moral inquiry itself, and the relationship between moral inquiry and human experience. I also challenge the now familiar assumption that rationally irresolvable moral disagreement is an unavoidable fact of human experience. Relativists and emotivists are, to be sure, the most prominent proponents of this thesis. But a variety of other theoretical stances have been thought to be compatible with—or even to require—its acceptance. Chapter 3 focuses in particular on non-relativistic pluralists such as Isaiah Berlin, who reject many of the skepticisms of emotivism, but who nonetheless defend the idea that rationally irresolvable moral conflict is inevitable. Such defenses, I argue, embody an impatience with the very processes of moral argument most likely to make it possible to resolve serious moral conflicts. Although I do not pursue the obvious links between impatience with moral argument and developments in contemporary political philosophy, in challenging this kind of impatience I challenge the usual grounds for the view that citizens of pluralist democracies must keep serious moral disagreements—such as disputes about the morality of abortion—off the political agenda. Inattention to the genuine nature of moral argument and inquiry has hindered our appreciation of the methods by which serious moral conflicts might be reasonably adjudicated.

In Chapter 4 I attempt to develop a richer conception of the link between philosophical moral inquiry and everyday moral inquiry than that informing most contemporary discussion. I argue that philosophical moral inquiry is a species of a very familiar genus: the critical, often unsystematic reflection on the kind of life worth living, which is an unavoidable part of everyday experience. Whereas much recent moral philosophy has sought to sever the link between everyday moral argument and philosophical moral inquiry, I argue that philosophy can make a genuine contribution to serious moral inquiry only if philosophers actively seek to reverse this trend. This means, among other things, relinquishing the influential conception of philosophy as capable of authoritatively "validating" claims to moral knowledge—or even authoritatively challenging the very possibility of moral knowledge. It also means accepting that moral philosophy is an interpretive discipline—more broadly, that interpretation is a fundamental characteristic of moral inquiry in general. By emphasizing the connections between interpretation and moral argument, I develop a suggestion first made by Michael Walzer in *Interpretation and Social Criticism*, but I depart from Walzer's skepticism about the value of philosophical moral inquiry. Everyday moral argument and philosophical moral inquiry are, on my view, simply species of the same generic interpretive enterprise. Philosophers, I argue further, must return to an essentially Socratic conception of moral inquiry: philosophers, that is, must be recognized as one (admittedly distinctive) set of participants in moral inquiry along with a vast community of other moral inquirers. Those who lament this conception of moral philosophy may assume that it is the task of moral philosophy somehow to solve the "problem of moral objectivity." But such claims, I argue, rest on misunderstandings of objectivity—in science as well as moral inquiry. Once these misunderstandings are recognized, skepticism about the objectivity of morality can be shown to rest on a series of mistakes about the nature of agreement and disagreement in science and in moral inquiry. On a revised understanding of objectivity, moral objectivity does not constitute a problem for philosophy to "solve." At the same time, my account sets the stage for the claim (in Chapter 5) that it is necessary to resist the skeptical approaches of philosophers such as Richard Rorty and Bernard Williams, who seek to show that moral inquirers might be able to relinquish their aspirations for objectivity in moral inquiry.

I argue in Chapter 5 that a defensible moral philosophy will demand a richer understanding of moral inquiry than has been provided on conventional accounts. In terminology borrowed from the anthropology of Clifford Geertz—and ultimately from the philosophy of Gilbert Ryle—I provide in Chapter 5 a "thick description" of moral inquiry, and of the cultures within which, and sometimes across which, moral inquiry takes place. Finally, I show what it really means to take seriously the complex connections between morality, culture, and philosophy in a non-skeptical and non-relativistic way, as those connections inform some matters of contemporary urgency, such as the question of the most appropriate way to respond to cross-cultural disagreement. Although inhabitants of different cultures admittedly have different experiences, they can nonetheless contribute to a cross-cultural moral conversation. Once this conversation begins, it becomes clear that the whole truth about morality can emerge only when the last person—like the last culture—has, in James's words, "had his experience and said his say." But it is also clear that philosophy is one important source of the "indispensable conditions" which determine what that "say" will be. There is thus room (despite the complexity of cultures and the existence of cultural disagreement) for philosophy to contribute to the collective self-scrutiny of culture, and even to scrutiny of assumptions about the nature and importance of culture itself.

Ultimately, I urge that moral philosophy, if it is to take moral disagreement seriously, may itself need to undertake fieldwork in familiar places. Although there is perhaps a place for continued philosophical debate about the structure of moral theories, there is often more to be learned from what Walzer calls the "workmanlike" moral inquiries of everyday agents and inquirers than from the disengaged speculation so common in contemporary moral philosophy. Any human being who seeks to understand and pursue a life worth living contributes to that ongoing moral inquiry of which moral philosophy is only one small part. Of course, this approach to moral philosophy requires relinquishing the notion that philosophy is in any way authoritative in moral inquiry. For many contemporary moral philosophers this will seem a self-destructive heresy. Those philosophers who believe that the fundamental task of moral philosophy is to "validate" moral conceptions, or (more skeptically) to demonstrate that no such conception can be rationally validated, will insist that I am arguing for the end of the discipline. But this is not a call for an end to philosophy—and certainly not a demand that it be replaced, as Rorty might argue, by some successor subject that eschews any theorizing at all. Rather, my aim is to suggest how contemporary moral philosophy might recapture the attention of sincere moral agents seeking aids to rational reflection about the structure of moral experience—about, that is, the life worth living and how human beings might attain it.

1 TAKING DISAGREEMENT SERIOUSLY

The social world does not divide at its joints into per-
spicuous we's with whom we can empathize, however
much we differ with *them, and enigmatical they's with*
whom we cannot, however much we defend to the
death their right to differ from *us.*

Clifford Geertz, *"The Uses of Diversity"*

MAPPING THE RELATIVIST DOMAIN

"Each man calls barbarism whatever is not his own practice," Montaigne claimed, because "we have no other test of truth and reason than
the example and pattern of the opinions and customs of the country we
live in" (Montaigne [1580] 1958, 152). Montaigne's observation reminds us that relativism about diverse moral practices is not a new
development. In recent decades, however, such relativism has taken on
extraordinary vigor across a range of disciplines. Predictably, many
contemporary anthropologists assert its merits, though with varying
degrees of conviction. Even Clifford Geertz, who is reluctant to defend
relativism, nonetheless insists that proponents of "anti-relativism"
wrongly attempt to place morality beyond culture. He therefore defends an "anti anti-relativism" as a means of preserving the link between culture and morality—denying that the double negative works in
the "usual way" (Geertz 1984, 276; 264). Other anthropologists make
stronger claims. Anthropological relativism, according to Richard
Shweder, is best able to grant "permission to diversity and difference"
because it assumes "the coequality or noncomparability of divergent
forms" (Shweder 1991, 27; 29). Philosophical defenses of relativism
have been equally varied. According to Gilbert Harman, for instance,
relativism best explains "the place of value and obligation in the world
of facts as revealed by science" (Harman 1989, 365). It also makes
sense, he continues, of "our" intuitions about the limited "motivational
reach" of our moral practices (Harman 1975, 5–8; cf. 1977, 105–110).

On the relativism Harman defends, "it makes no sense to ask whether an action is wrong, period," apart from its relation to a group's implicit agreement to accept certain moral rules (Harman 1975, 4). In a more qualified stance, David Wong seeks to combine relativist intuitions with recognition of the fact that "many of us" take at least some moral duties to transcend implicit agreements on rules of conduct. He nonetheless contends that some serious moral disagreements can be understood only on the assumption that there is "no single true morality." Moral principles can sometimes be true and justified in one society but not in another (Wong 1984, 24–25; 188).

Proponents of such views are remarkably sanguine about the coherence of their central claims. But at least three main difficulties deserve mention in any preliminary consideration of the merits of relativist views. First, what can it really mean to assert the "coequality" of ways of life, or the equal "validity" or justifiability of apparently conflicting moral practices and principles? Does the relativist have access to some standard for determining the adequacy or validity of moral principles and ways of life that allows independent assessment from the outside? If so, then it is unclear how a contentful moral relativism ever gets off the ground. Second, assertions of the "noncomparability" of different ways of life simply explain away moral disagreement. As Bernard Williams expresses this objection, any relativism that requires each ostensibly conflicting claim to be treated "as acceptable in its own place" seems committed to denying that moral conflict between diverse groups ever occurs at all (Williams 1985, 156). The assumption of noncomparability is sometimes defended as a methodological principle which aids the relativist anthropologist in "documenting the significance, relevance, and importance . . . of the differences between apparently divergent" cultural practices (Shweder 1991, 32). But such documentation presupposes the possibility of comparative studies of culture. If ways of life are truly "noncomparable," how might it be possible to conduct any such studies? Problems about the comparability of cultures generate a third important difficulty: the inherent weakness of any argument for relativism that relies on intuitions shaped by local moral concepts and practices. One starting point for many relativist views in philosophy—including the views of Harman and Wong—is a series of claims about "our" moral intuitions, and about moral concepts and judgments which relativists presume that "we" will find familiar. Yet if morality were truly relative, surely our intuitions about morality, and the concepts which express them, would be relative too. Relativist anthropologists similarly root arguments for relativism in claims about what "we" find unfamiliar or astonishing in the moral practices of particular groups. But, like relativist philosophers, they are never very clear about who "we" might be. Even if it were possible to agree on the proper scope of notions such as "our" and "we," arguments depending on such appeals would still be of dubious force. Indeed it is unclear how arguments of this kind could ever be more than ethnocentric curiosities.[1]

But in addition to these familiar difficulties with relativist views, there is a fourth, even more fundamental difficulty which has rarely been discussed. The problem is that the most compelling arguments for relativism rest on an implausible assumption about the nature of moral disagreement between diverse human groups—an assumption that, following R. B. Brandt and William Frankena, I call *descriptive cultural relativism* (Brandt 1967; Frankena 1973). Descriptive cultural relativism is the claim that differences in the moral practices of diverse social groups generate "ultimate" or "fundamental" moral disputes, disputes that are neither reducible to non-moral disagreement nor susceptible of rational resolution—disputes, that is, that are in principle irresolvable.[2] The thesis is best treated as a descriptive claim because it purports to state an observable fact. Further, the word *cultural* is used here in its most basic sociological and anthropological sense: a culture is simply any social group's more or less distinctive way of life.[3] Of course, in order to constitute a culture, a set of practices and beliefs must be fairly comprehensive in helping to shape a group's way of life. But a culture need not be marked off from other cultures by any particular geographical boundaries, nor need a group be particularly large in order to have a distinctive culture. A modern nation-state, for instance, may contain several cultures, some of which will be associated with relatively small groups of people. Descriptive cultural relativism, if true, might thus be an aid in analyzing the serious moral conflicts internal to many complex societies. Still further, since a person who belongs to more than one social group may be subject to multiple cultural influences, descriptive cultural relativism, if true, could also be an aid in understanding some of an individual agent's internal moral conflicts. I will show, however, that descriptive cultural relativism is empirically underdetermined and that even the best arguments for the thesis fail to support it. The object of this chapter is thus to defend one very simple claim: descriptive cultural relativism is unproven and implausible.

My challenge to descriptive cultural relativism is not a denial that differences in the moral practices and beliefs of different cultures may generate *serious* moral disagreements. But, as I argue in Chapters 1 and 2, serious moral disagreements—if they are genuinely moral disagreements—will always be disagreements in the secondary "details" of morality, not in ultimate or fundamental principles and beliefs. I show that it would not be possible even to recognize some dispute as a *moral* disagreement if "ultimate" or "fundamental" moral disagreement were really occurring. To be sure, there is a widespread tendency—within philosophy as well as outside of it—to treat descriptive cultural relativism as obviously true. Thus J. L. Mackie, who maintains that the "argument from relativity" grounds a powerful argument against the "objectivity of values," asserts that descriptive cultural relativism is "merely a truth of descriptive morality, a fact of anthropology" (Mackie 1977, 36). John Ladd, who is far more cautious in proclaiming the philosophical—and practical—importance of descriptive relativism, nonetheless characterizes the thesis as "a scientific and empirical" doctrine that is "neutral as far as evaluations are concerned" (Ladd 1985, 109). Yet descriptive cultural relativism is anything *but* a "neutral" account of the facts of cultural diversity, and in order to take moral disagreement seriously, it is necessary to reject its assumptions about moral conflicts between diverse human groups.

This challenge to the thesis of descriptive cultural relativism is crucial to my defense of moral objectivity because that thesis is an important premise of the most compelling defenses of *meta-ethical relativism*. Some of these meta-ethical views consist of a purely negative thesis about argument and justification in moral inquiry, or about the nature of moral language. But the negative claim of meta-ethical relativism may take any of a variety of forms: it may be argued, for instance, that no moral principle(s) can be shown to apply to everyone, or that there is no rational way to adjudicate between the conflicting claims of different cultures or persons, or even that there is "no single true morality." Yet while some theorists defend only a negative meta-ethical claim, others combine a negative thesis with some sort of positive claim. Formulations of the positive claims of meta-ethical relativism typically contend that at least some moral judgments are true, justified, or "valid" only relative to the practices or conventions of some society or cultural group. But if I am right, any meta-ethical relativism relying on the doctrine of descriptive cultural relativism simply cannot survive serious scrutiny.

Some relativists attempt to base a *normative ethical relativism*, in addition to a meta-ethical relativism, on the claims of descriptive cultural relativism. Normative ethical relativism has generally been formulated in one of two familiar ways. The normative claim defended by relativists who optimistically assert the "equivalence" of all practices and ways of life typically demands toleration of all ways of life as equally valid. More measured approaches demand that we simply "withhold judgment" about unfamiliar practices. Criticism of normative relativism's familiar inconsistencies has gradually undermined such views. How, for instance, does a normative relativist show a demand for toleration or for withholding judgment to be transculturally "valid"? Unfortunately, the difficulties of answering such questions have not hindered efforts to defend a related stance that Mary Midgley aptly describes as "moral isolationism." Relying primarily on the notion that not criticizing another culture is an important way of demonstrating respect for that culture, moral isolationists attempt to seal off unfamiliar practices from any critical reflection by cultural "outsiders" (Midgley 1981). Moral isolationism has gradually assumed a life of its own—independent of normative relativism's more conventional demands for toleration. I challenge moral isolationism, and the misconceptions about culture on which it is based, in subsequent chapters. But, more generally, if the claims of descriptive cultural relativism cannot be defended, neither can any normative view that presupposes them.

Of course, some meta-ethical relativisms, and even some normative ethical relativisms, do not presuppose descriptive cultural relativism as a fundamental premise. But those theories are not at issue here. In particular, I do not discuss the individualistic moral subjectivism commonly thought to support meta-ethical claims that morality is "always relative to the individual." Such claims often figure in a surprisingly successful rhetorical gambit whereby impatient participants in moral disputes attempt to silence moral discussion by insisting that morality is just a matter of opinion. Yet the success of such claims in ending moral debate has little to do with the quality of the arguments on which they rest. After all, people come to possess and understand the concept of morality only by learning a natural human language; the socializing processes that make language learning possible will partly shape at least some of a person's important personal tastes and preferences—if that is what moral principles are. Individualist accounts of the validity of moral principles pose no serious threat to the idea of moral objectivity since it is difficult to defend a consistent individualism about the validity of moral principles. A defense of moral objectivity can safely ignore meta-ethical relativisms premised on such accounts; meta-ethical claims grounded in descriptive cultural relativism simply pose the more genuine threat.

The link between descriptive cultural relativism and meta-ethical relativism is so strong, in fact, that it is difficult to present a consistent case for meta-ethical relativism without appealing to facts about cultural diversity. Harman's philosophical argument for relativism—supposedly based on a "soberly logical" analysis of moral judgments rather than on claims about cultural diversity—provides an instructive example of this difficulty.[4] Harman's main meta-ethical claim is that "there are no substantive moral demands that everyone has a reason to accept" (Harman 1978b, 110; cf. 1982, 571–572). Harman contends, for instance, that if Hitler "was willing to exterminate a whole people, there was no reason for him not to do so" (Harman 1977, 108–199; cf. 1975, 9). Similarly, he asserts that if a group of cannibals "see nothing wrong with eating people . . . there is no obvious reason why they should" (Harman 1977, 106; cf. 1975, 5). But Harman believes that moral relativism also "begins at home," in the behavior of "more or less professional criminals," of "simple egoists who think only of themselves," and of "ordinary people" who "have and act on certain moral principles but see nothing wrong with stealing from their employers . . . lying to an insurance company . . . or ignoring accident victims they pass on the road" (Harman 1982, 572). If such people "see no reason" to behave differently, Harman maintains, the truth of relativism is that there is no such reason. On the analysis that is supposed to establish this conclusion, to say that someone morally "ought" to do something is to imply that he "has reasons" to do it (Harman 1975, 8). Reasons, for Harman, are "considerations that could influence someone in the relevant way, considerations that would have an influence if fully appreciated, and if there were no (non-moral) defects in the person's reasoning" (Harman 1982, 573). But we cannot always find an argument or piece of reasoning, Harman observes, to lead someone such as Hitler, or even "ordinary people" who steal from their employers, "to appreciate their error if they were fully to understand this reasoning."[5] It is then "unclear," he urges, "what sort of reason they might have not to lie or steal or whatever" (Harman 1982, 572). From this supposed unclarity Harman then infers that there are no substantive moral demands that everyone has reason to accept. Yet no mere analysis of moral "oughts" can support this inference. In fact, the only consistent case that Harman can make for his meta-ethical views presupposes descriptive cultural relativism.

Two simple considerations show why. First, though Harman never uses the word *culture*, the ways of life implicit in all of his examples are most plausibly understood as cultures. Harman believes, as I have noted, that the validity of moral rules is always relative to a group's implicit agreements (Harman 1975, 4). Therefore his view is consistent only if the moral principles (if any) accepted by Hitler, by "more or less professional criminals," or by "ordinary people" are elements of some group's implicit agreement on moral rules.[6] But a group's implicit agreement to accept moral rules would surely be a central element of the practices which shape their way of life, and the practices which shape a group's way of life constitute their culture. Even the principles of Harman's "simple egoists" must be part of a group's implicit agreement, and ultimately part of a culture. Harman allows for a "limiting case" of group morality in which "the group has only one member"; in fact, he relies on this notion to explain the asymmetrical moral principles of a pacifist who condemns herself, but not others, for acts of violent self-defense (Harman 1975, 21–22; cf. 1978a, 117). The moral principles of the egoist might well be understood in similar terms. Moreover, the comprehensive way of life accepted by any single person—including an egoist—can be plausibly understood as a culture.[7] Edward Sapir once speculated that culture may, in some sense, always be individual. He observed that even in large social groups individuals must modify and revise group practices and beliefs in order to perpetuate them, and this observation led him to posit a sense in which each individual always has her own culture.[8]

But second, it is Harman's conception of moral motivation that leads most directly to his meta-ethical conclusion, yet the only argument he has for this conception implicitly posits descriptive cultural relativism. Harman claims of Hitler, for instance, that "in acting as he did he shows that he could not have been susceptible" to the moral considerations implicit in the "ought" judgments used to condemn him (Harman 1975, 7; cf. 1977, 109).[9] But what would count as evidence for such a claim? Surely it is more reasonable to suppose that Hitler did not care about conforming to principles he rejected. Harman allows that even when a person thinks something is morally right, she will not always be motivated to do it: "Sometimes we are tempted to do something else and sometimes we just do not care" (Harman 1977, 91–92).[10] At the very least, then, the moral backsliding of Harman's "ordinary people" seems to need no relativist explanation. For instance, an ordinary person who makes long-distance calls at her employer's expense most likely does not care—or does not care enough—that her actions violate her moral principles. To be sure, Hitler's choices are not plausibly explained as moral backsliding. They rested on a terrifying rejection of moral standards that condemn the murderous expression of hatred and prejudice. Yet the moral evil in this rejection is fully intelligible only in the context of the massive social evil embodied in the Holocaust, and this social evil is so vast that many believe it defies understanding. Relativism has often been a tempting response to conduct that appears incomprehensible or in any important dimension unfamiliar. But Stanley Milgram's investigations of obedience to authority revealed that the potential willingness to cause—and actively ignore—great suffering may be latent even in the most "ordinary" or respectable person.[11] Even when the readiness to act on this potential is "beyond the pale," the capacity to do so is not. This is why an understanding of the Holocaust (if possible) will come not from relativism but from efforts to discover how the willingness to cause and ignore human suffering could have become so widespread.[12]

Harman makes the familiar relativist assumption that we can understand Hitler only if he is construed as (in some way) an "outsider" who is therefore "beyond the motivational reach" of certain moral principles (Harman 1975, 8–10; 1977, 109). The implications of this assumption are made clearer in Harman's *Gedankenexperiment* about a society of professional criminals ("Murder Incorporated") in which the process of being educated into the criminal way of life somehow impairs the criminals' capacities to act on moral principles they reject.[13] Yet the process of being educated into a way of life is simply what an anthropologist would call *enculturation*, and any assumption that enculturation places one beyond the motivational reach of certain moral principles presupposes cultural determinism. Cultural determinist claims about limitations on our capacities for moral motivation obviously rely on assumptions about the implications of cultural diversity. Still further, cultural determinism implies that enculturation can place certain moral considerations beyond our conceptual (as well as motivational) reach, and that some moral conflicts will be "fundamental" or "ultimate." The cultural determinism implicit in Harman's view thus leads inevitably to descriptive cultural relativism. The implicit presuppositions of Harman's argument, which unsuccessfully seeks to avoid claims about the diversity of cultures, clearly confirm my claim that descriptive cultural relativism is crucial to any thoughtful defense of meta-ethical relativism.

Relativists who more willingly avow the significance of descriptive cultural relativism—especially in cultural and social anthropology—attempt to defend the doctrine by appeal to several assumptions about the fundamental characteristics of human cultures. In this chapter and the next I challenge influential formulations of three such assumptions: that cultures are internally integrated wholes, that cultures are fundamentally self-contained and isolable sets of practices and beliefs, and that cultural influence on belief and action must be understood deterministically. My criticisms of these assumptions are intended to challenge the empirical credentials—and thus the fundamental plausibility—of descriptive cultural relativism. Yet the doctrine might well be defended independently of these assumptions: its main claim is simply that cultural differences among the practices of human groups are sometimes a source of "irresolvable"—because "fundamental"—moral disagreement. Any view which depends on this claim relies on descriptive cultural relativism and is thus a target of the arguments in this chapter.

RELATIVISM, ETHNOCENTRISM, AND THE DECLINE OF MORAL CONFIDENCE

I have claimed that a challenge to descriptive cultural relativism is a crucial element of any anti-relativist defense of moral objectivity. Yet for many thoughtful people any such challenge is doomed from the start. No persuasive anti-relativism can ignore the origins and implications of this stance that Geertz aptly calls "anti anti-relativism." Thus, I briefly discuss a few influential assumptions about anti-relativism's failings in order to incorporate an informed response to their implications in my challenge to descriptive cultural relativism.

Critics of anti-relativism typically assume, first, that to rebut successfully any form of relativism one would need to prove the existence of "absolute" moral values, or a "single true morality," the principles of which legitimately apply to all persons, in all circumstances, without exception. It is then assumed, second, that every attempt to offer such proof has failed and that the only alternative to failed absolutism is some kind of relativism. Even philosophers who reject what might be called *rationality relativism*—who believe, as Harman has expressed it, that "in the end the same basic principles" underlie everyone's nonmoral reasoning—may insist that it is the failure of moral absolutism that makes moral relativism especially plausible (Harman 1982, 571–573). Melville Herskovits's anthropological account is equally striking in this regard.[14] According to Herskovits, absolutism *must* fail in the face of empirical observation: to describe some value as "absolute" is to claim it to be "fixed," and to deny that there is variation in evaluative practices from culture to culture or from epoch to epoch (Herskovits 1972, 31). Those who "hold for the existence of fixed values," he contends, "will find materials in other societies that necessitate a re-investigation of their assumptions" (Herskovits 1972, 15). Moral evaluations, like *all* evaluations, are "always relative to the cultural background out of which they arise" (Herskovits 1972, 14; 15). Relativism, Herskovits continues, is the only way to capture adequately the importance of culture and upbringing. A failure to acknowledge that moral evaluations are culturally relative ignores the force of enculturation in shaping thought and behavior—a phenomenon which produces patterns of conduct that are simply "automatic" and patterns of thought and belief that are often "below the level of consciousness" (Herskovits 1972, 76–77). Indeed, for Herskovits the belief that it might be legitimate to treat some particular value or standard as objectively valid— even for those who reject it—is simply another product of enculturation: a peculiar "ethnocentric" bias of a particular historical moment in the "Euroamerican tradition" (Herskovits 1972, 22).

What Herskovits views as "ethnocentric" bias has sometimes been thought—rightly or wrongly—to be a condition of the possibility of engaging in non-coercive action in a culturally complex world. That condition might be called *moral confidence:* confidence both in the making of moral judgments that purport to apply, legitimately, across cultures, and in the worth of trying to convince others of their legitimacy. Clifford Geertz has shown, however, that even when anthropologists do not interpret the data of cultural diversity in relativist terms, those data are nonetheless taken by a broader audience to show that both "our confidence in our seeings and doings" and "our resolve to bring others around to sharing them" are poorly supported (Geertz 1984, 264). It is little wonder, then, that explicitly relativist accounts of moral diversity will be perceived as even greater threats to moral confidence. Thus, Mary Warnock expresses the concerns of many when she laments the destructive "practical effects" of relativism, and insists that philosophers and non-philosophers alike will have to confront the challenges that relativism continues to pose to moral confidence: "for if the central problem is to find justification for asserting that anything is positively and absolutely right or wrong, to be pursued or avoided, the argument will inevitably be about the foundation of morality" (Warnock 1978, 143). Of course, in this passage Warnock seems to assume that moral confidence is linked to the plausibility of some form of absolutism—something, the relativist will claim, that the facts of moral experience always render impossible.

Relativists have often urged that relativism would ultimately generate a new kind of optimism about practical political affairs—one that would eventually replace the demand for moral confidence linked to a plausible moral absolutism. This optimism often informs the appeal of relativism, and relativist anthropologists have tended to be its most influential proponents. Herskovits believed, for instance, that with the decline of imperialism and colonialism, cultural groups with widely differing values and practices would increasingly be required to confront one another as political equals; in such conditions global peace would depend on a widespread readiness not only to recognize but also to respect unfamiliar practices. It was understandably tempting to assume that relativist anthropology might provide the theoretical resources for understanding the terms of that respect. The cultural evolutionism associated with much nineteenth-century anthropology—for instance, in the work of E. B. Tylor in *Primitive Culture* (1871)—typically implied that non-Western ways of life were worthy of respect just to the extent that they did not differ very much from supposedly "higher" ways of life familiar to European anthropologists. From the beginning, American anthropologists such as Franz Boas, Ruth Benedict, and Margaret Mead viewed cultural relativism as a powerful theoretical weapon against the excesses of cultural evolutionism.[15] Shweder echoes this view in his assurance about the "permission" that relativists give to diversity (Shweder 1991). Yet Herskovits was a particularly canny proponent of relativist optimism. He wisely resisted the tendency—famously displayed in the concluding paragraphs of Benedict's *Patterns of Culture* (1934)—to defend a potentially self-refuting *normative* principle prescribing toleration of coexisting and "equally valid" ways of life. He also denied that cultural relativism should be interpreted as "a doctrine of ethical indifference"; properly understood, he claimed, the doctrine simply showed that mutual respect for all cultural practices is a *prudential* concern (Herskovits 1972, 59). But he retained the view that non-relativist confidence in the possibility of objectively justifying moral judgments could never be more than a smug, and ultimately imprudent, cultural self-righteousness.

Such optimism does not adequately address concerns, such as Warnock's, about the destructive practical effects of relativism. Nor is it clear that relativism has had, or will have, the practical consequences that Herskovits envisions. First of all, it is doubtful that an acceptance of relativism could ever be shown to be *necessary* to ensuring respect for unfamiliar practices. Relativists often worry that a willingness to engage in moral criticism of another culture may be the entering edge of the imperialist wedge—the beginning of an attempt to *impose* disputed values forcefully on those who accept that culture (Herskovits 1964, 68–70; cf. 1972, 22–23). But the mere expression of moral criticism should not be conflated with violence or coercion. I argue more fully in Chapter 5, that a readiness to engage in open and uncoerced argument about particular moral practices is in fact palpable evidence of respect for those who must decide how, and whether, to perpetuate some aspect of their culture. Second, it is equally doubtful that a commitment to relativism could ever be *sufficient* to ensure mutual respect for cultures. Thrasymachus' chilling insistence in the *Republic* that justice is simply 'the interest of the stronger' surely gives the lie to any claim that relativists are more likely than non-relativists to favor a general policy of non-interference. Even if relativism could be shown to require rationally a preference for non-interference in other cultures, a generalized disposition toward non-interference will sometimes be antithetical to respect for culture. When the defining principles of one culture prescribe the forceful elimination of another—such as by means of forced expatriation or mass killing—the readiness to withhold judgment will, at the very least, aid and abet the destruction of cultures. Of course, the question of whether, and under what conditions, it might be defensible to *act* on a particular judgment that condemns some aspect of another culture is exceedingly complex. The dialectical value of the relativist stance on this matter cannot be overlooked, for relativism forces non-relativists to reflect on just how complex such matters really are. But twentieth-century history in particular should provide an important counterweight to optimism about the efficacy of relativist conclusions in the face of such events.

Merely to challenge assertions about the practical effects of relativism, however, does not undermine relativist claims that only relativism takes disagreement seriously. Nor, it is important to note, does it meet the relativist challenge to belief in the objective validity of cross-cultural moral judgments. Richard Rorty has attempted to take this challenge seriously without, he asserts, relinquishing anything essential for moral confidence. In language remarkably similar to that of many arguments for relativism, Rorty insists that there is no "supercultural observation platform" from which to assess the merits of diverse values (Rorty 1991a, 213). All human beings accept some "final vocabulary" in which they express praise, and contempt, as well as their "long-term projects . . . and highest hopes," yet there is nothing beyond these vocabularies to serve as a criterion of choice between them (Rorty 1989, 73; 80). How, then, does Rorty avoid the collapse of moral confidence? He is a self-described "ethnocentrist" who simply insists that "ideals may be local and culture-bound, and nevertheless be the best hope of the species" (Rorty 1991a, 208). And he is unapologetic in his conviction that the "best hope of the species" lies in the liberal democratic virtues: in the tolerance for diversity and in the preference for persuasion rather than force as way of coping with diversity (Rorty 1991a, 14–15; 214). For Rorty, then, ethnocentrism seems to be a way of steering a middle course between the Scylla of absolutism and the Charybdis of relativism.

Yet to be ethnocentric, on Rorty's scheme, is "to divide the human race into the people to whom one must justify one's beliefs and the others" (Rorty 1991a, 30). It is to relinquish the desire for objectivity in favor of a desire for "solidarity" with the members of one's *ethnos*— those who, Rorty contends, share enough of one's beliefs to make "fruitful conversation" possible. Thus,

> moral justification of the institutions and practices of one's group . . . is mostly a matter of historical narratives (including scenarios about what is likely to happen in certain future contingencies), rather than of philosophical metanarratives. The principal backup for historiography is not philosophy but the arts, which serve to develop and modify a group's self-image by, for example, apotheosizing its heroes, diabolizing its enemies, mounting dialogues among its members, and refocusing its attention. (Rorty 1991a, 200)

There is a curious irony in all this: assumptions underwriting a relativist stance somehow issue in a decidedly non-relativist confidence in one set of "local" moral values. As Geertz has suggested, this confidence has the air of a "relax-and-enjoy-it ethnocentrism" (Geertz 1986, 259) which may result in the very condescension and cultural self-righteousness that relativism sought to avoid.

Moreover, even if Rorty's moral ethnocentrism is an understandably tempting response to a "collapse of moral self-confidence" in Western liberal democracies (Rorty 1991a, 203), it is fraught with difficulties. To begin with, no human community—whether a small tribal village or a modern nation-state—is a windowless monad; every such community must, to some degree, face the likelihood of encounters with other communities whose beliefs, values, and practices will place varying degrees of pressure on the calm pursuit of any local way of life.[16] Although these encounters may sometimes be benign, history reveals that many are not. Moreover, even initially benign or accidental encounters between diverse human communities may generate dangerous conflicts. When the diverse groups concerned are unwilling, or even unable, to find neutral and *uncoerced* conversational ground, the human costs of such failures can be devastating. But in actual practice, diverse groups do sometimes agree (even if only implicitly) to accept some "vocabulary" as, at least for a time, neutral between previously competing vocabularies. Moreover, the possibility of such agreement presupposes a mutual readiness to see initially unfamiliar "others" as capable of sharing, or perhaps even *already* sharing, at least some of the beliefs and values of one's current *ethnos*. It presupposes, that is, the ability to see every "other" as—at the same time—a member of some further community of which one is at least potentially, and perhaps in actuality, a part. Rortean ethnocentrism, however, dangerously divides the world into "us" and the "others" in a way that renders fruitful *cross*-cultural conversation difficult if not impossible because it assumes that one can say in advance who is a member of one's *ethnos* and who is simply beyond the pale. As I will show, it is not only implausible but potentially self-destructive to assume that on matters of any moral significance there might be some antecedently given "fact of the matter" about the most appropriate way to draw the boundaries between one's own way of life and that of the "other."

The moral self-absorption of Rortean ethnocentrism poses a special threat to the social institutions in which liberal democratic ideals take shape (Moody-Adams, 1994b). The virtue of tolerance, for instance, makes complex demands on the liberal democratic institutions in which it is embodied. As Judith Shklar once argued, "Tolerance consistently applied is more difficult and morally more demanding than repression" (Shklar 1984, 4–5). In particular, one must confront the notoriously challenging question of whether, and to what extent, it is necessary for a liberal society to tolerate intolerance. A defensible answer must draw on a reflective and critical understanding of the nature and limits of tolerance; and while debates internal to liberal democracies may assist in forming that understanding, familiar debates about tolerance may also wind up at an equally familiar impasse. In such circumstances the richest sources for the appropriate reflection will often be the experience of societies in which tolerance is less secure. To be sure, such reflection may simply confirm the liberal democratic conviction that tolerance—even of the intolerant—is generally more important than concern about the substantial costs attending such tolerance. But even that conviction, and the cultural perspective of which it is a part, will have been subtly reshaped by the very process of sincere reflection on serious alternatives. Such reflection is possible only where there is readiness to engage in unself-righteous comparisons of ways of life—comparisons which the root-level assumptions of Rortean ethnocentrism rule out from the start. Given the difficulty of sustaining democratic political institutions, the moral self-absorption of Rortean ethnocentrism could be a suicidal prescription for liberal democracies.

Yet despite these difficulties, Rorty's "ethnocentric turn" exemplifies widely felt concern about the decline of moral confidence, and hence the need to reexamine the relativist challenge. If there is merit in the relativist's challenge to the possibility of securing cross-cultural moral agreement from an objective standpoint, it will seem difficult to meet that challenge without resorting to something quite close to Rortean moral ethnocentrism. However morally self-absorbed that stance may be, those who are troubled by the persistence of deep disagreements between human communities, and who are concerned that absolutist arguments have failed to challenge relativist responses, may view ethnocentrism as the last defense against a complete collapse of moral confidence. I argue in Chapters 4 and 5 that there is a non-ethnocentrist alternative to the excesses of absolutism, on the one hand, and relativism, on the other. It is possible, that is, to defend a non-ethnocentrist rebuttal of relativism that does not seek to prove the existence of a "single true morality" whose truth is guaranteed by a realm of "absolute moral values." Yet any successful rebuttal of relativism must first ask whether relativism is correct in claiming that disagreement seriously *necessitates* relinquishing the idea that morality and moral inquiry can be objective.

THE EMPIRICAL UNDERDETERMINATION OF DESCRIPTIVE CULTURAL RELATIVISM

Many theorists in philosophy and anthropology, as well as many thoughtful people in everyday life, find some version of meta-ethical relativism compelling because they take it to involve a series of virtually irresistible inferences from experience—a series of inferences that allegedly support the claims of descriptive cultural relativism. Herskovits claimed, for instance, that a simple understanding of a few basic facts about cultural diversity in moral practices would eventually issue in a potent relativism about justification and about the nature of morality. He insisted that relativism is simply "a scientific, inductive attack on an age-old philosophical problem, using fresh, cross-cultural data, hitherto not available to scholars, gained from the study of the underlying value-systems of societies having the most diverse customs"(Herskovits 1972, 14). Borrowing liberally from the terminology of William James, Herskovits characterizes his relativism as simply a "tough-minded"—that is, truly empirical—approach to understanding the "nature and role of values in culture." This "tough-minded" anthropology, as I have noted, leads to the claim that moral evaluations are "always relative to the cultural background out of which they arise" (Herskovits 1972, 37–38; 14; cf. 1964, 61–78). But what does this claim really come to?

Descriptive cultural relativism, to reiterate the point I made earlier, is anything *but* a "neutral" account of the facts of cultural diversity. To be sure, all empirical hypotheses are underdetermined by available data; the acceptance of empirical hypotheses involves implicit commitments to explanatory and predictive virtues that function—in Quine's phrase—as "guides to the framing of hypotheses" (Quine and Ullian 1978, 64–82). Considerations such as the simplicity of a new hypothesis, or the extent to which a hypothesis might maximize the conservation of current beliefs or offer generality of explanation, figure as important non-empirical constraints on the choice of empirical theories. Moreover, while the epistemological values presupposed by reliance on these virtues differ in kind from those values presupposed by the acceptance of particular *moral* virtues, descriptive cultural relativism clearly cannot be evaluatively neutral. Yet descriptive relativism is in need of special scrutiny since empirical generalizations about moral practices are quite special instances of the general phenomenon of underdetermination. Of course, any such generalization will embody complex judgments that draw comparisons, and especially contrasts, between the moral practices of different human groups. But these contrastive and comparative judgments imply—and rely on—descriptive claims about moral practices that are also underdetermined by available data.

To understand the importance of this underdetermination, consider that the effort to construct empirical hypotheses about the data of moral experience, even in observing a familiar group, is thoroughly structured by an elaborate set of non-empirical assumptions even about what is to count as data. Familiar debates in contemporary moral philosophy between Kantians and non-Kantians who disagree about the moral status of emotions provide an important example of the sorts of questions at issue. Matters become even more complex when hypotheses concern the moral practices of unfamiliar groups. Ironically, moral relativists seldom hesitate to assume that the natural languages of the groups they encounter contain a concept of morality—or, more precisely, some concept that plays a role very much like that which the concept of morality plays in the language of the typical anthropologist-observer. But this assumption (however plausible) presupposes a sophisticated judgment about a concept—the concept of morality—so complex that its content is "essentially contested," in W. B. Gallie's phrase, even by speakers of the same language.[17]

Decisions about how to determine precisely *which* phenomena constitute the moral data of a particular way of life create special difficulties. John Ladd's account of his efforts to describe Navajo ethics, detailed in *The Structure of a Moral Code* (1957), provides useful (if unwitting) testimony to the extent of these difficulties. Ladd criticizes methods relied on by R. B. Brandt, in his *Hopi Ethics* (1954), which also offered a descriptive account of the morality of a Native American community. Ladd contends, for instance, that Brandt's methods were insufficiently attentive to the Hopi perspective, and that they could really yield only a study of the extent to which the Hopi accept "principles like our own" (Ladd 1957, 316). Yet Ladd's own account shows that determining what constitutes *sufficient* attention to a group's perspective on their own morality is a vexing problem. Thus, for example (in what Ladd himself recognizes is a problematic feature of his account), he relies principally on interviews (through interpreters) with only two Navajo informants (Ladd 1957, 335–425). Of course, his decision to use such a small number of informants probably rested on a judgment from someone familiar with the Navajo, or perhaps even a member of the Navajo, that certain people would be more likely than others to provide an "authoritative" version of Navajo values and practices. Yet it is no easy matter to justify this kind of confidence in authoritative versions.

Any such confidence embodies a complex evaluative stance that will sometimes prove neither methodologically nor morally benign. Very often such confidence overlooks the possibility of internal conflict, as when a community practice has been subjected to criticism from within. Imagine, for example, that in some community a certain common practice has been the subject of intense criticism from a small but forceful group within that community. An outside observer who undertakes to describe this community's moral practices may well be told that the internal critics are not authoritative voices but mere aberrations. But a failure to record the substance of the internal criticism will issue in a description that is false to the internal complexity of the community's way of life. What is more, this very complexity may itself be of supreme *moral* importance for the culture, for sometimes a critic is a vehicle for the kind of self-scrutiny that reveals an accepted practice to be incompatible with some deep commitment of the group. This is, after all, the Socratic view of moral reasoning which gave such force to the stance of nonviolent civil disobedience in the American South.[18] For an ethnographer to participate—knowingly or unknowingly—in potentially silencing such reflection is to give legitimacy to an evaluatively non-neutral version of the moral practices of the group. Indeed, perhaps no attempt to describe a group's moral practices and beliefs can be a morally neutral act, especially given the artificiality of the anthropologist's "ethnographic present," which fails to suggest the inherent potential for ongoing evolution of complex moral practices. But the constant danger that any description may fail at neutrality is ignored by claims such as those of Brandt, for example, who at one point argues that the beliefs of "the average member" of a group are central to an adequate empirical study of that group's ethics (Brandt 1959, 89). Even if it were possible to identify a clear referent of the term "average member," there will always be important moral questions on which the perspective of the person who is *not* average, or even the person who is in some way "marginal," is equally important—if not more so—to a sufficiently informative account of the moral principles of a culture (Scheper-Hughes 1984, 90). What would it mean, for example, to try to describe the moral import of homelessness in America by interviewing only the "average American," who is unlikely to be homeless?

The non-empirical and evaluative commitments of any attempt to describe a people's moral practices are thus quite numerous, and quite obviously in need of close scrutiny. Likewise, descriptive cultural relativism, which makes an empirical generalization about the actual moral practices *of all human beings*, is in need of even greater scrutiny. Yet little philosophical attention has been devoted to this task. Many philosophers would simply defend the non-empirical commitments embodied in descriptive cultural relativism without further ado, because for them the doctrine is just an influential confirmation of the view that fundamental conflicts are an essential feature of morality itself. Thus, for instance, Stuart Hampshire has claimed that there "must" always be moral conflicts which "cannot" be resolved "by any constant and generally acknowledged method of reasoning." Indeed, according to Hampshire, morality "has its sources in conflicts"—conflicts "in the divided soul and between contrary claims" (Hampshire 1983, 152). David Wong makes a similar claim: if one takes moral disagreement seriously, one simply recognizes that there will always be "irresolvable" moral disagreements. Wong also takes the inevitability of such disagreements to support a "limited" meta-ethical relativism on which "there is no single true morality" (Wong 1986, 95; cf. 1984).[19] Hampshire vehemently denies that he is arguing, in Herskovits's apt phrase, for the relativism of "ethical indifference" (Hampshire 1983, 154). Yet he never considers the possibility that his view of the "sources" of morality—which is remarkably similar to Wong's view that the principal "point" of morality is to regulate conflicts—might implicitly commit him to a weak meta-ethical relativism.[20] Instead, he simply urges that his principal concern is to warn of the "harm" that moral philosophy can do if it implies that "there ought to be, and that there can be, fundamental agreement on, or convergence in, moral ideals." His avowed purpose is to chide the moral theorist who would look for "an underlying harmony and unity behind the facts of moral experience" (Hampshire 1983, 155; 151).

The view that fundamental conflict is intrinsic to morality has become so widespread that it appears in the most unexpected quarters. It has been claimed, for example, that even a robust moral realism—on which there are moral facts and real moral properties whose existence and nature are independent of "our beliefs" about right and wrong—must allow for the inevitability of fundamental moral disagreement (Brink 1989, 7–8; 202). Thus, David Brink argues for a realism about moral facts and properties that also accepts the persistence of disputes involving "incommensurable" (but, in his view, equally "objectively valuable") considerations, as well as "moral ties"—disputes, that is, all of which have "no uniquely correct answers" (Brink 1989, 202). Of course, even Brink acknowledges that there "are limits" (though he does not define them) to how often one can construe moral disputes as fundamental—as "not resolvable even in principle"—and yet also defend the independent existence of moral facts and properties (Brink 1989, 202). Brink is somewhat too sanguine about how easy it might be to establish these limits. But my point is simply that even robust moral realists have come to expect that they must accommodate belief in the inevitability of fundamental moral conflicts. This is a particularly striking example of how profoundly philosophy's supposed insensitivity to moral disagreement has influenced contemporary philosophical thinking about morality.

But what element of human experience could encourage the belief that fundamental moral conflict is an ineliminable feature of the social world? For many—both in philosophy as well as outside it—the data of cultural diversity provide the best evidence of moral conflicts which allegedly cannot be reduced to non-moral disagreement and cannot be resolved by reasoning and argument. One society defends polygamy while another rejects such arrangements as morally unacceptable; one group practices female circumcision and infibulation while another rejects it and the assumptions that seem to underlie it; one culture appears to approve ritual headhunting while members of other cultures would condemn the practice: such disputes are often cited as paradigmatic cases of fundamental moral conflict. Yet though these differences are real, and though the conflicts they sometimes generate are quite serious, it is not clear why it *must* be assumed that such conflicts cannot be reduced to non-moral disagreement and—in Hampshire's phrase—are not susceptible of resolution "by any constant and generally recognized method of reasoning" (Hampshire 1983, 152). Comparative anthropology provides obvious evidence of cultural variability in moral practices, but why should it be assumed that the moral disagreements sometimes occasioned by that variability are also *fundamental*—rationally irresolvable—moral conflicts?

In the first part of the twentieth century, a number of Gestalt psychologists who were dissatisfied with relativism—thinkers such as Karl Duncker, Max Wertheimer, and later Solomon Asch, among others—posed the very same question. These theorists then went on to challenge the empirical basis of descriptive relativism, effectively denying the reasonableness of the move from the fact of cultural variability to the doctrine of descriptive cultural relativism.[21] A central positive aim of these views was to argue that all purportedly fundamental moral disagreements might be shown ultimately to reduce to disagreements in beliefs about the non-moral properties of the actions or practices under consideration. Moreover, many Gestalt theorists (especially Duncker) made still stronger claims, attempting to demonstrate the existence of "invariant" laws of ethical valuation. The challenge that the Gestalt critique might pose to descriptive cultural relativism is seldom given sufficient attention, but as psychologists such as Asch maintained—and as philosophers such as Brandt and Frankena ultimately recognized—its challenge to the evidential basis for descriptive ethical relativism can be detached from the controversial aspects of the Gestalt theorist's positive commitments.[22] Moreover, that challenge is of great value. First, it helps reveal the precise ways in which descriptive ethical relativism is not a neutral description of the data of cultural diversity, and how, as Asch once remarked, it presupposes an ultimately insupportable conception of the radical "alienness" of diverse cultural traditions (Asch 1952, 381–383). Second, and equally important, the Gestalt theorist's challenge helps show how descriptive cultural relativism actually hinders a serious understanding of the conditions under which *real*—not simply apparent—moral disagreement is possible at all.

In an important article in *Mind*, entitled "Ethical Relativity? (An Inquiry into the Psychology of Ethics)" (1939), Karl Duncker discussed the philosophical relevance of Gestalt psychology's criticisms of relativism. Duncker began by identifying important features of the "psychological situation" with reference to which participants in any social practice actually behave: the "situational meanings" of the practice. The situational meaning of any practice, as he and other Gestalt theorists understood that notion, would typically include a complex set of non-moral beliefs about both the "objective" (especially causal) properties and the "subjective" features (or affective associations) of the action (Duncker 1939, 43–44). Duncker then claimed that moral judgments "on the whole" are based on socially developed patterns of situational meaning that vary widely from one culture to another, and that anthropological reports are insufficiently attentive to important variations in the situational meanings of the practices they purport to describe. One of his most important examples concerned possible variations in the situational meaning of the practice of killing superannuated parents. Disputes about the implications of this practice (famously described, for instance, in early accounts of the pursuit of the Northwest Passage) had historically played an important role in philosophical exchanges about the nature of morality.

Duncker's contribution to the debate was really quite simple. He argued, first, that where killing one's aged parents is understood, for example, as a means of sparing them the misery of a lingering death, or of increasing their chances of getting into a promised heaven, the situational meaning of the practice could be expected to give it "a quality of benevolence" (Duncker 1939, 42). He then contrasted such cases with those in which it would be denied that the killing of aged parents has any such properties. Here, he contended, the practice would quite expectedly be the object of extreme disapproval. Now, descriptive cultural relativism claims that different cultures connect "different and even opposed evaluations" to the *same* action (Asch 1952, 376). But, on Duncker's view, killing one's aged parents where that practice has the socially sanctioned meaning of sparing them a lingering death simply *is not* the same action as killing aged parents where this would be viewed as causing the early and unnecessary death of innocent persons. Ethical valuation, he argued, "is not concerned with acts as abstract events in space-time. The ethical essence of an act depends upon its concrete pattern of situational meanings" (Duncker 1939, 43).

Duncker went on to claim—quite controversially—that "the same act, being the same" has never been observed to have different moral valuations, and then to attribute this presumed fact to the existence of invariant "inner laws" of ethical valuation (Duncker 1939, 50–51). There are indeed serious obstacles in the way of proving the truth of these claims, but my aim is not to resuscitate the Gestalt theorist's positive account of morality. I simply want to show that recognizing the importance of situational meanings reveals serious methodological obstacles to proving the truth of descriptive relativism about morality. And these obstacles may be insuperable. As Brandt once observed, it is difficult (at best) to establish that one has indeed *found* a genuine instance of fundamental moral diversity (Brandt 1967, 76). In order to do so, it would be necessary to produce two people, or two cultures, who attribute identical non-moral properties to an action that they nonetheless appraise differently—and it is extremely difficult, Brandt argues, to accomplish this. Moreover, the nature and extent of the difficulty can even be discerned in familiar moral disputes. Debates about abortion, for instance, typically turn on quite complex relationships between situational meanings, on the one hand, and moral evaluations, on the other. Competing positions on abortion are often linked to patterns of situational meaning structured around disputed understandings of the properties of the fetus, and (implicitly) even of the pregnant woman. Such debates thus provide quite palpable evidence of the importance of Duncker's notion of situational meanings.

But the Gestalt theorist's insistence on the importance of socially determined differences between situational meanings might seem to concede too much to the relativist. For anthropologists such as Herskovits typically argue that relativism is just an inescapable consequence of giving due recognition to "the force of enculturative conditioning in shaping thought and behavior" in general (Herskovits 1972, 32). Enculturation, as Herskovits conceived of it, is the "all-pervasive," largely "unconscious" process of "conditioning" by which one learns a culture. Moreover, the force of that conditioning, he argued, would be felt as powerfully in the realm of factual beliefs (and hence in socially sanctioned patterns of situational meanings) as in the realm of moral evaluations themselves. Duncker vehemently asserts that the "ethical essence" of an act depends on "concrete" patterns of situational meanings. But an astute relativist would surely respond that variation in these concrete patterns must be recognized as an important methodological obstacle to establishing the existence—at least empirically—of the Gestalt theorist's invariant laws of moral valuation.[23]

Yet while the dependence of moral valuation on situational meanings may be an important obstacle to establishing empirically the positive claims of Gestalt theory, pointing out those obstacles simply produces a theoretical standoff—not a conclusive victory for descriptive relativism. Moreover, even if there is little hope for positive proof that there are invariant laws of ethical valuation, Duncker's criticisms pose a particularly serious challenge to a doctrine whose proponents appeal to its superior empirical credentials. Anthropologists such as Herskovits, Benedict, and Boas, as well as philosophers such as Ladd and Mackie, want to maintain that descriptive relativism is simply a plausible "inductive attack" on the problem of moral valuation. If that is the case, however, it should be possible to show how a careful descriptive relativism might convincingly overcome its admitted methodological difficulties.

An illuminating and important attempt to show just this is contained in Brandt's discussions of relativism in *Ethical Theory* (1959). These are of particular interest, since his study of Hopi ethics seems to have provided numerous occasions for reflecting on the potential obstacles to describing adequately the moral practices and beliefs of an unfamiliar culture. Moreover, several contemporary discussions of relativism, in both philosophy and anthropology, continue to treat Brandt's claims about descriptive relativism as authoritative.[24] Brandt begins by acknowledging how difficult it is to determine whether there is ever fundamental—or "ultimate"—moral disagreement between different cultures; he then criticizes what he sees as the shortcomings of standard anthropological treatments of the issues. Relying on familiar features of the Gestalt theorist's critique, he argues that

> most of the comparative material assembled . . . tells us . . . simply whether various peoples approve or condemn lying, suicide, industry, cleanliness, adultery, homosexuality, cannibalism, and so on. But this is not enough. We need, for our purpose, to know how various people conceive of these things. Do they eat human flesh because they like its taste, and do they kill these slaves merely for the sake of a feast? Or do they eat flesh because they

think this is necessary for tribal fertility, or because they think they will then participate in the manliness of the person eaten? (Brandt 1959, 101–102)

Brandt even posits, somewhat unexpectedly, that those who currently condemn cannibalism might relinquish their condemnation were the socially accepted situational meaning to undergo sufficient change. Thus, "perhaps those who condemn cannibalism would not do so if they thought that eating the flesh of an enemy is necessary for the survival of the group. If we are to estimate whether there is ultimate disagreement of ethical principle, we must have information about this, about the beliefs, more or less conscious, of various peoples about what they do" (Brandt 1959, 102–103). This concern with the "more or less conscious" beliefs about the situational meanings of a practice even leads Brandt to take a position on parricide that is remarkably like that of Duncker (Brandt 1959, 99–100).

Brandt thus eschews appeals to the sorts of practices typically claimed to embody attitudes and assumptions that are "noncomparable" or "incommensurable" with "our" attitudes and assumptions about the world—practices such as socially sanctioned parricide, cannibalism, and witchcraft. A more typical treatment of these issues appears in Harman's "soberly logical" defense of relativism (Harman 1975, 3). Harman constructs a hypothetical example of a group of cannibals attacking the lone survivor of a shipwreck, in an effort to illuminate "our" intuitive conviction that a social practice of cannibalism would be evidence of "a primitive morality" held by "savages" best assumed to be "beyond the motivational reach" of "our" moral judgments (Harman 1975, 8). Harman's claims for moral relativism, as one commentator has argued, thus appeal to figures imagined as entirely beyond the pale—as utterly alien and "other" (Matilal 1989, 345–346). Evans-Pritchard's ethnographic study *Witchcraft, Oracles, and Magic among the Azande* (1937) contains a similar emphasis. His account continues to generate philosophical debate about the extent to which—in Peter Winch's words—the Azande "hold beliefs that we cannot possibly share and engage in practices which it is peculiarly difficult for us to comprehend. They believe that certain of their numbers are witches, exercising a malignant occult influence on the lives of their fellows. They engage in rites to counteract witchcraft; they consult oracles and use magic medicines to protect themselves from harm" (Winch 1972, 78). It is a matter of some importance that Brandt avoids these fairly standard ways of attempting to establish fundamental ethical disagreement between "us" and "them." His resistance to these approaches draws on his conviction that comparative surveys have provided insufficient data about the non-moral beliefs associated with social practices. "We must concede," he asserts, that anthropology has not provided "an adequate account of a single case, clearly showing that there is ultimate disagreement in ethical principle" (Brandt 1959, 102).

Given this last concession, however, it is startling that just a few paragraphs later Brandt himself claims to have found one example capable of establishing that there is *in fact* ultimate disagreement between cultures. At one point he even contends (on the basis of that example) that the case for fundamental disagreement is "well-established," though he later retreats from this stance, asserting more hesitantly that "probably—we must admit the case is not definitively closed—there is at least one ultimate difference of ethical principle" (Brandt 1959, 102; 103). More surprising still is the substance of the example that he takes to establish the reality of fundamental moral disagreement. It is "notorious," Brandt begins, that "many peoples seem quite indifferent to the suffering of animals." He then describes the practices of certain groups in Latin America who, he contends, sometimes pluck chickens alive "so that they will be more succulent on the table," and, later, a Hopi Indian children's game in which "children often catch birds and make 'pets' of them. A string is tied to their legs, and they are then 'played' with. The birds seldom survive this 'play' for long: their legs are broken, their wings pulled off, and so on. One informant put it: 'Sometimes they get tired and die. Nobody objects to this.' Another informant said: 'My boy sometimes brings in birds, but there is nothing to feed them and they die'" (Brandt 1959, 102–103).[25] At this point, however, the discussion takes a remarkable turn. For Brandt's argument to establish the existence of an ultimate ethical difference between *cultures* comes down to a series of open-ended rhetorical challenges to "the reader": "The reader is invited to ask himself whether he would consider it justified to pluck a chicken alive for this purpose"; "Would the reader approve of this [Hopi game], or permit his children to do this sort of thing?"; and so on (Brandt 1959, 102; 103). That such rhetorical appeals might be thought to lend empirical support to the doctrine of descriptive relativism seems to *this* reader to rest on a number of curious and ultimately implausible assumptions.[26] That they have not been criticized as such may suggest how axiomatic descriptive relativism has come to seem. Curious as they are, these assumptions are worth examining in detail because they commonly underwrite attempts to generalize about the nature and extent of cross-cultural moral disagreement, and they are usually implicit in influential attempts—both relativist and ethnocentrist—to challenge the objectivity of morality. I intend to show that these assumptions cannot be defended, and ultimately that they obstruct attention to any plausible defense of the objectivity of morality and moral inquiry.

Brandt's discussion presumes, to begin with, not only that "the reader" will in fact disapprove of the described practices, but also that this disapproval should be taken to manifest a general *cultural* sensitivity to the suffering of animals. But why should it be assumed that there will be some *one* kind of response from all imaginable readers of Brandt's *Ethical Theory*, and that such a response could legitimately be taken to represent a monolithic moral concern for animals in those readers' culture(s)? To be sure, many people reading the relevant passage might well disapprove of the described practices; they might even recoil in horror at the idea of plucking a chicken alive or carelessly breaking the wings of a small bird. Brandt goes on to report his "decided impression" that Hopi disapproval of causing pain to animals was "milder than he would suppose typical in suburban Philadelphia—certainly much milder than he would feel himself" (Brandt 1959, 102). Nevertheless, even if one concedes Brandt special insight into the culture of "suburban Philadelphia," such responses could not prove the existence of a general concern for animal suffering in his readers' culture(s)—unless of course, all his readers were assumed to inhabit suburban Philadelphia. Indeed, a substantial subset of Brandt's readers would be markedly indifferent to forms of animal suffering that are regularly sanctioned by their own culture(s). Thus, for example, the suburban American parents who unthinkingly give animals as "presents" to children who are unprepared to care for them are not so different from the Hopi parents in Brandt's example, as the continued existence of societies for the prevention of cruelty to animals reminds us. Even further, anyone teaching a course in contemporary moral problems to a large group of American undergraduates may encounter a surprising number of students who report difficulty in sharing concern about the suffering of animals in slaughterhouses and factory farms. Given all these considerations, just how great an ethical difference could there really be between the attitude toward animal suffering in the culture of "the reader," on the one hand, and that attitude in the Hopi and Latin American cultures described, on the other?

Brandt returns to the disputed example in a later chapter, and the resulting discussion reveals his own dissatisfaction with his initial argument. But his attempts to strengthen the case are even more problematic than his earlier appeals to the evaluative responses of "the reader." He contends that "on the whole, primitive groups show little feeling that it is wrong to cause pain to animals, whereas the columns of the *New York Times* are testimony to the fact that many persons in the U.S.A. take a vigorous interest in what goes on in slaughterhouses . . . There is at least some question whether [primitive groups] have a vivid imagination of what the suffering of an animal is like, comparable to that of the authors of letters to the *Times*" (Brandt 1959, 284–285). Why should the imaginative powers allegedly displayed by a subset of authors of letters to the *New York Times* be taken to reveal an entire culture's moral convictions? Moreover, why does Brandt consider it unimportant that—even according to his own example—not everyone in the United States objects to the existence of slaughterhouses? The internal complexity of American attitudes about animal suffering cannot be irrelevant to understanding "the morality" of American culture, nor can it be irrelevant to any defensible attempt to contrast that morality with the indifference to animal suffering suggested by Brandt's examples. More generally, if descriptive cultural relativism is just a "tough-minded" account of the facts, it ought to be possible to say how the descriptive relativist knows what those facts really are.

The problem is that it is profoundly difficult to construct a reliable description of the moral practices of an entire *culture*—a description of the sort that could license judgments contrasting one culture's basic moral beliefs with those of other cultures. To be sure, some of the difficulties in formulating the contrastive judgments needed to defend descriptive relativism reflect methodological obstacles that plague the construction of *any* reliable descriptive morality and not simply a description of the moral practices of a given culture. Well-known controversies generated by the claims of empirical psychologists attempting to describe patterns of moral reasoning—such as the controversy surrounding the debate between Carol Gilligan and Lawrence Kohlberg— point to some of the central difficulties.[27] Thus, for instance, a psychologist typically relies on verbal reports that are subject to self-deception, or even to intentional attempts to deceive a researcher. Further, the design of any study intended to elicit the verbal data to be interpreted may itself be subject to markedly non-neutral assumptions about what is appropriately construed as a moral conviction. Finally, even if neutrality in the design of an empirical study of moral reasoning is a realizable goal, there is still the question of how to produce a neutral *interpretation* of the data obtained in such a study.

Special concerns arise when, as in the case of ethnography, the study of verbal responses is combined with the observation of nonverbal behavior, whose interpretation is fraught with peculiar difficulties. Some of these difficulties are a function of the complex relation between judgment and action. If, for instance, weakness of the will is a genuine feature of human behavior—if, that is, human beings sometimes fail to conform their conduct to moral convictions that they truly accept—this fact will surely complicate the interpretation of behavior. But even where there is no reason to presume weakness of the will, it is remarkably difficult to read off correctly unstated moral beliefs and attitudes (or even non-moral beliefs about situational meanings) from behavior. At one point Brandt implicitly concedes this when he assures the reader that he tried to discover some belief "in the Hopi subconscious" that might make it possible to say that Hopi practices did not reveal some ultimate difference in ethical principle between the Hopi and "the reader" (Brandt 1959, 103).[28] Yet the notion that there might be some psychological monolith called "the Hopi subconscious," which is capable of revealing hidden truths about Hopi practices when their "more or less conscious beliefs" would not, is just as problematic as Brandt's accompanying readiness to overlook the existence of socially sanctioned indifference to animal suffering in the larger American culture.

The most serious obstacles to formulating contrastive judgments about the moral practices of particular human groups, and to establishing the truth of descriptive relativism, reflect a difficulty peculiar to the study of cultures: that of deciding who—if anyone—has the "authority" to represent the defining principles, especially the basic moral principles, of a given culture. Should the undergraduate who is unwilling seriously to contemplate arguments about animal rights or interests, for example, be treated as representative of the American moral stance toward animals? Or is the moral fervor of the animal rights activist who periodically fires off a letter to the *New York Times* perhaps more representative? Of course, neither stance adequately represents the moral convictions of American culture as a whole. But if it is reasonable to expect in the culture of a large industrialized nation-state moral complexity of the sort that might frustrate the attempt to formulate meaningful generalizations about moral beliefs, would it then be reasonable to expect the same kind of complexity in the culture of small, preindustrial, and often "preliterate" communities? If not, why not? The answers to such questions have important implications for deciding whether descriptive cultural relativism yields a plausible picture of the social world. I will argue that a careful accounting of the facts of cultural complexity, and the associated difficulty in establishing moral authority, makes it difficult (if not impossible) for descriptive cultural relativism—and the various skepticisms about moral objectivity often alleged to follow from it—ever to get off the ground.

CULTURAL AUTHORITY, CULTURAL COMPLEXITY, AND THE DOCTRINE OF CULTURAL INTEGRATION

I have tried to show that even Brandt's careful attempt to defend descriptive relativism founders on important facts about the opacity of human conduct, the complexity of cultures, and the resultant difficulties of determining who has authority to represent the defining moral principles of a culture. He fails to find in Hopi culture an indifference to animal suffering that could not also be found—on a fairly large scale—in that segment of American culture he attempted to hold up as a contrast. In this section I argue for a set of more general claims that shows why the problems of cultural complexity and moral authority must always prove vexing to the proponent of descriptive relativism. The descriptive relativist claims that it is possible to identify at least some instances of fundamental or ultimate moral disagreement between the moral practices of particular cultures. I contend that the moral practices of particular cultures are, in general, simply resistant to the kinds of generalizations needed to figure in the contrastive judgments implied by descriptive relativism. Descriptive relativism claims to account for certain kinds of contrasts ("fundamental" conflicts) between the moral practices of particular human communities, but the alleged contrasts cannot be plausibly or reliably formulated. The moral practices of real human communities—unlike the ideal moral systems constructed by moral philosophers, often in an effort to reconstruct rationally a given set of moral practices—exhibit a fundamentally non-integrated complexity that renders them resistant to the kinds of judgments that must figure in the descriptive relativist's contrasts.

Such claims will seem heretical to many within philosophy as well as outside of it, and indeed to many of those who reject meta-ethical relativism, as well as to many who would defend it. For on the orthodox view of the matter, although cultures are composed of a complex—and, initially, seemingly disparate—array of uniformities in beliefs, values, and practices, cultures are nonetheless amenable to both individuation and description, principally because they exhibit a high degree of internal, and generally coherent, integration. According to this influential doctrine of cultural integration, the seemingly disparate elements of the way of life of any group—its culture—can always be understood to form a generally coherent whole (which is somehow more than the mere sum of its parts). The doctrine of cultural integration typically also implies that any significant element in that whole can be expected to exhibit a fair degree of integration, both internally and relative to other elements in the culture. Still further, the beliefs, values, and practices that (among other things) have a special importance in maintaining the continued life of the group—its morality—are normally construed as "significant" in the relevant sense. Now, it is interesting and important (if the standard histories of the evolution of the culture concept are correct) that

the notion of cultural integration was initially a product of the philosophical antecedents of anthropology—especially in the writings of
J. G. Herder—and thus had questionable empirical credentials from the
beginning.[29] But many social scientists now consider the notion to be a
prerequisite to the scientific study of culture. The doctrine has played
a particularly prominent role in relativist claims that it is "impossible"
to understand some particular belief or practice apart from the cultural
context in which it is found (Benedict 1934b). Yet the notion of cultural
integration is widely influential in the empirical study of cultures primarily because it is neutral between the various definitions of culture
that now compete for acceptance in the social sciences (Herbert 1991).

The heterodox view that I defend, by contrast, recommends rejecting the notion of cultural integration because it is incapable of generating a plausible picture of the social world, and thus prevents real
understanding of the complex relation between morality and culture.
Consider a classic statement of cultural integration in Evans-Pritchard's
discussion of Zande witchcraft. He insists of the Azande that "all their
beliefs hang together, and were a Zande to give up faith in witch-
doctorhood he would have to surrender equally his belief in witchcraft
and oracles . . . In this web of belief every strand depends upon every
other strand, and a Zande cannot get out of its meshes because this is
the only world he knows. The web is not an external structure in which
he is enclosed. It is the texture of his thought and he cannot think that
his thought is wrong" (Evans-Pritchard 1937, 194–195). This is an
extraordinary passage in many respects, but what is perhaps most extraordinary is that there is no way to verify its central claims empirically. As Dan Sperber has argued, ethnographic evidence alone could
not support any assertion that a particular array of beliefs is truly integrated into a coherent whole (Sperber 1985, 46). Moreover, the insistence on "finding" a set of essentially coherent and integrated beliefs
often leads an ethnographer to ignore empirical evidence that might
show just how complex, and occasionally inconsistent, the beliefs of any
culture may be. It is thus that Evans-Pritchard's many claims that "the
Zande" are trapped in a "web of belief" are called into question, for
they are not easily reconciled with his reports of "a considerable body
of sceptical opinion in many departments of Zande culture, and especially in regard to their witch-doctors" (Evans-Pritchard 1937, 183).

Evans-Pritchard's willingness to generalize about "the Zande mind," in spite of the complexity of Zande beliefs—like Brandt's speculations about the "Hopi subconscious"—rather mysteriously suggests that there might be some one entity that believes, thinks, and reacts as an integral whole, in accordance with some fixed cultural pattern. If this sort of mystical stance about the possibility of group minds is a prerequisite to the doctrine of descriptive cultural relativism, it becomes less and less clear why so many thinkers have taken that doctrine to be a simple "scientific" and "empirical" one. For such claims clearly conflict with obvious and important facts about social differentiation and differences in belief.

An illuminating discussion by the linguist and anthropologist Edward Sapir helps to clarify the cultural importance of social differentiation. Sapir had attempted to make sense of a curious feature of a once quite influential ethnographic study, titled *Omaha Sociology* (1884), by J. O. Dorsey. In several passages of the study, Dorsey would first describe some custom, belief, or attitude that virtually all of his informants wholeheartedly agreed upon, only to go on to indicate that one reliable and authoritative informant did not agree: again and again Dorsey felt moved to inform the reader that "Two Crows denies this" (Sapir 1985, 569–570). Sapir speculated that the ethnographer must have confronted circumstances that made it reasonable to conclude not that Two Crows did not know his culture, or that his testimony was somehow unreliable, but that Two Crows had his own version of Omaha culture. Sapir went on to stress the importance of recognizing in every culture—even in the "preliterate," "premodern" societies that anthropologists so commonly studied at the time—the existence of unique individual human beings whose knowledge of a culture would always be mediated by a variety of institutions. He even contemplated the possibility that, in a sense, each individual has her own culture—or perhaps her own subculture (Sapir 1985, 321; 515). Sapir seems to have thought that cultures, so understood, might still manifest a high degree of integration (Sapir 1985, 515–522). But even if it were reasonable to maintain that each person's culture—or version of a culture—manifests a high degree of internal integration, Sapir's view would still require far more attention to facts about social differentiation than either Evans-Pritchard or Brandt appears ready to allow.

But the existence of reliable informants who plausibly deny particular assertions from other reliable informants poses an even more serious challenge to the idea of cultural integration than Sapir acknowledged. It is on this basis, for instance, that some anthropologists have challenged influential ethnographies which virtually exclude the testimony of the women in a culture. These theorists sometimes simply emphasize the distorting consequences of such neglect, which presumes that the experience and cultural understanding of women is only incidental to obtaining a complete picture of a culture (Scheper-Hughes 1984, 91; Weiner 1976; Ardener 1975). But they have also noted that in follow-up studies, carried out with the intention to redress the balance between the testimony of women and men informants, women informants in some cultures have sometimes produced versions of important cultural practices that are vastly different from, and sometimes even incompatible with, those offered by men (Weiner 1976; Scheper-Hughes 1984). Such results raise serious concerns about the selectiveness, the incompleteness, and ultimately the unreliability of ethnographies that depend only (or even principally) on the testimony of particular social groups (McCarthy 1992).

Yet by far the most important catalyst for reflection on these matters is that ethnographers have *themselves* produced conflicting accounts of various cultures. This is a phenomenon that many ethnographers have come to describe as the "Rashomon Effect," after Kurosawa's 1950 film *Rashomon*, which depicts four quite different, and in many ways conflicting, accounts of a single encounter in the woods of twelfth-century Japan—and which never endorses any of the four as the correct account (Heider 1988). The Rashomon Effect in ethnography has involved disagreement over significant elements of some particularly well studied cultures, and it has involved the work of extremely important figures in anthropology. For instance, central features of Benedict's account of the culture of the Zuni of the American Southwest faced a significant challenge in the late 1930s (Herskovits 1964, 51–52). More recently, Malinowski's claims about the applicability of Freudian psychology to cultural phenomena in the Trobriand Islands—specifically his insistence that the Oedipus complex is absent in the Trobriand archipelago—have been criticized by the contemporary American anthropologist Melford Spiro (Spiro

1982).[30] But perhaps the most famous—and in many respects the most accessible and instructive—controversy is that generated in response to Derek Freeman's attack, in *Margaret Mead and Samoa* (1983), on Mead's claims in *Coming of Age in Samoa* (1928). For philosophers interested in the relevance of anthropology to philosophy, this debate suggests that the Rashomon Effect should raise important doubts about the doctrine of cultural integration.

As is well known, Mead had defended several generalizations about the attitude toward sexuality among her Samoan informants—for whom, she claimed, sex was free of guilt and repression. She had also argued that the results of her Samoan research provided an "anthropological veto" of a then-influential hypothesis that there is a biological basis for the Sturm und Drang of adolescence (Mead 1961, 1–5). She even based an eloquent and influential plea for American educational reform on her claims about the relation between adolescent stress and cultural conditions. More than fifty years later Freeman vehemently rejected virtually all of Mead's claims. He insisted, for instance, not simply that Mead's generalizations were wrong, but that they also manifested an unacknowledged readiness to confirm "cultural determinist" theories at the price of empirical accuracy. But some of his most pointed objections concerned Mead's descriptive claims about Samoan behavior and attitudes, especially attitudes toward sexuality. Freeman contended that his findings revealed that Samoans actually accepted quite puritanical, guilt-ridden, and repressive attitudes that shaped particularly rigid cultural expectations about the control of adolescent sexuality (Freeman 1983). He claimed, in effect, to have discovered a set of traits, beliefs, and practices concerning Samoan sexuality that were just the reverse of those that Mead had claimed to find.

It is neither possible nor relevant to try to settle here some of the thornier questions surrounding the correct evaluation of the work of Mead and Freeman. Yet crucial facts about the different circumstances under which they obtained their respective data are central to my discussion. As the anthropologist Nancy Scheper-Hughes has suggested, those circumstances—and the social differentiation and cultural complexity they reveal—make it implausible that Freeman's data could have been a corrective to Mead's (Scheper-Hughes 1984). It is significant, for example, that Mead's fieldwork was done when she was a twenty-three-year-old graduate student, and that she relied primarily (and deliberately) on data collected from about fifty adolescent Samoan females—of principally non-titled social status—ranging in age from eight to twenty. Several commentators have noted that the picture of Samoan culture likely to emerge from data obtained by a young female graduate student interviewing adolescent girls of modest social status should be expected to differ from the picture that a mature male could obtain from his middle-aged and socially well placed male informants.[31] Even further, Mead obtained her data during a nine-month stay on the island of Ta'u in the Manu'a island group of American Samoa, while Freeman's data were obtained primarily from Western Samoa. The quite different colonial histories of these two regions would surely have been registered in the cultural phenomena that each ethnographer encountered (Weiner 1983). Finally, much of Freeman's data was obtained several years after Mead's 1925 fieldwork, and all cultures change over time.

Mead's answers to some of her Samoan critics, in her prefaces to later editions of *Coming of Age in Samoa*, indicate that debate about Mead's portrayal eventually became an important element of the culture it claimed only to describe. Of course, it is important to ask whether Freeman and Mead provide an accurate account of the interviews and the other data that each relied on—though this inquiry raises issues that cannot be treated here. Yet, given well-known facts about the extent to which different social groups tend to produce strikingly different accounts of the culture they presumably share, it is simply implausible that Freeman's data could yield a more accurate account of Samoan culture *in its entirety* than Mead's data could. Scheper-Hughes goes on to argue that the more fundamental error—and perhaps an important shortcoming of Mead's own early work, as of Freeman's response to Mead's work on Samoa—is the notion that Samoan culture might be a "single integrated reality somewhere 'out there' waiting to be accurately described" (Scheper-Hughes 1984, 91). I have already indicated how the phenomenon of social differentiation yields important reasons for thinking that Scheper-Hughes is right.

But it is important to consider in more detail how the assumption of cultural integration leads ethnographers to ignore internal skepticism about—as well as epistemological and behavioral distance from—a given set of cultural forms. Evans-Pritchard's impatience with those Azande whose skeptical attitudes might have challenged his claims about the Zande "web of belief" is a particularly striking instance of this phenomenon. He frequently complains about Zande royalty, for instance, whom he found distant and unforthcoming, and thus "with rare exceptions . . . useless as informants" (Evans-Pritchard 1937, 13–14). Further, after discussing the attitudes of several informants whom he believed to have been "closely associated with court life" and thus to have acquired the "detached attitude of the nobles towards Zande (commoner) practices," he contends that his "informant, Kuagbiaru, had the same detached viewpoint as a result of even closer association with court life. He was never deeply moved by revelations of witch-doctors, and even treated them with a measure of open contempt" (Evans-Pritchard 1937, 184). Yet he then claims to know that Kuagbiaru's mockery was "only half serious," and he goes on to insist that the reader must not "get the impression that there is anyone who disbelieves in witch-doctorhood." The ethnographer's apparent disdain, and even personal dislike, for the "detached attitude" of the uncooperative royal class—whose attitudes seemed to pose a problem for his web-of-belief account—is an important and disturbing element in explaining his curious readiness virtually to dismiss a "considerable body" of skeptical opinion (Evans-Pritchard 1937, 184–185). Moreover, had Evans-Pritchard explored the implications of the links between Zande social class, on the one hand, and commitment to witchcraft and magic, on the other, he might have provided an intriguing contribution to the sociology of knowledge. Writing at roughly the same time, Robert Lowie insisted that variations in class position, and especially in experience, could be reliably counted on to create "primitive skeptics" (Lowie 1933).

Other aspects of Evans-Pritchard's treatment of Zande thought merit even closer attention. In the very same paragraph in which the reader is informed that a Zande "cannot think that his thought is wrong," Evans-Pritchard unexpectedly observes: "Nevertheless, his beliefs are not absolutely set but are variable and fluctuating to allow for different situations and to permit empirical observations and even doubts" (Evans-Pritchard 1937, 195). Here, as elsewhere, Evans-Pritchard acknowledges the existence of doubt. Yet the passage also attempts to render the existence of that doubt compatible with his assertions about the Zande "web" of belief by suggesting that the Azande have an unfailing tendency to *adapt* their doubts so as to preserve maximum coherence among their beliefs. But Evans-Pritchard offers no *argument* to support these claims (Archer 1988, 8–9). Once one admits the possibility of internal skepticism and doubt in a culture, there is no obvious reason to assume that this skepticism is unproblematically reintegrated into some new form of cultural coherence (Archer 1988, 9). Equally important, in many of those passages which reiterate this assumption, Evans-Pritchard makes some curiously inconsistent generalizations about the temperament of the Azande. He contends, for instance, that the Azande are "almost always cheerful and sociable . . . [T]hey adapt themselves without undue difficulty to new conditions of life and are always ready to copy the behaviour of those they regard as their superiors in culture" (Evans-Pritchard 1937, 13). Later he adds that the Azande are "always laughing and joking" (Evans-Pritchard 1937, 148). But this picture of a people always "cheerful" and always "laughing and joking" does not square with much of what Evans-Pritchard claims elsewhere in the book. In an extended discussion of the circumstances in which accusations of witchcraft are generally made, the reader is informed that "in the daily tasks of life there is ample scope for friction. In the household there is frequent occasion for ill-feeling between husband and wife and between wife and co-wife arising from division of labour and sexual jealousies. Among his neighbours a man is sure to have both secret and open enemies . . . One man may have uttered unguarded words which have been repeated to another . . . All unkind words and malicious actions and innuendoes are stored in the memory for retaliation" (Evans-Pritchard 1937, 101). Even if this passage contains its own exaggerations, if it is even partially true, it cannot then be the case that the Azande "are always laughing and joking." Evans-Pritchard's efforts to defend the "seamless web" account of Zande beliefs against such obvious counterevidence leads him to reassert some familiar prejudices about the temperament of African peoples—prejudices whose crudeness runs contrary to the usual complexity of his observations about the frictions of daily life. Commentators rightly argue that, in general, Evans-Pritchard's concern to represent the fully developed humanity of his subjects was unusual among ethnographers of his day.[32] This is why it is particularly striking that he must not only endanger the consistency and believability of his ethnography but also relinquish his usual respect for the humanity of his subjects in order to preserve the myth of cultural integration.

Evans-Pritchard seems to have thought that the doctrine of cultural integration provided a means to counter the once influential view that there is a radical difference between the "prelogical," fundamentally mystical mental habits of the "primitive" (those allegedly indifferent to the law of contradiction) and the supposedly more rational, "scientific" mind of the "modern." In his foreword to the English translation of Lévy-Bruhl's *"Soul" of the Primitive*, for instance, Evans-Pritchard insisted that Lévy-Bruhl had "overstated the case" about "primitive mentality" (Evans-Pritchard 1966, 5–6). The "web of belief" account is presumably Evans-Pritchard's attempt to avoid the excesses of Lévy-Bruhl's view. He tries to show that, interpreted within the context of that "web" (and the practices governed by it), Zande beliefs have a coherence—and hence an order—that could not be discerned from without. Yet some sympathetic critics have argued that Evans-Pritchard's view does not go far enough. Thus, Winch insists that Evans-Pritchard failed to recognize how completely "the concepts used by primitive peoples can only be interpreted in the context of the way of life of those peoples" (Winch 1972, 28). Unfortunately, Winch never acknowledges that this prescription raises questions about how the very task of ethnography is possible. Such questions seldom trouble those relativist anthropologists who defend the doctrine of cultural integration as a means (in Shweder's phrase) of giving "permission" to unfamiliar ways of life—often by asserting the "noncomparability" of ways of life. Yet while theorists such as Shweder and Winch, among others, envision the doctrine as a way of narrowing the gulf between the unfamiliar ways of various "others" and that way of life allegedly accepted by "us," reliance on the doctrine actually widens the gulf between cultures by encouraging an ultimately implausible conception of the epistemological, moral, and attitudinal *exclusivity* of ways of life.

A typical manifestation of this conception of exclusivity can be found in Winch's insistence that the Azande engage in practices that it is "peculiarly" difficult for "us" to understand. Another instance of this way of thinking is Bernard Williams's contention that some ways of life are not "a real option for us" (Williams 1981; 1985). Williams has never been terribly precise about what makes a way of life a "real option," though he offers a few examples of "outlooks" that he believes are no longer real options for "us," such as the life of a Bronze Age chief or a medieval samurai (Williams 1985, 161). Moreover, he has complicated the discussion by maintaining that "today" all confrontations between existing cultures (even between modern technological societies and "exotic traditional" groups) must be real, and not merely "notional," confrontations. Yet his fundamental point is that whenever some way of life can offer "us" a merely notional confrontation, the "language of appraisal—good, bad, right, wrong" is not applicable to that way of life (Williams 1985, 163; 160–161). But such claims are most curious in light of Williams's simultaneous defense of a view that undermines attempts to draw sharp boundaries between "us" and various cultural "others." In the relevant passages he argues quite convincingly that because cultures "constantly meet one another and exchange and modify practices," it is implausible that social practices might "come forward with a certificate saying that they belonged to a genuinely different culture" and might thereby be insulated from "alien" judgments and responses (Williams 1985, 158). These passages offer a more plausible account of the terms under which cultures confront one another. For as Clifford Geertz has argued, "The social world does not divide at its joints into perspicuous we's with whom we can empathize, however much we differ *with* them, and enigmatical they's with whom we cannot, however much we defend to the death their right to differ *from* us" (Geertz 1986, 262). Winch typically defends the alternative conception by reference to the uniquely "mystical" nature of the "primitive" (Winch 1972). Williams's account, by contrast, tends to gives greater emphasis to the "unreflective" nature of life in "traditional" societies (Williams 1985, 163–164). But both views are implicated in a powerful irony: there is no conception more mystical or unreflective than the doctrine of cultural integration, along with its usual companion, the assumption that beliefs and values of "traditional" or "primitive" societies must be *more* integrated than those of any other.

Contemporary anthropologists have finally begun to question whether making sense of cultural differences requires that any culture be designed like a seamless web.[33] Some anthropologists even suggest that it is only by rejecting the doctrine of cultural integration and accepting a more complex view of cultures and the social world in general that a plausible anthropology is possible (Carrithers 1992; cf. Turner 1974, 13–14). A more complex view of the social world helps explain Brandt's difficulties in establishing the existence of fundamental ethical disagreement. For however "notorious" (in Brandt's phrase) or "peculiar" (in Winch's) some practice found in an unfamiliar culture might seem from any particular point *outside* that culture, it is always possible to find a similar manifestation of such behavior from some point *within* one's own, more familiar culture. Thus, for instance, to the American activist who believes (and acts on the belief) that the interests of non-human animals deserve equal consideration with those of human beings, the behavior of a fellow American who consistently rejects this conception will seem as notorious as any described in Brandt's examples. Similarly, to the religious atheist or the agnostic, various components of the religious devotee's beliefs will seem markedly peculiar. Anyone not convinced of this point need only consider the vehemence of various eighteenth- and nineteenth-century debates about the doctrine of transubstantiation. Further, even if a particular kind of behavior to be found in the familiar place is not a socially sanctioned practice, it may still play the sort of role envisioned here: in societies that do not sanction cannibalism, the survivors of a plane crash who sustain themselves by consuming human flesh become objects of widespread fascination. Finally, in many societies the children of ill, aged parents may sometimes contemplate the moral acceptability of euthanasia, in spite of often widespread social disapproval of the practice.

When Brandt acknowledges that there actually might be some socially sanctioned circumstances under which whole communities who condemn cannibalism might modify their condemnation (and even change their behavior), he makes an important concession to my claim about the most plausible picture of the social world. Attributions—or, more to the point, *accusations*—of socially sanctioned cannibalism have historically been powerful rhetorical devices for characterizing ways of life that are not "real" options for "us" (Arens 1970, 7–9).[34] Brandt's confidence that his readers might find the beliefs that underwrite a social practice of cannibalism intelligible and accessible—even if not wholly comfortable—is thus quite extraordinary. Given that confidence, it is difficult to fathom his assumption that the indifference to animal suffering that he found in certain "primitive" societies would somehow be uniquely unfamiliar to members of "modern" societies. But the doctrine of cultural integration embodies a potent mythology, and the descriptive cultural relativism that presupposes that mythology has come to have so great a hold on thinking about culture and morality that even the most reflective treatments of the central issues will give way in the face of it. Brandt's account embodies one of the most plausible and reflective attempts to locate "one ultimate difference" in ethical principle between cultures. His failure to find fundamental conflict thus suggests that the doctrine of descriptive relativism is in serious trouble.

An examination of the precise way in which Brandt's view fails yields important insights about the methodology of moral interpretation. It reveals that the interpretation of unfamiliar moral practices must proceed on the assumption that there is a way, in language familiar to the interpreter, to supply a pattern of situational meaning (not only factual beliefs but also affective associations) that might explain why the people concerned value the action or practice under consideration. This is not a denial of moral diversity and disagreement. A vehement defender of monogamy who disapproves of polygamy, for instance, can supply a set of factual beliefs and affective associations that make sense of a group's defense of the practice of polygamy without relinquishing her disapproval. But I contend that moral disagreement is possible only where there is quite substantial agreement about many of the basic concepts that are relevant to moral reflection. If these claims make the Gestalt theorist's insistence on the importance of situational meanings sound like a proto-Davidsonian view of moral interpretation, then that is all to the good.[35] As David Cooper has argued, central features of Donald Davidson's claims about interpretation are likely to make better sense of moral disagreement than any moral relativisms that claim to take disagreement seriously (Cooper 1978). Ladd was critical of Brandt's descriptive ethics because it appeared likely to yield a study of the extent to which the Hopi accepted "principles like our own." Yet a judgment or belief can be a moral judgment or belief only if it fits into a complex of beliefs and judgments that, to a substantial degree, resemble one's own moral beliefs and judgments.[36] The interpretation of unfamiliar moral practices is possible only because "ultimate" or "fundamental" moral disagreement is not.

THE PERSPICUOUS "OTHER": RELATIVISM "GROWN TAME AND SLEEK"

Meta-ethical relativists who take some version of descriptive cultural relativism to be an important foundation for their views will be especially impatient with these claims. They are likely to insist that my arguments about the methodological obstacles to descriptive cultural relativism, and about the way in which the doctrine of cultural integration obscures social differentiation and cultural complexity, simply ignore the most important contributions of relativism. Herskovits, for instance, often characterized relativism as the inescapable consequence of recognizing the force of "enculturative conditioning" (Herskovits 1972, 32; 56). Relativists may thus cite the theory of enculturation as one of their most important contributions to thinking about morality. They will probably insist that an understanding of enculturation is most likely to reveal precisely *how* relativism takes disagreement seriously, and thereby makes better sense of the social world than alternative views. Yet it is not clear why accepting the fact of enculturation— acknowledging the role of culture in influencing belief and behavior— must commit one to any relativist conclusions, even the supposedly "simple" empirical doctrine of descriptive cultural relativism. It is certainly true that every culture develops patterns of normative expectations about emotion, thought, and action which help to structure the formative experiences of each person in a given culture-bearing group. Moreover, an upbringing in accordance with these normative expectations will profoundly influence the character of even the most fundamental desires and purposes likely to be manifested in human action. But these facts do not prove anything about the correctness of either descriptive or meta-ethical relativism.

Consider one of Herskovits's most important examples claiming an inescapable link between the fact of enculturation and more robust relativist doctrines: the polygamous family structure of the West African nation of Dahomey, which he encountered during his fieldwork in the 1930s. Herskovits rightly contends that he is giving the reader a chance to look at Dahomean family life "from the point of view of those who practice it" (Herskovits 1972, 14). What Herskovits offers is thus a sympathetic description—or redescription—of an unfamiliar practice. Yet that redescription actually confirms my claims about the methodology of moral interpretation—that such an account, in order to be accessible to an outsider, must appeal (in part) to values that are in some respect familiar to the presumed audience. Herskovits first describes the ways in which the Dahomean family structure allowed parents to perform a variety of familiar economic and social tasks bound up with raising children (Herskovits 1972, 13–14). He then shows how Dahomean approval of the polygamous family as a central social and economic unit revealed their acceptance of an important—and once again *familiar*—distinction between "serious" and "casual" sexual relations. He even emphasizes that when Dahomeans "who know European culture . . . argue for their system," they contend that it permits individual wives to space their children "in accord with the best precepts of modern gynecology." But this, too, only strengthens my case. In trying to make their practice of polygamy intelligible to outsiders by means of concepts familiar to those outsiders, Dahomean men were in fact relying on some of the most basic principles of moral interpretation. In so doing, they recognized the importance of a fact that the relativist (like the Rortean ethnocentrist) is reluctant to acknowledge: cultural understanding is possible precisely because no culture is a windowless monad.

The explanatory posture of those Dahomeans—and of Herskovits, in his most careful moments—also shows why Winch's account of cultural understanding ultimately goes awry. Winch argues at one point that "seriously to study another way of life is necessarily to seek to extend our own—not simply to bring the other way within the already existing boundaries of our own, because the point about the latter in their present form, is that they *ex hypothesi* exclude the other" (Winch 1972, 33). He rightly observes that studying an unfamiliar way of life extends one's own: learning, for instance, that more than one mode of family organization may promote values that one takes to be important will indeed extend one's understanding both of those values themselves and of the unfamiliar practices that seek to promote them. But this extended understanding would not be possible if the practices, beliefs, and values which a particular observer finds familiar truly did completely "exclude" those of an unfamiliar way of life. It is because the Dahomean culture described by Herskovits manifests a quite familiar concern for the care of children, for instance, that it is possible to understand how Dahomean marriage practices embodied important features of that concern. Winch simply fails to appreciate the circumstances that make it possible to understand an unfamiliar way of life. Moreover, as I have tried to show, even the characteristics of so-called "traditional" or "primitive" societies cannot make Winch's account any more plausible. Every society—even in the industrialized Western world—contains complex cultural phenomena that display profound mysticism, unreflectiveness, and even deep inconsistencies. These phenomena can be potent forces in shaping the beliefs and practices of social groups—such as social scientists and philosophers—who are allegedly least likely to be affected by them. Indeed, as I have suggested, some of the most mystical elements of Western cultures are revealed in widespread assumptions about the notion of culture itself.

Few critics of polygamy would be converted to approval of the practice solely on the strength of Herskovits's account of it. Probably most would not be converted even on the strength of several even more sympathetic accounts, such as Herskovits himself tries to provide. At one point, for instance, he urges that the polygamous family has economic resources and a degree of stability "that might well be envied" by outsiders (Herskovits 1972, 14). Someone who is particularly enamored of economic and social stability, to the exclusion of other considerations, might be a candidate to make the evaluative leap capable of transforming understanding into approval. But others who come to understand polygamy as an alternative way of expressing concern for some values that they prize may nonetheless insist that the practice embodies other values (concerning the status of women, perhaps) that they simply will not embrace as an alternative for themselves. But there is nothing mysterious in this. In the language of the Gestalt theorist, those who fail to make the evaluative leap simply continue to disagree about the situational meaning of polygamy. The importance of enculturation to understanding their tendency to accept a particular pattern of situational meanings is justly stressed by anthropologists, relativist and non-relativist alike.

Herskovits rightly would insist that it was never the purpose of relativism to create converts to unfamiliar practices, even though early accounts of the doctrine stressed the practical benefits of the relativist view that much of human life (including a preference for polygamy or monogamy) is a product of "culture" and not of "nature." Herskovits would claim, instead, that relativism is "in essence a new approach to the question of the nature and role of values in culture": relativism reveals, he argues, that when an unfamiliar practice is examined *from the point of view of those who practice it*, it can be "seen to hold values that are not apparent from the outside" (Herskovits 1972, 14). Indeed, though he makes a special effort to display the hitherto unseen values of polygamy, he also emphasizes that a "similar" case can be made for monogamy "when it is attacked by those who are enculturated to a different kind of family structure" (Herskovits 1972, 14). But—to borrow D. G. Ritchie's apt characterization of Henry Sidgwick's utilitarianism—what Herskovits has offered here is a relativism "grown tame and sleek."[37] While stressing the influence of enculturation, this tame and sleek relativism also incorporates the quite plausible hypothesis that unfamiliar practices can be seen to "hold values that are not apparent from the outside." And ethnographic activity premised on this hypothesis implicitly assumes the potentially perspicuous "other": it assumes that it is often possible to understand the point of view of those who have unfamiliar practices. In fact, the identification and interpretation of unfamiliar practices essentially depends on an observer's ability to make important elements of an unfamiliar way of life intelligible in familiar terms.

But the hypothesis of the potentially perspicuous other challenges the notion that one might understand ways of life that are essentially "noncomparable" with, or radically alien to, the way of life with which one is familiar. Indeed, it points to the fact that the identification and interpretation of moral practices is particularly dependent on the "comparability" of ways of life. As my analysis of Herskovits's example reveals, it is possible to recognize and describe a *moral* disagreement between cultures—however imperfectly and provisionally—only when it is also possible to find familiar moral values on which the cultures in question agree. But how could it be possible to find familiar moral values to serve as the basis of moral disagreement unless judgments of moral value simply cannot be confined to one culturally or socially bounded "place"? The same processes that create cultural space for "modern" mystics and "primitive" skeptics leave room for substantial moral complexity within cultures, and it is the complexity of human cultures that consistently thwarts relativist efforts to confine moral judgments to any one culturally bounded "place." Relativism simply ignores the internal complexity of cultures which makes cross-cultural moral disagreement possible. One who would take moral disagreement *seriously* should thus reject the relativist's understanding of cultural diversity in moral practices.

2

THE USE
AND ABUSE
OF HISTORY

To me the most important question, is a methodological one: whether social anthropology, for all its present disregard of history, is not itself a kind of historiography.

E. E. Evans-Pritchard,
Social Anthropology and Other Essays

The culture of any society at any moment is more like the debris, or "fall-out," of past ideological systems, than it is itself a system, a coherent whole.

Victor Turner, Dramas, Fields, and Metaphors

HISTORY, ETHNOGRAPHY, AND THE BLURRING OF CULTURAL BOUNDARIES

The internal complexity of cultures, I have argued, consistently thwarts relativist efforts to confine moral judgments to a single culture. Any conception of cultural diversity in moral practices that is invoked to license such efforts embodies an inadequate understanding of culture. Cultural boundaries are not morally impenetrable walls. Neither, however, are the boundaries of historical eras. Any human being who learns a natural language, I argue in this chapter, is capable of reinterpreting moral conceptions, beliefs, and sentiments revealed in reflection on some past era, thereby becoming a morally credentialed "insider" of the most serious kind. I thus reject what might be called—adapting a phrase from Bernard Williams—the relativism of historical distance, which denies that moral judgments made by contemporary critics can legitimately apply to the past. It is sometimes thought that this kind of relativism can be independent of the broader claims of meta-ethical relativism. This is the stance, for instance, of those who decry the "relativism" of multiculturalist challenges to the conventional history curriculum, yet insist that it is illegitimate to criticize figures such as Jefferson for failing to uphold the moral standards "of our time." But claims about the limited historical reach of moral judgments rest on the same problematic presuppositions as does meta-ethical relativism about contemporaneous cultures. A consistent anti-relativism, as I show here, demands the rejection of historical relativism.

Yet the relativism of historical distance represents a distinctive application of the claims of meta-ethical relativism in two respects. First, unlike relativism about contemporaneous cultures, the relativism of historical distance typically presumes that the history of moral thinking is a history of progress driven by the emergence of new moral ideas. In this chapter I provide the groundwork for challenging this view. I deny that there is ever anything really "new" in moral thinking—as a prelude to more extensive discussion, in Chapter 4, of the interpretive nature of moral argument and inquiry. But the relativism of historical distance is distinctive in a second way: it reveals more fully than other forms of meta-ethical relativism just how weak the empirical credentials of descriptive cultural relativism really are. The descriptive cultural relativism underwriting most meta-ethical relativisms, I have argued, presupposes the doctrine of cultural integration. But the doctrine of cultural integration seldom stands alone. It is typically linked, implicitly or explicitly, with two other assumptions: first, the notion that cultures are fully individuable, self-contained wholes, and second, the view that the capacity for moral agency is culturally determined. The tendency to connect the doctrine of cultural integration with the concepts of fully individuable cultures and cultural determinism can be found in relativist treatments of moral conflicts between contemporaneous cultures. It is especially pronounced, however, in relativist efforts to challenge the application of "contemporary" moral judgments to the past. But moral relativism, as I show, simply makes bad historiography. The idea of fully individuable cultures fails to acknowledge the historical interconnection of cultures. Moreover, cultural determinism embodies an implausible moral psychology: it is an empirically underdetermined, and fundamentally indefensible, account of the relationship between culture and moral agency.

The assumption of cultural integration, I have suggested, tends to be conjoined with the notion that it is possible to locate and describe fully individuable, self-contained cultural wholes. The methodology of relativist anthropology, in particular, often links these claims. Thus, Benedict's *Patterns of Culture* purports to describe societies that are both internally integrated and fully self-contained: "A culture, like an individual, is a more or less consistent pattern of thought and action" (Benedict 1934b, 46). Each of the "primitive societies" described, according to Benedict, contains a single uniform cultural tradition; in each society "the manners and morals of the group" are molded to "one well-defined general pattern" that is "simple enough to be contained within the knowledge of individual adults" (Benedict 1934b, 17–18).[1] In relativist understandings of culture, however—in philosophy as well as anthropology—the notion of cultures as fully individuable is the more fundamental concept. Even Benedict believed that not all cultures actually achieve internal integration. "Like certain individuals," she contends, "certain social orders do not subordinate activities to a ruling motivation" (Benedict 1934b, 223). She continued to maintain, however, that all cultures are nonetheless fully individuable "articulated wholes." This is why, on her view, one can thoroughly participate in a culture only if one "has been brought up and lived according to its forms" (Benedict 1934b, 37; 48).

Evans-Pritchard's development of such views, though not rooted in an explicitly relativist methodology, has helped to shape contemporary philosophical understandings of culture and history. That he thought of existing cultures as fully individuable and self-contained wholes is amply illustrated in his contention, discussed in Chapter 1, that the Azande were inextricably enmeshed in a "web of belief." The conception of culture underlying such claims has been especially influential in those varieties of moral philosophy, and the philosophy of social explanation, influenced by Wittgenstein's later writings. As Jonathan Lear has shown, proponents of these views commonly argue for the "autonomy" of existing cultures, and then rely on the notion of cultural autonomy to argue that cultures are ultimately immune from the evaluation and criticism of cultural "outsiders" (Lear 1984, 144–146). Evans-Pritchard's anthropology retains a central place in philosophical debates about the merits of relativism because it helps support such claims about cultural autonomy.[2] But Evans-Pritchard actively extends the conception of cultures as internally integrated and fully individuable to the study of history. In some of his later theoretical essays, he claims that there is a special relationship between the anthropological study of "primitive cultures," on the one hand, and historical research into the past of modern Western societies, on the other hand. Wherever historical documents are "not too vast to be grasped and assimilated by a single mind," he contends, the "total culture can be studied as a whole and contained in a single mind, as primitive cultures can be studied and contained" (Evans-Pritchard 1962, 151). Evans-Pritchard's commitment to the idea of fully individuable cultures is thus of special interest to relativists of historical distance.

Yet sympathetic critics of relativism have cautioned against excessive confidence in the idea of fully individuable cultures. As I noted in Chapter 1, Bernard Williams rightly warns that a fully self-contained culture is "at best a rare thing." His warning is rooted in the recognition that vast continuities and similarities between the practices of diverse cultures substantially complicate any effort to draw determinate boundaries around each culture. Williams's view thus signals a fundamental shortcoming of standard relativist views: their tendency to concentrate on the *differences* between cultures at the expense of facts about cultural overlap, continuity, and similarity. The pursuit of difference, moreover, suggests how powerfully relativism may be fueled by exoticism—by a fascination with practices that are (allegedly) most unlike those in the theorist's own culture. From Herodotus' claims that "custom is king" to Shweder's "post-Nietzschean" celebrations of the anthropologist's "astonishment" at diversity and difference, a veritable fetishism of strangeness has helped to shape relativist accounts of cultural practices. Some theorists have even assumed that establishing a way of life as a "genuine" culture actually *requires* an effort to preserve the purported strangeness of its practices. Evans-Pritchard underscores this point:

> Magic and oracles are more difficult for us to understand than most other primitive practices and therefore more profitable a subject for study than customs which invite easy explanations. Any European can at once comprehend, and even respect, a cult of the dead, but when presented with an account of African magic it appears to him as so much nonsense . . . For our own culture comprises notions of the soul and of life after death and Gods, so that we are at once able to translate Zande beliefs about these entities into terms of our own culture and to find them reasonable, if mistaken. (Evans-Pritchard 1937, 313)

But the presuppositions of this passage are deeply problematic. For what could justify the claim that a cult of the dead "invites easy explanation" while a belief in witches does not? Agnostics, atheists, and behaviorists in Evans-Pritchard's own Britain might have found several aspects of a cult of the dead to be as "difficult" as any notion bound up with Zande belief in witchcraft. Peter Winch, in his analysis of the philosophical relevance of Evans-Pritchard's claims, confidently asserts the "peculiarity" of Zande beliefs that "certain of their members are witches, exercising a malignant occult influence on the lives of their fellows" (Winch 1972, 8). Yet such beliefs have familiar analogues even in the practices of contemporary Western liberal democracies. The demonization of Communists and their "sympathizers" in the United States—reaching a fever pitch in the McCarthy era—certainly borders on an appeal to occult influence. More recent efforts to demonize homosexuals, or feminists, or even (in the American context) "liberals," are likewise not terribly far removed from Zande beliefs in witchcraft. Still further, even if it were possible to explain the distinction between customs that invite easy explanation and those that do not, why should customs deemed *most difficult* to explain be thought the best subjects for the formal study of cultures?

Evans-Pritchard claims that the difficulty of some alien views will obstruct attempts to assimilate them to "our own": "Along this path lie many pitfalls, because the desire to assimilate primitive notions to kindred notions of our own tempts us . . . to read into their beliefs concepts peculiar to our own, and . . . to interpret their beliefs by introspection or in terms of our own sentiments" (Evans-Pritchard 1937, 313). Yet he later contends that the first "main phase" of the anthropologist's task is precisely "to understand the significant overt features of a culture and to translate them into terms of his own culture" (Evans-Pritchard 1962, 149). The irony in this stance is instructive: it shows the implausibility of the notion that any culture might really be a fully self-contained whole, whose practices can be understood only in terms of their relation to that whole. Familiar ethnographic methods—learning a language, interrogating informants, engaging in participant observation—are feasible means of learning about a culture only if cultures are not fully self-contained entities. The ethnographic endeavor itself thus quickly defeats any claim to have identified a fully self-contained culture. But the irony of Evans-Pritchard's stance also suggests that something more than exoticism motivates continued commitment to the idea of fully self-contained cultures. Even Evans-Pritchard continued to defend the idea long after recognizing that his ethnographies had made several previously unfamiliar practices at least moderately accessible to outside audiences.

What ultimately sustains the idea of fully self-contained cultures is a profoundly ahistorical view of the nature and development of cultures. Indeed, the most serious difficulties with this notion emerge most clearly at the intersection of the study of history and the study of culture. For a genuine appreciation of history would show that complex processes of historical interchange and interconnection among cultures have produced the kind of overlap and continuity between cultures that always blur cultural boundaries. Moreover, the interconnection and interdependence of cultures—though intensified in recent history—are in no way new, nor are they confined to the cultures of societies that have experienced lengthy historical connections with the West (Midgley 1991, 90). There is thus no ground for supposing that the cultures of "primitive" societies might provide special exceptions to phenomena associated with the historical interconnection of cultures (Midgley 1991, 90–92). To be sure, nonliterate societies typically preserve their histories in ritualistic (and often nonlinear) oral traditions that baffle the historian or ethnographer looking for a simple linear account (Vansina 1985). But even Evans-Pritchard insisted that such difficulties do not license any conclusions that such societies have no history (Evans-Pritchard 1962, 146–147). Still further, though the conventions of ethnographic writing seem almost designed to obscure this fact, the now classic ethnographies that shaped twentieth-century anthropology—and continue to shape contemporary philosophical discussion about relativism—were not produced in a historical vacuum. Real and complicated histories of religious proselytism, colonialism, and economic expansion typically created the conditions in which ethnographic work was actually carried out. These histories, moreover, often profoundly altered the historical self-consciousness of the societies under study.[3]

The relativist tendency to ignore, or overlook, the historical interconnection of cultures may reflect the continued appeal of the familiar postulate that cultures originated as "distinct answers" to common problems posed by human biology and the human condition (Kroeber and Kluckhohn 1963, 348). This postulate inevitably discourages attention to the facts of cultural interconnection over time. Yet many anthropologists who accept the separate origins doctrine nonetheless find good evidence for the theory of historical interconnection. A. L. Kroeber and Clyde Kluckhohn, for instance, once speculated that were it possible to recover sufficient "ancient and lost evidence," even relativists would have to concede that "every culture shares some of its content, through derivation, with every other on earth" (Kroeber and Kluckhohn 1963, 347n). Of course, this kind of speculation about the ultimate interconnection of all cultures is essentially unfalsifiable, and will seem empirically suspect even to relativism's unsympathetic critics. But known facts about the complex ways in which particular cultures have actually come into contact, and "exchanged" or borrowed customs and traditions, offer general support for such speculation. Not all of the relevant cultural exchanges have been voluntary or deliberate. Some have resulted from large-scale social, political, and economic disruptions: colonization, conquest, and slavery and the expansion of economic trade. Still others flow from small-scale cultural "border crossings" by mobile groups and individuals—including, of course, the activities of anthropologists engaged in fieldwork.[4] But whatever the causes of the relevant contacts between cultures, their effects ultimately undermine attempts to draw exclusive or impenetrable boundaries around any single culture (Midgley 1991). To be sure, a penetrable boundary is still a boundary; I do not deny that the concept of identifiable cultures makes sense. Indeed, that concept provides a reasonable means of recognizing what James Clifford describes as collective articulations of human diversity.[5] Moreover, I do not deny that some elements of every such articulation will be local in origin, and that even "borrowed" traditions are often combined with existing elements in locally distinctive patterns. But the local distinctiveness of cultural practices does not entail that cultural boundaries are impenetrable walls. Admittedly, this fact sometimes makes it difficult—as Midgley has suggested—to determine the precise "extent" of a culture. This is why on many issues, not just in moral reflection, there is no antecedently given fact of the matter about how best to demarcate a particular community of belief and valuing—a particular culture.

The blurring of cultural boundaries by historical interconnection is intensified by quite different processes that belong to the complex *internal* histories of cultures. Relativist anthropology, like its analogue in the work of Evans-Pritchard, is unable to recognize and understand these processes because it tends to take a synchronic approach to the study of cultures. But historical processes internal to cultures generate conditions that render implausible, for instance, Benedict's expectation that any culture might consist of a single pattern of thought and action. After all, even in traditional societies a person occupies more than one social role, and the social institutions that define these roles serve as varied paths by which culturally shaped patterns of belief and behavior are transmitted. These paths for the transmission of culture ultimately generate a wide variety of "positions" or perspectives, both inside and outside any culture, from which it is possible to reflect on the elements of that culture.[6] Some quite simple facts about social differentiation illuminate these processes. Men and women, for instance, may develop different understandings of central cultural phenomena. But social differentiation is far more complex than this, even in traditional societies. Differences in material well-being, in political or religious authority, even in age, will be linked to varied and sometimes quite elaborate overlapping patterns of normative expectations about behavior. The universality of social differentiation simply renders implausible the idea that there might be a single integrated and consistent "internal point of view" on any culture. In any society—simply by virtue of social differentiation and its historical effects—there are always multiple and distinct ways of being a cultural "insider."

Equally important, every society in some way confines some persons or groups to its margins, creating what I call "internal outsiders." Slave societies are one obvious and extreme example. But persons may be consigned to the social margins in a variety of ways: by virtue of economic status, gender, physical appearance, behavior, sexual preference, or age. In a more complex way, some properties, such as gender, may confer marginal status in one social realm but not in another. A middle-class woman in nineteenth-century England, for example, could be culturally celebrated as the "angel in the house" yet be denied suffrage and essentially excluded from the economic realm outside the house. The existence of internal outsiders not only guarantees internal cultural complexity in unexpected ways but also works to blur further any boundaries drawn around a set of cultural practices. In particular, there is often cross-cultural overlap in the experiences of internal outsiders, which create unexpected possibilities for cross-cultural understanding and for cross-cultural moral argument. Even within a single society, divisions of class and race may be complicated by the complex experiences of different *kinds* of internal outsiders: Mark Twain's *Huckleberry Finn* richly exploits the moral knowledge shared by those (such as Huck Finn and the runaway slave Jim) who inhabit different spaces on the margins of American slave-owning society.[7] Relativists commonly argue that in criticizing the practices of an unfamiliar group, cultural "outsiders" necessarily encroach on some monolithic cultural preserve that they simply "cannot understand." But cultural "credentials"—by which I mean access to the kind of understanding of a culture that might license moral criticism—are not simple tokens of membership. The existence of people who are in varied ways confined to the margins prevents the development of moral monoliths, and thus consistently undermines relativist attempts to render cultural practices immune to cross-cultural criticism.

Yet social differentiation, however complex, is not the only basis for challenging the conception of culture typically embodied in relativism. Moreover, social differentiation focuses attention only on processes related to (more or less) fixed social and cultural positions. But every society creates conditions in which individuals and groups are somehow able, in the words of Victor Turner, to "slip through the network of classifications that normally locate states and positions in cultural space" (Turner 1969, 95). Turner adopts the notion of "liminality" to describe this phenomenon, relying on a concept developed by Arnold van Gennep to describe the rites of passage found in tribal societies. In these studies—as in Turner's own work on ritual processes—it was observed that persons on the threshold *(limen)* of initiation into new social positions (a condition which might last for some time) temporarily existed "between" clearly defined cultural positions. The liminal condition, as Turner characterizes it, is a "gap between ordered worlds" (Turner 1974, 13–14). Liminality is a state of liberation, usually temporary, from all the varied normative demands of a culture. Turner goes on to argue that there are "liminoid" phenomena in all human societies; even industrialized societies contain "liminoid" analogues of the liminal processes found in tribal and early agrarian societies.[8] Some occupations—for instance, that of artist or writer, sometimes even philosopher—make what Turner calls "liminoid gestures" in modern industrialized societies (Turner 1974, 15–17). But Turner is adamant that in preliterate tribal societies the liminal periods in major rites of passage create opportunities for everyone, male and female, to stand temporarily outside their everyday structural positions in family, lineage, and clan and engage in critical reflection on features of their way of life (Turner 1974, 231–260; cf. 1969, 1–43). He thus rejects the widespread notion that traditional or preliterate tribal societies leave no "cultural space" for reflection. Turner acknowledges that the socially subversive potential of the liminal tends to generate powerful, and culturally complex, attempts to control it. Yet he suggests that controlled liminality may actually be essential to cultural survival in that it appears to leave space for the kind of criticism that is likely to allow culturally beneficial reform and revision of existing standards (Turner 1974, 13–15). If Turner is right about the universality of "liminoid" phenomena, the conception of culture implicit in views such as Benedict's and Evans-Pritchard's—and in any philosophical arguments that rely on them—simply will not survive scrutiny.

Even without relying on the concept of liminality, however, one can show that historical developments even in traditional societies undermine attempts to treat cultures—at any point in their history—as fully individuable wholes. For the survival of a culture over time depends on the ability of individuals who share a culture to modify, reshape, and sometimes even reject particular cultural practices. At the very least, every society will experience changes in material circumstances that place various stresses on existing cultural practices. In periods of environmental change, social upheaval, or economic instability, the survival of a culture may demand extraordinary inventiveness and spontaneity. Such periods require, even of everyday agents, the ability to modify existing cultural patterns in their own practice (if only incrementally). News reports, for instance, reveal that economic depression in regions of Appalachian Kentucky has produced profound tensions within family culture as the desire of many women in the region to help supplement (or replace) family incomes clashes with the local cultural prohibition against women taking employment outside their home. In the face of economic crises, however, this prohibition has gradually eroded. Recounting an emergency room visit after a miscarriage, one woman reports, "I got this bill for $1700 for 11 hours in the hospital . . . We had no insurance. That's when I started making my own decisions" (Kilborn 1991).

To be sure, a society may be overwhelmed by certain kinds of change: catastrophic climatic changes, earthquakes, economic emergencies, or wars may destroy a way of life. But I follow Turner in maintaining that no society can survive, even in ordinary circumstances, if its culture is insufficiently open-ended and labile (Turner 1974, 15). Indeed, a society which conformed to Benedict's conception of a single dominant cultural influence shaping individual personalities according to a single pattern of culturally approved behavior and belief would probably be a society in a state of irreversible decline. Turner offers a helpful alternative to the views of Benedict and Evans-Pritchard in thinking about culture. He claims that "the culture of any society at any moment is more like the debris, or 'fall-out,' of past ideological systems, than it is itself a system, a coherent whole. Coherent wholes may exist (but these tend to be lodged in individual heads, sometimes in those of obsessionals or paranoiacs), but human social groups tend to find their openness to the future in the variety of their metaphors for what may be the good life and in the contest of their paradigms" (Turner 1974, 14). Unfortunately, Turner did not develop the implications of this conception. But as I eventually argue (in Chapter 5), central components of this conception—especially its postulate of the *moral* "openness" of cultures to the future and its reminder of the historicity of cultural phenomena—yield a more plausible account of the connection between culture and morality than accounts implicit in influential relativist views.

RELATIVISM AS A "KIND OF HISTORIOGRAPHY"?

Benedict's "single dominant influence" view of culture eventually issued in a curious methodological assumption: that one might study the cultures of functioning societies "at a distance." She famously applied this method in her efforts to study Japanese culture in the early

1940s, as part of the American war effort. In the resulting monograph, *The Chrysanthemum and the Sword* (1946), she claimed to study culture (as national character) principally by studying the character of individuals—who, though living apart from the group, were assumed to be representatives of the culture. Research projects of the 1950s, eventually joined by anthropologists such as Mead, attempted to build on this notion.[9] Yet such projects were markedly incompatible with the commitment to anthropological fieldwork that, at least since Malinowski's work in the Trobriand Islands, had been deemed an essential advance over late Victorian armchair anthropology. Mead's observations on the methodological presuppositions of the study of culture "at a distance" underscore the depth of this incompatibility. Understanding culture "at a distance," Mead wrote, "can only be achieved within a frame of reference that recognizes the internal consistency of the premises of each human culture and also recognizes that much of this consistency is unconscious, that is, not available to the average member of the culture" (Mead and Metreaux 1953, 399–400). The empirical basis of "culture at a distance" studies is surely dubious if "much" of what the anthropologist seeks to study about a culture is "not available to the average member of the culture." Even more important, the very idea that one might profitably study a *functioning* culture at a distance—quite independent of problematic attendant assumptions about the cultural patterning of individual character—is simply oblivious to historical reality. Even in ordinary circumstances, cultural phenomena undergo subtle changes and revisions over time, and one might plausibly expect that catastrophic circumstances—such as a full-scale war—would produce at least some changes in central cultural phenomena. The project of studying the culture of functioning societies at a distance is ultimately committed to viewing cultures as unchanging realities somehow frozen in time. It is thus antithetical to a properly historical perspective on cultures, and its ahistoricity casts doubts on the plausibility of the assumptions that underlie it—especially the assumption that cultures are fully individuable, self-contained wholes.

Benedict's turn to the study of culture at a distance is not the only ethnographic endeavor that is rendered empirically suspect—and historically inaccurate—by a commitment to the idea of fully individuable, self-contained cultures. Some of Evans-Pritchard's claims about Zande witchcraft—many of which have been influential in philosophical discussions of moral and conceptual relativism—likewise rest on ahistorical assumptions. Ironically, Evans-Pritchard took his ethnographies to be especially sensitive to the dangers of an ahistorical anthropology. As I noted earlier, he argues for a crucial link between the anthropological study of "primitive cultures" and the historical study of the past of modern Western societies. Thus, for instance, he urges that historians of "early periods" might learn from the anthropologist's methods for studying the "total culture" of primitive societies (Evans-Pritchard 1962, 151). He also chides his mostly functionalist contemporaries in British social anthropology for not recognizing that the history of social and cultural institutions is central to anthropological understanding. "The past is contained in the present as the present is in the future," he claims; history cannot be irrelevant to the study of cultures (Evans-Pritchard 1962, 60). His advice to historians presupposes a familiar analogy between "primitive" cultures and "the past." But implicit in this familiar analogy is a series of assumptions about the cultures of *functioning* societies that are ultimately antithetical to a genuinely historical stance.

Evans-Pritchard's analogy obscures, perhaps even denies, the fact that the ethnographer exists at the same time, in the same historical present, as the inhabitants of the "primitive" society under study. The analogy is thus a powerful distancing device that functions, in a phrase coined by Johannes Fabian, as "a denial of coevalness" (Fabian 1983). Of course, Evans-Pritchard's stance toward the similarities and differences between his subjects and himself is far too complex to allow any simple account of the role that these distancing devices play in his own work. He was notably concerned, for instance, to compensate for the ways in which some ethnographers studying African peoples had failed to present them as fully realized human beings. But contemporary survivals of the distancing devices that are implicit in Evans-Pritchard's advice to historians—survivals in philosophy, anthropology, and everyday discourse—are clearly more problematic. They encourage a new kind of exoticism, on which the living cultures of non-industrialized societies become little more than artifacts in a kind of culture museum. This exoticism occasionally gives rise to interventionist efforts to preserve traditional societies from cultural change, where the principal motivation for such efforts is the desire to preserve for "us" (inhabitants of industrialized societies) some living specimens of a simpler, "nobler" existence.[10] In such circumstances, relativism and its analogues—far from being respectful antidotes to cultural imperialism and ethnocentrism—give rise to a new kind of cultural imperialism (Putnam 1983, 232–233). Instead of "giving permission" to cultural diversity and difference, these views simply refuse to allow others the prerogative of cultural self-definition (McCarthy, 1989, 269n).

Ironically, excessive reliance on the analogy between "primitive" cultures and the past threatens to turn fieldwork itself into a version of Benedict's study of culture at a distance. It encourages the ethnographer (and now the presumed audience of the ethnography) to overlook the fact that the cultures of functioning societies have *ongoing* histories. Yet the culture of a functioning society has not only a history that precedes any anthropological fieldwork, but also a history that (in all likelihood) will continue once that fieldwork has ended. An ethnographic study of a *functioning* society, even at its best, captures only a passing moment in the history of an ongoing way of life. This crucial fact is obscured by the standard reportorial technique of the most influential ethnographies, the "ethnographic present," a rhetorical device that aspires to a timeless, essentially synchronic record of cultural phenomena (Pratt 1986; Marcus and Fischer 1986). It has been suggested that early ethnographers might have found the ethnographic present unproblematic because fieldwork is "by its nature synchronic, conducted at a particular moment or point in time" (Marcus and Fischer 1986, 96). But this suggestion is clearly mistaken. In a particularly rich characterization of anthropological method, Evans-Pritchard reveals why: "The anthropologist goes to live for some months or years among a primitive people . . . [H]e learns to speak their language, to think in their concepts and to feel in their values. He then lives the experiences over again critically and interpretatively in the conceptual categories and values of his own culture and in terms of the general body of knowledge of his discipline. In other words, he translates from one culture into another." The activity of the ethnographer during fieldwork and after is "itself a kind of historiography" (Evans-Pritchard 1962, 148). This warning—that anthropology is a "kind of historiography"—suggests an extraordinary ethnographic self-awareness. But what kind of historiography does Evans-Pritchard's work actually embody?

At crucial places in his work on the Azande, Evans-Pritchard retreats to an ethnographic stance that completely negates the importance of history. The examples I discuss ignore, in particular, the possibility that the recent *colonial* history of the Azande might have had a profound impact on the cultural phenomena that Evans-Pritchard sought to study. These details are of special significance for assessing familiar claims that philosophers, as well as sociologists of knowledge, have made about the theoretical importance of Evans-Pritchard's observations concerning Zande beliefs and practices. In a defense of moral relativism, for instance, David Wong contends that Zande magical rites described by Evans-Pritchard establish the possibility of "relativity in ideals of human flourishing," and hence help make the case for moral relativism (Wong 1986, 103). In a defense of relativism about standards of rationality, David Bloor contends that Evans-Pritchard's *Witchcraft, Oracles, and Magic among the Azande* (1937) describes a society that is "profoundly different from ours" (Bloor 1991, 138). Developing an explicitly relativist interpretation of Evans-Pritchard's work, Bloor claims that the Azande accept a "different logic" not comparable to "the Western perspective" (Bloor 1991, 140). Yet the deeply problematic character of Evans-Pritchard's characterizations of the Azande should trouble such contemporary proponents of relativism who rely on his work to support their claims.

To be fair, Evans-Pritchard eventually published a collection of essays, *The Azande: History and Political Institutions* (1971), that offered a detailed—if partial—reconstruction of Zande history. Still further, even in 1937, in *Witchcraft, Oracles, and Magic among the Azande*, he was careful to point out that by 1926, when he began research in the southern Sudan, the British administration of the region (which had begun in 1898) had gone some way toward dismantling the political kingdom of the Azande. An early passage in that work briefly describes this dismantling process, which included undermining the power of the Zande royal class, enacting new legal codes concerning witchcraft, and concentrating the Azande into new settlements "in order to combat sleeping sickness" (Evans-Pritchard 1937, 18). These changes meant, of course, that Evans-Pritchard's fieldwork on the Azande—as he admits—

was carried out in these new settlements. Inexplicably, however, he never asks whether the resettlements might have had discernible effects on the cultural phenomena that most interested him: magic, witchcraft, and oracles. Indeed at one point he simply asserts his (unexplained) certainty that the resettlements "have not produced any great change in the life of the Azande" (Evans-Pritchard 1937, 15). But even sympathetic critics have wondered whether changes in the distribution of people in physical space might have had important effects, for instance, on the frequency and vehemence of accusations of witchcraft.[11] According to Evans-Pritchard, the concept of witchcraft provided the Azande with both "a natural philosophy" by which "the relations between men and unfortunate events are explained" and "a ready and stereotyped means of reacting to such events" (Evans-Pritchard 1937, 62). Yet wouldn't the hardships of physical resettlement, which he recognizes to have disturbed traditional Zande family life and economic activity, also have been likely to affect the extent of daily charges of witchcraft?

The most basic facts of Zande history, which Evans-Pritchard simply ignores at crucial moments, suggest that Zande practices may have been in a state of extreme flux when he studied them—in even greater flux than cultural practices usually are, even on the Turner-like model that I defend. Relativist proponents of the "strong programme" in the sociology of knowledge, including Bloor, have special reason to question Evans-Pritchard's claims in view of the methodological commitments they believe to be implicit in a plausible cognitive relativism. For they invoke as support for their relativism several claims about Zande culture that their relativist methodology should lead them to question. In a jointly written essay, "Relativism, Rationalism, and the Sociology of Knowledge," Barry Barnes and David Bloor discuss important elements of that methodology (Barnes and Bloor 1982). They contend that the incidence of particular beliefs must be accounted for by investigating the "specific, local causes" of their credibility. One must inquire, for instance, whether a belief "is part of the routine cognitive and technical competences handed down from generation to generation . . . Is it transmitted by established institutions of socialization or supported by accepted agencies of social control?" (Barnes and Bloor 1982, 23). Yet Evans-Pritchard's stance toward Zande history seems to have rendered such investigation impossible.

A second, related instance should further shake the confidence of contemporary relativists that Evans-Pritchard has described a society "profoundly different" from their own. Evans-Pritchard's "outline of Zande culture," which introduces the 1937 monograph, notes the 1905 killing of a powerful Zande leader, King Gbudwe, and then states that the dismantling of the Zande political kingdom was in many ways an important consequence of this event. Indeed, although he is normally critical of the "crude teleology" he associated with the functionalism of Radcliffe-Brown and Malinowski (Evans-Pritchard 1962, 146), Evans-Pritchard describes these events with uncharacteristically teleological zeal: after the killing of King Gbudwe, he writes, Zandeland was "finally" brought under Anglo-Egyptian rule (Evans-Pritchard 1937, 18). Yet he goes on to observe that, even in 1926, many of his Zande informants had begun to characterize the death of King Gbudwe as a "catastrophe that had changed the whole order of things" (Evans-Pritchard 1937, 19). In a later essay, "Zande Kings and Princes," Evans-Pritchard reevaluates this period of his fieldwork.[12] He adds, for instance, that his informants described the death of Gbudwe as the start of a "deep moral cleavage." The memory of their king represented "all that they are proud of in their past and all that they have lost by European conquest: their independence and the stability of their political and domestic institutions" (Evans-Pritchard 1962, 217). Given such observations, it is implausible—to put it mildly—that twenty years of British colonial rule could have had *no* significant effect on those cultural practices Evans-Pritchard hoped to describe. It is hard not to conclude that his methods for studying those practices simply failed to do justice to their complexities.

In "Zande Kings and Princes" Evans-Pritchard responds to his informants' concerns by attempting to discredit their testimony: they had been "educated in the old traditions," he claims, and this "may have led them to paint the past in too rosy a hue" (Evans-Pritchard 1962, 217). Near the end of his 1971 account of Zande history, moreover, he insists that Zande versions of this period are "peripheral" to the main story (Evans-Pritchard 1971, 395). Such claims invite unsympathetic charges (which I shall not pursue here) that the development of British social anthropology was fueled as much by colonialist designs as by disinterested observation and theory.[13] But even on a sympathetic reading, Evans-Pritchard's resistance to his informants is incompatible with his axiom that "the past is contained in the present." The historiography implicit in this claim recognizes that at any point in time, even long-standing cultural phenomena are partly shaped, and re-shaped, by the historical fortunes and misfortunes of the society in which they emerge. The historiography implicit in Evans-Pritchard's account of Zande practices is curiously impervious to this fact. Those who are genuinely concerned about the significance of ethnographic data for moral reflection should be more than a bit wary of an account that ignores informants' claims about a recent "deep moral cleavage" in their culture.

Of course, the question whether a given culture can contain the resources with which to understand its own practices adequately has long been at the center of important controversies in the philosophy of social science (Wilson 1970, viii–xii). Adjudication of the complex issues underlying the larger controversies in this area is beyond the scope of this study. Yet Evans-Pritchard's statements on the relevant issues bear importantly on my criticisms of the assumptions underlying his ethnography. He argues, for instance, that while there is one kind of understanding at "the level of consciousness and action" which is open to members of a culture, or to foreigners who have learned that culture's customs and participate in its life, there is another level of understanding accessible only to the trained observer. The social anthropologist, he contends, "discovers in a native society what no native can explain to him and what no layman, however conversant with the culture, can perceive—its basic structure" (Evans-Pritchard 1962, 148–149). But the notion that one might understand another way of life by summarily disregarding important resources *internal* to the culture—in this case by attempting to discredit informants' claims about their own recent history—embodies an extraordinary and epistemologically indefensible arrogance. An ethnographer is never more than an especially astute resident alien—unless, of course, she decides to become a cultural émigré. Familiar ethnographic methods—such as interviewing of informants and participant observation—thus make sense because it is reasonable to assume that a group's consensus about its own culture is central to any adequate understanding of that culture. Of course, some informants may be ignorant of important details about their culture. They may be unaware, for instance, of the existence of powerful secret societies or potentially dangerous subcultures. Informants may also be subject to self-deception, or for some reason they simply may wish to deceive an interlocutor. The dangers of self-deception—individually and collectively—present special methodological challenges. They suggest, in particular, that the best possible account of a culture is never *simply* an interpretation of a group's overlapping consensus about it. But the dangers of self-deception on the part of the ethnographic interpreter are no less significant. Contemporary anthropological debates about the "self-reflexive" character of the ethnographic enterprise are compelling because they recognize that an ethnographer's cultural self-understanding is almost always at stake—even in a supposedly "objective" empirical study of another culture. Indeed, in some instances what an ethnographer singles out for emphasis may reveal less about the culture under study than about the ethnographer herself. This why an informant's understanding of her own culture should be assumed to be at least *in principle* capable of defeating some element of an ethnographic account. Evans-Pritchard's attempts to discredit the testimony that implicitly criticized British colonial rule in the Sudan should concern even a sympathetic reader of his work.

To reiterate, then, the intersections of ethnography and historiography that I have discussed reveal three serious flaws inherent in construals of functioning cultures as fully individuable, self-contained wholes. First, such construals ignore facts about the historical interconnection of cultures. Second, they presuppose an inadequate conception of how cultures (even relatively "isolated" cultures) develop *internally* over time. Third, they are incapable of giving due weight to the continuing histories—both before and after the anthropologist's fieldwork—of those cultures that they attempt to isolate from all others. Anyone not yet convinced of the importance of these ongoing histories should consider one final example. Participants in philosophical debates about relativism and moral objectivity continue to cite as examples of "cultural divergence" Colin Turnbull's study *The Mountain People* (Turnbull 1973).[14] Turnbull insists that "those positive qualities that we value so highly"—qualities such as kindness, generosity, and honesty—"are no longer functional for the Ik" of northern

Uganda (Turnbull 1973, 27). Yet just a few years after the appearance of *The Mountain People*, knowledgeable anthropologists questioned both Turnbull's methods and his conclusions.[15] Equally interesting, the Ik themselves were at one point ready to challenge some of Turnbull's claims as potentially libelous—and some anthropologists seconded their contentions that their way of life had indeed been drastically misrepresented.[16] This challenge is a vivid reminder that the ahistorical conventions of ethnographic description were developed on the assumption that ethnography would not be read by the people it describes. But it also shows that ethnographic accounts have typically been driven by an embedded rhetoric of comparison: the conventional ethnography was written for some group of "us" about a "them" whose culture had, somehow, to be represented as a fundamentally different way of life (Marcus and Fischer 1986). This same rhetoric informs philosophical forays into empirical anthropology. Brandt's attempt to establish the truth of descriptive cultural relativism by comparing and contrasting "our" attitudes about animals with those of "the Hopi" is an instructive reminder (as I argued in Chapter 1) of the dangers in this rhetoric. It is a basic prerequisite of cultural interpretation that the ways of life of the interpreter and the interpreted cannot be *fundamentally* different—however much difference there may be in the details. The determined insistence that, nonetheless, an interpreted culture is "really" a fully individuable, self-contained whole is simply an unreflective refuge against this basic fact of cultural interpretation.

At this point some theorists may insist that despite the ahistoricity of the assumption that cultures might be self-contained wholes, there is surely a truth in relativism when it comes to assessing cultures that existed in the past. This is precisely the stance of Bernard Williams. Williams concedes that particular practices cannot, for the most part, have "immunity" to the judgment of outsiders; but he remains convinced that there have been some fully individuable—and morally impenetrable—"traditional" cultures with which "we" outsiders can have only "notional" confrontations.[17] A "notional" confrontation occurs when an unfamiliar way of life is not a "real option" for the people considering it—that is, if they could not "live inside it in their actual historical circumstances and retain their hold on reality, not engage in extensive self-deception, and so on" (Williams 1985, 160–161). What makes confrontation between cultures notional for Williams is "distance"—usually distance in time. Yet despite issuing a few warnings about the dangers of utopianism, Williams's "relativism of distance" is principally reserved for certain realized ways of life in the past. But a relativistic suspension of evaluative judgment is apparently not required for every past way of life. Williams's relativism of distance presumes that some cultures are fully individuable *wholes,* whereas others are not. The relativism of distance applies, he argues, only to societies in which everyone—except the occasional "criminal" or "dissenter"—must be understood to have lived "entirely by the local values" (Williams 1985, 162). It applies, that is, where "we . . . conceive of the society in question as a whole." Finally, he claims that "our" modern language of moral appraisal does not apply, for instance, to the lives of Bronze Age chiefs or medieval samurai (Williams 1985, 158–161; 1974, 140).

But what evidence is there that the lives of Bronze Age chiefs or medieval samurai must be understood to have been lived "entirely" by a uniform set of "local values?"[18] Diaries and records kept by court nobles and Buddhist priests in late fifteenth-century Japan suggest that the medieval period in Japanese history was a time of great social and political upheaval, not a morally monolithic cultural whole (Varley 1970). This may explain David Wong's suggestion that by contrast to medieval Japan, "the differences among North Americans on most moral issues" would seem relatively minor (Wong 1992, 769). In a very different context, Mary Midgley has challenged relativist assumptions about moral uniformity by reflecting on the medieval samurai practice of *tsujigiri,* or "trying out" their new swords at the expense of unsuspecting passersby. The practice involved "testing" the sword's fitness (prior to battle) to sever a person in half in one blow. Now, a relativist of distance might well consign those random passersby (along with the warriors themselves) to a realm of impenetrable cultural "others" whose way of life does not constitute a "real option for us." Some less subtle relativists will even claim a special *understanding* of the "other" that has somehow eluded potential critics of the practice: to question the morality of samurai practice, they will assert, is to challenge the integrity of uniform cultural approval of the practice. But, as Midgley suggests, the assumption that there was uniform cultural approval of the practice requires a further, problematic assumption: that endangered passersby would have generally *consented* to be sacrificed to the ritual (Midgley 1981). Midgley wisely urges her readers to consider whether this is a plausible result. Contemporary readers may lack sufficient evidence to license a determinate claim on the matter, yet the familiar human distaste for unnecessary suffering suggests several responses. Surely at least some potential victims of the practice would have objected to it. If so, it is reasonable to suggest that their perspective would have created "cultural space" in medieval Japan for internal criticism of samurai practices.

The idea of fully individuable cultural wholes (whether or not such wholes are taken to be internally integrated) tends to be associated with a cultural determinism on which enculturation—particularly in traditional societies—inescapably molds belief and behavior to a single uniform cultural pattern. This is the account of enculturation presented in the most influential defenses of anthropological relativism—in the work of Benedict and Herskovits, for instance. On the basis of such views, meta-ethical relativists may be tempted to deny that such societies might possibly leave cultural space for internal criticism. Or, when they do recognize the possibility of internal criticism, they sometimes assume that such criticism can be viewed only from within the culture as a kind of *madness*—a characteristic of those whose "peculiarities" relative to the (putatively) dominant personality type ultimately place them outside the bounds of normality in the culture. The last chapter of Benedict's *Patterns of Culture* contains some intriguing claims about just such a conception of cultural criticism—a conception which, as I will show, has recently been echoed in Rorty's implicitly relativist approach to history. But all such appeals to the notion of inescapable dominant cultural influences are profoundly, and therefore disablingly, ahistorical.

Relativists rightly assert the formative importance of enculturation as initiation into culturally shaped patterns of belief, emotion, and action. Even before the rise of modern social science, informal (and largely anecdotal) evidence of the so-called feral or "wild child" phenomenon suggested that being encultured is in fact a condition of the possibility of responsible agency. And a growing consensus in social science, especially in anthropology, underscores the importance of such evidence (Geertz 1973, 74–75). Every culture develops intricate patterns of normative expectations about emotion, thought, and action—expectations that not only help structure each person's formative experiences but also help shape many of the fundamental desires and purposes that influence action. Further, the distinctive economic, social, and political institutions that structure a group's collective life will broadly determine the boundaries within which culturally sanctioned behavior takes place (Moody-Adams 1994a). But no culture of a functioning society can be perpetuated over time without some modification of cultural patterns in the lives of individual agents. In order to survive, cultural processes must allow the transmission of cultural patterns to agents on terms that leave these agents capable of modifying, revising, and occasionally rejecting elements of the cultural patterns by which they are initially shaped. Cultural survival thus depends on the preservation, and even enhancement, of the capacities of individuals for creativity and spontaneity in emotion, thought, and action. It depends, that is, on individuals' developing the capacities for self-evaluation and self-correction.

The idealist strain in much contemporary moral and political philosophy—especially in communitarian criticisms of various unreflective individualisms—provides wise counsel of restraint in any attempt to say what self-evaluation and self-correction might come to. It is crucial, that is, to respect the ways in which individual identity is initially constituted and partly shaped by cultural upbringing. Otto Neurath's image of the mariner who must repair his vessel while at the same time staying afloat on the open sea is thus an instructive emblem of the self-reflection that makes cultural survival possible. Since the evaluating self is always constituted—at least in part—by desires, values, and purposes under evaluation, one can examine one's most fundamental constitutive ends only one "plank" at a time (Moody-Adams 1990b, 127–129). But a culture that worked to impair capacities for self-evaluation and self-correction would be creating the conditions for its own demise. Moreover, not only does the external environment generate pressure to preserve individual abilities for self-reflection, but also the internal "effects" of culture are always mediated though a variety of persons, institutions, and personal experiences. Even in a traditional society there are thus *internal* pressures against narrow and confining patterns of enculturation. The variety of mediating influences in any society simply renders implausible any notion that some dominant cultural influence inescapably shapes the individual personality.

To be sure, processes and institutions that one might find in the "culture" of a concentration camp or a torture chamber, for instance, would be substantially different from those that I attribute to the culture of a functioning society. In such settings the manipulative exercise of power typically limits, or effectively eliminates, variety in internal institutions, and works (to varying degrees) to prevent external conditions from impinging on internal experience. The resultant conditions of control, surveillance, and standardization of the rhythms of daily life are aptly captured in Erving Goffman's notion of the "total institution" (Goffman 1961). But even here, generalizations about the effects of such institutions will sometimes be unreliable. First, not every total institution is equally "total"; there is an important difference between a maximum security prison and a minimum security detention camp designed for white-collar criminals. Second, and even more vividly, not every total institution is brutal: there is a world of difference between a convent and a Nazi concentration camp. Third, even the most brutal total institution may fail to eliminate altogether individual capacities for self-reflection and self-evaluation. Of course, lively debates about the psychological effects of total institutions have been stimulated by Bruno Bettelheim's accounts of life in a Nazi concentration camp and Stanley Elkins's contentions about the psychological effects of American slavery.[19] But blanket generalizations about the effects of such institutions must account for the narratives written by nineteenth-century African American slaves, and the varied testimonies in novels and memoirs of survivors of concentration camps, which suggest that even the most brutal total institutions do not always stifle or silence resistance. Of course, some postmodern theorists—especially those influenced by the writings of Michel Foucault—claim to find virtually everywhere in daily life evidence of the coercion, surveillance, and confining standardization usually associated with total institutions. But this stance minimizes crucial differences between different kinds, and different uses, of coercive power. Most important, it trivializes the suffering of those who experience life (and often the threat of death, whether actual or "social") in the most brutal total institutions.

Rejecting relativism's denial of internal complexity, and its inordinately confining conception of enculturation, leaves room for a simple alternative to its flawed conception of cultural criticism. The culture of a particular society has "space"—logical or conceptual—for questioning the morality of a given practice if that society satisfies two rather simple criteria. First, there must be at least one class of people in that society that suffers hardships as a result of the practice in question while receiving comparatively few of its benefits. Second, there must be good reason to presume that most of those who generally reap some of the benefits of the practice would not have chosen to be members of groups that suffer most of the burdens. These criteria allow me to challenge two widespread assumptions generally thought to strengthen the claims of the relativism of distance: an assumption of the allegedly "superior" reflectiveness of modern as opposed to traditional societies, and an assumption that, in general, even the people who principally bear the burdens of particular cultural practices become somehow unable to voice resistance to them. A variety of contemporary historicisms, as well as more radically perspectival "postmodernisms," are currently ranged in support of these assumptions. Yet even traditional societies can meet the two criteria I have described and thus be assumed to allow "cultural space" for criticism of existing practices. Even traditional societies generate multiple perspectives within their cultures, and those perspectives that are in some way marginal—especially the positions of those people I have called internal outsiders—will prove to be particularly important in this regard. But also, and equally crucial, even traditional societies generate "liminal" space (however ritually structured) that creates room for various kinds of cultural criticism. Any effort at transhistorical moral inquiry and reflection implicity appeals to this liminal "cultural space" for moral criticism. Relativists—especially relativists of historical distance—tend to deny the cultural and moral importance of the marginality and liminality that create this cultural space. Thus, they cannot understand the basis for legitimate cross-cultural and transhistorical criticism.

MORAL DEBATE, CONCEPTUAL SPACE, AND THE RELATIVISM OF DISTANCE

Relativists of distance, I have claimed, are especially likely to deny that historically distant societies might have generated cultural space for internal moral criticism of social practices. This is an implausible conception of any society complex enough to have left traces of once functioning cultures. But many contemporary philosophers, social scientists, and historians take some variant of the relativism of distance to be a reasonable, or even necessary, presupposition of historical reflection. In fact, even theorists who claim to reject relativist accounts of moral debate between contemporary cultures—including Williams and, in a different way, Rorty—nonetheless accept (if sometimes only implicitly) a relativist suspension of judgment for certain ways of life in the past. Proponents of this view typically share three basic claims. They agree, first, that the practices and institutions of past epochs must sometimes (on some versions always) be granted immunity from criticism on the basis of "our" moral notions. Second, in particular cases (on some versions all) social institutions and practices must be viewed as integral parts of a "whole" way of life (a culture) that failed to provide logical or conceptual space for moral criticism or debate. Finally, this limitation of logical or conceptual space is assumed to affect the motivational and conceptual capacities of persons, principally by making members of the culture unable to refrain from participation in certain practices and institutions. Different versions of the view go on to offer distinctive accounts of the precise manner in which the cultural limitation of space for moral debate supposedly occurs. I will briefly discuss the details of three influential versions of the relativism of distance before noting the general difficulties with the view, as well as more specific problems raised by each version.

One influential version appeals to the notion of a culturally induced "moral blindness" that renders persons unable to see what is wrong with a particular practice, or to recognize the possibility of alternative social and cultural arrangements, or sometimes both. Relying on this conception, philosophers in particular have effectively exempted a wide variety of historical periods from contemporary moral criticism. Michael Slote, for example, has argued that ancient Greek slave owners were "unable to see what virtue required in regard to slavery," and that this inability "was not due to personal limitations (alone) but requires some explanation by social and historical forces, by cultural limitations" (Slote 1982, 102). The Greeks were "blinded to the injustice of slavery," according to Slote, because their "ignorance of alternatives" worked to instill the belief that slavery was "natural and inevitable and thus beyond the possibility of radical moral criticism." What they lacked, in his view, was something that "we" have: a knowledge of " 'experiments' in living without slavery." "We" have made sufficient moral progress to "see the wrongness of slavery," Slote claims, because of (non-moral) knowledge of societies in which slavery has been absent and people have nonetheless flourished and survived (Slote 1982, 102). Moral philosophy, Slote believes, has a special contribution to make to moral progress by inventively using historically accumulated non-moral knowledge to produce "new and better moral knowledge" (Slote 1982, 104–105).

Bernard Williams has urged that while the notion of culturally induced moral blindness illuminates the moral circumstances of some "isolated and nonliterate" traditional societies, the relativism of distance sometimes applies to societies that cannot be understood in such terms. It may be appropriate, he argues, to adopt a relativist suspension of moral judgment even in assessing societies where the moral concepts and categories needed to condemn and reject a practice were, after all, culturally "available" (Williams 1985, 164). This conviction issues in a second version of the relativism of distance, one that Williams intends to apply to cases where the members of some society had widespread knowledge of alternative social arrangements but for some reason failed to appreciate that there were "alternatives for them" (Williams 1985, 164). He argues in *Shame and Necessity* that ancient Greece provides just such a context. His analysis of Greek poetry, drama, and philosophy leads him to conclude, for instance, that most ancient Greeks recognized the arbitrariness and violence involved in slavery and saw it as a "paradigm" of bad luck (Williams 1993, 123–124). He believes, further, that the complaints of slaves themselves—"frequent in drama and, certainly, in everyday life"—would have revealed the position of the slave as "an arbitrary calamity" (Williams 1993, 112). Still further, he contends that although the Greeks generally conceived of slavery as "necessary" to sustain the life enjoyed by free (male) Greeks, only Aristotle thought that this "necessity" might ground an argument that slavery is just. For most Greeks, Williams claims, "the effect of the necessity was, rather, that life proceeded on the basis of slavery, and left no space, effectively, for the question of its justice to be raised. Once the question is raised, it is quite hard not to see slavery as unjust, indeed as a paradigm of injustice, in the light of considerations basically available to the Greeks themselves" (Williams 1993, 124). The relativist suspension of judgment is appropriate, this passage argues, because the widespread belief that slavery was necessary to the Greek way of life left no space for moral debate. Considerations of justice and injustice, Williams continues, were "immobilised by the demands of what was seen as social and economic necessity" (Williams 1993, 125).

This version of the relativism of distance thus rejects "progressivist" accounts of "our" relation to the Greeks. Proponents of such accounts often maintain that the Greeks had morally "primitive" conceptions of justice, agency, and responsibility, which have gradually been replaced by progressively refined and complex notions (Williams 1993, 4–5). In rejecting such accounts, Williams resists the Whiggish temptation to interpret the end of slavery as a testimony to the superiority of modern moral consciousness—despite his belief that attitudes toward slavery constitute one of "the most fundamental and striking contrasts" between the Greeks and "ourselves." "We" may marshal ethical arguments against slavery "that the Greeks did not have," he maintains, but we need not do so in order to condemn it (Williams 1993, 127; 124). Although they did not use the Enlightenment language of human rights, neither did they have a "morally primitive" belief that slavery was just. In a final blow to progressivist accounts, he concludes that the immobilization of moral debate by conceptions of social and economic necessity has not disappeared from modern life but simply "shifted to different places" (Williams 1993, 125).

There is yet a third influential formulation of the relativism of distance, a formulation which ultimately challenges some fundamental assumptions of Williams's appeal to the immobilization of debate and Slote's notion of moral blindness. Proponents of this version would accept the presupposition—common to the accounts defended by Williams and Slote—that the ancient Greeks in some way believed in the "necessity" of slavery. They would argue, however, that concepts required to condemn and reject a practice such as slavery would not have been—on some views, could not have been—"available" to those who believed in the necessity of that practice. Some proponents of this view might want to resist the label "relativism of distance." This seems the case with Rorty, who defends a particularly vehement example of the view. But insofar as this view involves a commitment to the moral boundedness of particular historical epochs, it is properly treated as a relativism of distance. Further, although Rorty does not specifically discuss ancient Greek slavery (nor does he specifically discuss very much about evaluating any past epochs), his account ultimately provides an important and influential alternative to the views defended by Slote and Williams. According to Rorty, serious moral criticism of firmly entrenched social practices always requires a prior effort to expand the "logical space necessary for moral deliberation" (Rorty 1991b, 231–232). Yet expanding the space for moral debate, he continues, requires the ability to expose current and (allegedly) unquestioned assumptions about a particular practice as, in fact, assumptions. This is difficult to accomplish, in his view, since "injustices may not be perceived as injustices, even by those who suffer them" (Rorty 1991b, 232). Indeed, Rorty claims that "only if somebody has a dream, and a voice to describe that dream, does what looked like nature begin to look like culture, what looked like fate begin to look like a moral abomination. For until then only the language of the oppressor is available, and most oppressors have had the wit to teach the oppressed a language in which the oppressed will sound crazy—even to themselves—if they describe themselves as oppressed" (Rorty 1991b, 232). Rorty's stance in this passage clearly echoes Benedict's likening of some forms of cultural criticism to madness. Sometimes Rorty retreats from this stance, as when he claims that "a talent for speaking differently rather than arguing well is the chief instrument of cultural change" (Rorty 1989, 7). But, in general, he seems to believe that a sufficiently powerful moral criticism of existing practices must usually involve using familiar words in ways that initially "sound crazy."

Rorty's account implicitly grounds his relativism of distance in two theses about persons and their psychological states. He accepts a "nonreductive physicalism" (Rorty 1991a, 113–125) which he typically combines with an especially strong cultural determinism. Thus he argues, for instance, that people who are suffering "do not have much in the way of a language" (Rorty 1989, 94) because persons are "centerless networks" of beliefs and desires whose vocabularies are "determined by historical circumstances" (Rorty 1991a, 191). Elsewhere he insists that the human subject "is simply whatever acculturation makes of it" (Rorty

1989, 64). Applied to a social practice of slavery, Rorty's view thus posits that even slaves themselves could not have described their situation as an injustice without the aid of someone who possessed a "talent for speaking differently." More precisely, he believes that only some sort of radical disruption in conventional ways of describing the practice of slavery could have created the conceptual space for condemning slavery as an injustice.

Given this commitment to the idea that, morally speaking, there are radical discontinuities between historical periods, Rorty is unexpectedly reluctant to relinquish the notion of moral progress. He claims to side with historicists such as Hegel and Dewey, against "universalist" philosophers such as Kant, in saying that moral progress depends on expanding the logical space for moral deliberation (Rorty 1991b, 231–232). Yet progress, in the broadest sense, is surely some process of movement toward an end or goal that can be expressed (or at least imagined) prior to and independent of the process itself. Rorty is famously critical of an effort to defend such conceptions (Rorty 1991a, 7–28). How, then, should his references to moral progress be understood? Moral progress, he claims, is simply a matter of modifying practices "so as to take account of new descriptions" of cultural phenomena (Rorty 1991b, 234), not of conforming to any antecedently valid, historically transcendent standard according to which the rejected practices were "really" wrong. His advice to contemporary feminists is especially instructive in this regard. For he suggests "dropping the notion that the subordination of women is *intrinsically* abominable, dropping the claim that there is something called 'right' or 'justice' or 'humanity' which has always been on their side, making their claims true" (Rorty 1991b, 237). "Practical politics," he continues, may require reformers to "speak with the universalist vulgar," even though "vulgar" universalism—like its most sophisticated philosophical elaborations—is complicit in what he considers a "fantasy of escape . . . into an ahistoricist empyrean" (Rorty 1991b, 237). Unfortunately, Rorty's conception of progress contains its own fantasies of escape—fantasies that suppose there is nothing problematic about conflating a preference for linguistic novelty with an appreciation of moral reform.

More generally, the relativism of distance—particularly, but not only, in that form defended by Rorty—raises several unanswered questions. To begin with, its proponents never define the contemporary "we" whose judgments supposedly do not apply to the past; indeed, few relativists of distance even seem to recognize the need for such definition. Philosophy has long been preoccupied with the problem of the first-person singular, but the first-person plural—especially the unreflective use of the terms "we" and "us"—is no less problematic, and no less worthy of philosophical attention. In particular, a defensible formulation of the relativism of distance would have to contend with the fact that no culture—certainly not any contemporary culture from which relativist arguments typically emerge—is a moral monolith. Virtually every belief allegedly confined to some distant or "primitive" moral past could probably be found to have some important analogue, and a surprising number of adherents, in contemporary societies. Slavery, often held up as a paradigm of a practice that "we" all agree in rejecting, is not so clearly condemned by would-be Rhett Butlers and Scarlett O'Haras who continue to lament a way of life "gone with the wind."

Defenders of the relativism of distance, furthermore, almost never explain the grounds on which a particular moral concept should be embraced as "ours." This is especially problematic, since theorists claiming to have identified shared moral beliefs or intuitions are engaged in a kind of fieldwork—a fieldwork in familiar places—whose methodological assumptions should be open to scrutiny and debate. In Chapter 1, I discussed several difficulties related to the task of establishing who, if anyone, can be said to speak for a whole culture. Unfortunately, philosophers are altogether too prone to arrogate that authority. Henry Sidgwick shrewdly urged that the "larger part" of the philosopher's life is occupied with beliefs that he shares with the "unphilosophical majority"; this claim is especially plausible as an account of the preoccupations of moral philosophy (Sidgwick 1895, 150). Yet philosophy typically transforms commonsense concerns in quite extraordinary ways—sometimes in ways that create, among philosophers, suspicion and mistrust of the concerns with which philosophy began. Philosophers should thus be wary of the tendency to think that their intuitions necessarily have very much to do with the intuitions of the non-philosophical culture as a whole. But even apart from the dangers of relying on narrowly philosophical intuitions, any attempt to generalize about the content of "our" moral intuitions—as part of an attempt to contrast "us" with some group of cultural others—is prone to an artificially narrow conception of the intuitions current in a particular culture at a particular moment. The whole idea of "moral progress," or simply of radical change in moral beliefs, may well turn out to be rooted in just such artificially narrow conceptions of the boundaries between "us" and some historically distant "others."

Still further—and this is its third weakness—the relativism of distance fails to clarify how one might determine the identity of a particular "they" in the past whose practices are to be shielded from contemporary moral criticism. Relativists of distance often write as if those who suffer under a morally suspect practice had no identity at all. Williams's view at least allows that the complaints of Greek slaves had a culturally important role in Greek society itself. In this way he recovers the truth that even marginal persons—including slaves—have a complex cultural identity. He thus at least broaches the possibility that ancient Greece possessed the cultural space for moral criticism, according to the two criteria I outlined earlier. But this same awareness that Greek slaves in fact had genuine identities makes Williams's turn to the "immobilisation of debate" especially puzzling. Rorty's view, by contrast, involves the implausible claim that oppressive social practices generally destroy the critical capacities of their victims. But there is no reason to expect this. In the first place, it is unlikely that the experience of oppression necessarily affects all victims of oppression in the same way. Moreover, in the case of slavery, Orlando Patterson finds no historical evidence that any slaves ever acquiesced in the masters' efforts to degrade and dehumanize them. Where appropriate records can be found, Patterson urges, one discovers the remarkable regularity with which slaves have managed to preserve their sense of self-worth (Patterson 1982, 100–101). This is one subject on which Rorty's efforts to "naturalize" Hegel may have led him astray, for he seems to have overlooked the extraordinary richness of Hegel's discussion of the master-slave relation. Hegel's understanding of the asymmetry of this relation—and its tendency to produce in the slave the potential for a more sophisticated appreciation of freedom—might well yield a better understanding of the empirical reality of slavery than Rorty's culturally deterministic, "non-reductive" physicalism.

Of course, Rorty might object that my view presumes some "prelinguistic consciousness to which language needs to be adequate," some "deep sense of how things are" which it is the task of practical philosophy to attend to (Rorty 1989, 21). Such a notion is incompatible, he would continue, with a naturalistic explanatory scheme. Yet Rorty's own claims on this topic are inconsistent. In keeping with his "non-reductive" cultural determinism, Rorty has argued that "there is no such thing as 'the voice of the oppressed' or the 'language of the victim' " (Rorty 1989, 94). But this view underwrites the unsupportable generalization that the task of putting victims' experience into language must "be done for them by somebody else" (Rorty 1989, 94). That *every* human being is actually overwhelmed by suffering—even extreme suffering—is not only implausible but also inattentive to historical fact. Consider, for example, the role that nineteenth-century slave narratives—by Frederick Douglass and Harriet Jacobs, for instance—played in vividly rendering the evils of slavery.[20] Moreover, Rorty's view would entail that there is nothing for an external observer to write or speak about when considering an allegedly "voiceless" victim. On the one hand, Rorty insists that language is "ubiquitous," that there is nothing outside of language to which language must conform (Rorty 1982a, 346). But he also wants to maintain, on the other hand, that "pain is nonlinguistic" (Rorty 1989, 94). He seems to think that this notion of pain as "nonlinguistic" accords with his Darwinian convictions: "Pain is what we human beings have that ties us to the nonlanguage-using beasts" (Rorty 1989, 94). Yet this stance creates a disabling dilemma. If pain is really a "nonlinguistic" phenomenon, Rorty cannot really believe that language is ubiquitous. But if language is really ubiquitous, and pain is "nonlinguistic," then Rorty appears to deny the reality of pain. Perhaps Rorty's underlying allegiance to the Rylean conception of mind—with its implicit logical behaviorism—leaves him unable to provide a convincing understanding of the pain and suffering caused by severe oppression. In any event, Rorty's account simply fails to make sense of the concept of pain as it actually functions in language and in complex social practices.

Even within an essentially naturalistic framework, the "language of the oppressor"—that is, the array of concepts used by oppressors in the effort to legitimate their practice—can be seen to be far less important than Rorty thinks. Consider, first, Wittgenstein's familiar "reminder" (in *Zettel*) that it is possible to recognize that someone else is in pain, or to doubt whether some expression of pain is genuine, only if one has acquired the concept of pain (Wittgenstein 1970, sec. 545–549). Yet one can acquire the concepts that make such awareness possible only because there is a fundamental—Wittgenstein sometimes says "natural"—connection between pain and pain behavior. This is not to deny that there may be pain without pain behavior (or that there can be pain behavior without pain). Rather, the point is simply that a certain kind of cry, a wince, a limp, a reaching for one side of the jaw all constitute regular, even "natural," expressions of pain. As Wittgenstein uses the notion, an "expression" need not be a *statement* proclaiming that one is in pain; in fact, it need not involve any kind of verbalization at all. It is thus that limping or cradling one's jaw might be an expression of pain. Because some such expressions so transparently affirm or avow one's pain, Wittgenstein treats them as natural or "primitive" expressions of pain. Wittgenstein's claims about natural or primitive expressions are admittedly complex. Yet this point is quite simple: in certain circumstances some kinds of pain behavior (including, but not limited to, verbalizations) can be considered *transparent* affirmations of pain because they predictably elicit from observers an unreflective (or natural) readiness "to tend" to the party expressing pain (Wittgenstein 1970, sec. 540–541). Imagine what happens, for instance, when one recognizes that a newborn infant (or any being without language) is in pain. Of course, such recognition presupposes a complex social practice whereby some kinds of behavior are simply treated as unlearned expressions of pain. Wittgenstein's reliance on the word "natural" in these contexts may seem to ignore the conventional or social element underlying these processes of recognition. Yet the underlying point is surely incontestable: the practice of recognizing that an infant is in pain rests, at least in part, on "primitive" and originally prelinguistic phenomena such as crying and wincing. None of this actually licenses talk about a prelinguistic "consciousness," of course, and that notion is in no way essential to the view defended so far. Unlike many contemporary philosophers, however, I am not in principle opposed to the notion of a prelinguistic consciousness; indeed, I believe that it might plausibly explain why total institutions so often fail to crush the human spirit.

These considerations, taken together, help show why some people who suffer oppression do not need the "language of the oppressor" (or indeed any linguistic structures at all) to be able to express their pain and suffering. Admittedly, some kinds of pain (the pain of extreme humiliation, for instance) seem to have an irreducibly linguistic component. But even for these kinds of pain, it is reasonable to suppose that a range of natural expressions may yet be all that is needed to *express* such pain. It is important that such expressions may fail to elicit the "tending" reaction I have described, especially in persons who pride themselves on affecting ignorance of the pain and suffering inflicted on those they choose to harm. The records of Amnesty International, for instance, vividly portray the means by which torturers inure themselves to the suffering of their victims (Amnesty International 1973; 1984; cf. Scarry 1985). But the ability to inure oneself to another's expression of suffering, rather like the ability to fake pain, is parasitic on the more fundamental connection between the expression of pain and the eliciting of a response in observers. Rorty is unable to appreciate the force of such considerations. Instead, his conception embodies a profoundly non-naturalistic tendency to reify theoretical abstractions such as "culture" and "historical circumstances," and to treat them as though they might really function as causes of behavior. Yet at any given point in the history of a functioning society, facts about both internal complexity and external pressures on cultural survival suggest that being "determined" by historical circumstance or by a culture is never a simple phenomenon. In particular, the fact that no culture is an integrated, fully individuable whole undermines the very basis on which it makes sense to think of a culture (or "historical circumstances") as a single determinate cause of behavior. Of course, it may be possible to produce interpretations—or what philosophers might prefer to call rational reconstructions—that impose a unity and uniqueness on the various elements and processes that make up a way of life. Historians and philosophers of history were once principally concerned to do just this. But a rational reconstruction of a way of life is not itself a way of life. The concept of culture is a useful theoretical abstraction, but it outlives its usefulness when it is assumed that an abstraction might cause anything to happen. The relativist conception of culture—along with Rorty's appropriation of it—may be the last great survival of "enchantment" in the modern world.

The most serious difficulty with the relativism of distance, however, is that it simply presumes that it is reasonable to confine particular moral convictions to a single historically bounded time. This presumption serves to cordon off past eras from moral criticism by "outsiders," appealing to the need for a relativist suspension of judgment. On such views, determinate moral boundaries between epochs can be located by reference to some widespread change in behavior, or more broadly by reference to some notable change in social institutions. It is thus that debates about the historiography of slavery—as the views so far discussed reveal—provide a rich source of reflection on the commitments of a relativism of distance. Yet the mere fact that social institutions and cultural practices change cannot in itself count as evidence of general or widespread change in moral convictions. As Williams rightly argues, it is not at all obvious that the end of chattel slavery in the modern world is a sign of change in *fundamental* moral ideas from the time of ancient Greece (Williams 1993, 124–125). If Williams is right, Enlightenment notions of equality, for instance, might simply have cast the injustice of slavery in a new light, rather than suddenly embodying some new moral discovery or insight. Equally important, it is quite possible that most of the significant changes in human history have had less to do with "moral progress," or any spontaneous outburst of new humanitarian sentiments, or even a stimulation of moral debate, than with considerations of social expediency and enlightened self-interest (Asch 1952, 380).

It is worth considering in detail some of the difficulties attending those versions of the relativism of distance which suppose that a change in social institutions indicates a fundamental change in a group's social morality. To see why, it must be noted first that such theories should yield plausible explanations of how the alleged change in social institutions might have occurred. In a series of essays the historian Thomas Haskell has attempted to do just that with regard to New World slavery. Haskell contends that a new sentiment of "humanitarianism," or a "new moral consciousness," appeared in England, America, and Western Europe between about 1750 and 1850. Yet, like Williams, Haskell also believes that at least some of the concepts and categories needed to condemn and reject slavery morally have been culturally "available" for some time. Thus, for instance, he claims that the suffering of slaves had "long been recognized": even Locke, who wrote slavery into the Fundamental Constitutions of Carolina, seems to have thought that slavery was "a vile and miserable" state (Haskell 1987, 848). Indeed, Haskell insists that "in every slave regime some people were morally perceptive enough to recognize that slaves suffered ... even under the best of material conditions, simply because they were 'in the power of another' " (Haskell 1987, 849). But Haskell is perplexed by the apparent failure of those who recognized the sufferings caused by slavery to condemn it morally and then to reject it outright: "Why, in a culture that had long identified humanity with spiritual autonomy, and ethical conduct with reciprocity, did practically no one before the eighteenth century interpret the Golden Rule to require active opposition to the very institution of slavery? Or, to put it another way, why, in a culture that has long honored the Golden Rule, does recognition that slaves suffer have such a long history and opposition to slavery such a short one?" (Haskell 1987, 849).

In language that recalls the ethnographer's embedded rhetoric of comparison—and that clearly declares his allegiance to the relativism of historical distance—Haskell insists that a moral perspective "which recognized that slaves suffered and acknowledged that it was bad for people to suffer and yet tolerated slavery, seems alien to us" (Haskell 1987, 849). He goes on to claim that a "new," and purportedly more modern, moral sensibility—one that could turn "old" moral material like the Golden Rule to new purposes—required the appearance of new conceptions of "personal agency and moral responsibility" (Haskell 1987, 829). He then traces the origins of these new conceptions to the development of the capitalist market economy: the development of the market, he argues, helped expand the concept of causation and enlarge confidence in the power of individuals to intervene in the course of events (Haskell 1985b, 556–557; 562–563).

As Haskell's critics have noted, however, the development of the market is far more morally ambiguous than his account allows (Ashworth 1987, 817–818). Mandeville's famous insistence that private vices are sometimes public virtues is a vivid reminder of this ambiguity. Equally important, Haskell's view fails to solve other problems that confront the historian of New World slavery. In particular, he fails to make sense of the apparent selectiveness of English abolitionists, who seemed not to have recognized that some of their objections to chattel slavery might legitimately require greater concern for the miseries of the English working class.[21] Thus, even Haskell's subtle analysis proves unable to provide a plausible understanding of how a "new" moral sensibility might have developed—and still make sense of all the relevant details. As a result, one must ask whether there was really a new sensibility, or whether this was just a case of a familiar tendency to recognize a moral imperative and nonetheless fail to act on it. My view would best explain, for instance, how long after Britain outlawed the African slave trade in 1807—and emancipated more than 700,000 colonial slaves in 1833—some British factories continued to manufacture manacles and iron collars for the ongoing illegal slave trade (Davis 1984). David Brion Davis points out, further, that the cotton textile industry so central to the British industrial economy during this period continued to depend quite heavily on raw material produced in the slave states of America (Davis 1984, 108; 209). Relativists of distance are strangely unwilling to consider what such facts might really mean for efforts to exempt particular epochs from moral assessment.

Similar difficulties attend the efforts of contemporary moral realist philosophers who claim that there are moral facts, and that moral facts have important value in explanations of various natural facts. In a defense of moral realism, for instance, Nicholas Sturgeon argues that slavery simply had to become "more oppressive" (particularly in the United States) before its moral wrongness could really be perceived (Sturgeon 1988, 245). Sturgeon attempts to show not only that the wrongness of slavery is a natural fact like other facts, but also that the *discovery* of this fact, at some point in the late eighteenth or early nineteenth century, was a large part of the cause of slavery's eventual demise. Yet important comparative histories of slavery challenge the notion that slavery actually became more oppressive in the nineteenth century.[22] Moreover, Sturgeon's notion of "moral facts" radically, and even dangerously, detaches moral language from the contexts of inquiry and action in which they have a genuine place. The persistence of slavery in the New World, I contend, should be attributed not to a presumed failure to perceive a moral property of "wrongness," but to a widespread and morally culpable capacity to ignore willingly the suffering of human beings.

Rorty's view obviates the need to offer the sort of historical explanations offered by Haskell, on the one hand, and Sturgeon, on the other. But his view posits such radical discontinuities between shifting linguistic practices that it is unclear how it leaves any room for the very idea of *history* at all. Rorty is also committed to a fundamentally implausible conception of the moral critic of social practices. The person who is allegedly able to "expand" logical space for moral debate, Rorty contends, invents "previously unplayed" roles and describes "hitherto undreamt-of possibilities" (Rorty 1991b, 232; 236). On occasion Rorty even describes this person as a "prophet"; prophecy, he contends, is all that nonviolent movements can appeal to when argument fails (Rorty 1991b, 235). But, as Michael Walzer has argued, a prophetic message can be the basis for effective social criticism only insofar as it builds on previous messages. Rorty writes as though socially effective prophecy might simply be a matter of changing the subject. Walzer's conception is far more compelling: prophecy is social criticism only to the extent that it mounts a challenge to conventional practices by appeal to concepts and values already shared in that society (Walzer 1987, 89). The prophet is a social critic, Walzer stresses, only insofar as he "is not the first to find, nor does he make, the morality he expounds" (Walzer 1987, 71). Walzer thus maintains—I think rightly—that prophetic social criticism is not invention but interpretation. This, in fact, is why the most effective prophetic appeals of a secular kind so often signal, from the very outset, the link between the prophetic message and shared understandings. In the *Apology*, for example, Plato depicts Socrates prefacing his remarks by appeals to his fellow Athenians; so, too, in the "Letter from Birmingham Jail," Martin Luther King, Jr., begins his criticisms of segregation by appeals to his fellow Americans. Rorty's conception of social change by means of prophetic moral criticism implausibly construes that criticism as moral invention de novo. The actual practice of such criticism reveals the inadequacy of this conception.

Williams's analysis wisely avoids many of these difficulties, at least in the case of slavery. Indeed, he takes the provocative (and I think correct) view that it was not the moral condemnation of New World slavery that required "new materials," but rather the "scriptural and systematically racist . . . attempts to justify slavery . . . when the question of its justice had for a long time been raised" (Williams 1993,

124–125). Yet despite the many strengths of Williams's conception, his view retains one of the most serious flaws of the relativism of distance. He assumes that hypotheses about what some agents *could not* do can be based solely on observations about what they *did not* do. This assumption informs Williams's appeal to the idea that moral debate was "immobilised" by something independent of the choices of human agents—as it does Rorty's confining conception of linguistic practices and Slote's appeal to "moral blindness." But while it is plausible that the Greeks did not, in general, engage in widespread moral debate about slavery, it is not clear why the explanation for this fact must be sought in anything except the choices of human agents. What could count as evidence that the Greeks were *unable* to question the morality of slavery (on either Williams's or Rorty's terms) or *unable* to imagine alternative ways of life and thus recognize the wrongness of slavery (on Slote's terms)? Merely by virtue of learning a language—in particular, learning to form the negation of any statement—every human being has the capacity to question existing practices, and to imagine that one's social world might be other than it is. To be sure, some powers of imagination are richer than others. But any claim that one simply "couldn't imagine" an alternative way of life is at best a disguised admission that one has in fact imagined things being different (however prosaically) but found that imagined world unacceptable.

It is sometimes difficult to articulate what would be required to put an alternative way of life into practice. It may be equally (if not more) difficult to act on such a conception, even when it is richly articulated. Still further, these issues cannot be considered apart from the problems of collective rationality: even a morally reflective person may reasonably wonder about the possible futility of acting alone in some circumstances, and about the difficulty of persuading others of the need for reform. The relativist of distance may want to argue that such considerations make it inappropriate to blame members of past societies for their participation in practices such as slavery. Yet most arguments to exempt past societies from blame implicitly rely on one further assumption: that it is morally smug or self-righteous to blame, since "we" would not want to be condemned for failing to reject some established practice of "our" own. Relativism here gives way to a decidedly nonrelativistic reliance on evaluative notions—such as the moral unacceptability of smugness or self-righteousness—that *ought* to govern moral reflection on the past. Further, implicit in the demand to refrain from being morally smug or self-righteous is the notion that it is somehow not "fair" to blame those in a past epoch for the practices they observed and the institutions they accepted. But these claims sound suspiciously like the inconsistent demand made by normative relativists who call for the uncritical toleration of unfamiliar practices.

Relativists of distance are probably right to point out that the moral dimensions of slavery, for instance, were insufficiently debated by the ancient Greeks. But there is no convincing evidence that the blame for this should be traced to anything other than the affected ignorance, in Aquinas' phrase, of those who wanted to perpetuate the culture of slavery.[23] Affected ignorance—choosing not to know what one can and should know—is a complex phenomenon. But sometimes it simply involves refusing to consider whether some practice in which one participates might be wrong. Sometimes—perhaps much of the time— cultures are perpetuated by human beings who are uncritically committed to the continuance of a way of life. To be sure, there are degrees of responsibility for the continuance of any given way of life. A slave owner is more actively implicated in the continuance of a system of slavery, and hence bears far greater burdens of responsibility and blame, than a non–slave-owning freeperson. But, as K. J. Dover suggests, even the poorest Athenian citizen—who could vote, and who could expect certain kinds of legal protection from physical harm— might have had reason to see himself as a member of an elite group (Dover 1974). Even the poorest Athenian citizen could thus have been guilty of some degree of affected ignorance, and hence partly implicated in responsibility for the continuance of Athenian social practices.

Affected ignorance takes so many forms that any exhaustive taxonomy of its manifestations is elusive. Yet some kinds of affected ignorance are familiar in everyday life. Affected ignorance may involve asking not to be informed of the nature—or even the occurrence—of morally unacceptable actions or practices. The head of a brokerage house, for instance, may demand that her employees increase the firm's profits but insist that she wants to "know nothing" about how they do this. She is in some degree morally culpable if the firm is later implicated in insider-trading scandals.[24] In other cases, affected ignorance involves choosing to ignore the moral relevance of obvious facts. A father who accepts expensive gifts from a teenage son may prefer to "ask no questions" about the source of those gifts. But he is morally complicit (even if legally innocent) should those gifts turn out to have been purchased with money from the sale of illegal drugs. In a third kind of case, affected ignorance involves a more active refusal to accept the moral relevance of obvious facts, or even to accept an adequate description of the facts. Thus, a torturer who describes his violent methods by means of deceptively benign phrases—the "telephone," "the parrots' swing"—uses language to obscure the connection between his action and the suffering of his victims.[25] He is nonetheless responsible for choosing not to acknowledge the humanity of his victims. A fourth form of affected ignorance is common, for instance, in slave-owning societies where those who are not slaves learn to inure themselves to the complaints and discontents of those who are. Affected ignorance very likely takes additional forms, but in all of its manifestations it is morally culpable. It is morally culpable ignorance because it involves a choice not to know something that is morally important and that would be easy to know but for that choice. There is nothing extraordinary about the various behaviors that affirm such a choice: affected ignorance is a widespread and ordinary fact of everyday life. Precisely because it is so easy to choose affected ignorance, it is often very difficult to be moral.

Theorists who are troubled by the implications of my claims may wonder whether my conception too readily requires blaming people for what it is difficult not to do. But many moral theorists seem to assume that there are only two possible responses to behavior that we may want to condemn: a therapeutic model of behavior which effectively does away with the idea of moral blame, and a rigorously moralistic model which emphasizes blame and ignores the forgiveness that recognizes how hard it is to be moral. There is another possibility, however: a forgiving moralist's model of moral reflection, which acknowledges the ordinariness of affected ignorance and yet recognizes the serious effort required to adopt a critical stance toward everyday social practices (Moody-Adams 1994a). The attitude of forgiveness is, moreover, a crucial component of much sophisticated moral reflection. The most estimable of moral qualities in human beings will sometimes be revealed in the effort to forgive the wrongdoing of one's predecessors rather than simply exempt them from criticism. Efforts to forgive, however, make sense only in a context in which it is possible to recognize how some past society might in fact constitute one's cultural predecessors. The relativism of historical distance tends to license a self-deceptive detachment from morally relevant parts of a group's history, and it generally obscures the importance of many backward-looking moral judgments. But in Book 3 of the *Nichomachaean Ethics*, Aristotle emphasizes that some of the most important demands on moral reflection have an essentially backward-looking emphasis: these include determinations of moral praise and blame, determinations of the conditions under which it is appropriate to excuse or morally exonerate, and determinations of the conditions under which forgiveness—and sometimes simply the *effort* to forgive—might be appropriate. Much recent analytic moral philosophy, even of the non-relativist variety, assumes that moral judgment and moral reasoning are essentially forward-looking, principally a matter of finding adequate decision procedures to guide (future) action. Yet one's ability to be a moral person cannot be detached from the ability to learn from the past mistakes of those who share at least some of one's central cultural presuppositions. Most versions of the relativism of distance—including Slote's "moral blindness" account and Rorty's denial of moral continuity across epochs—overlook this fact, and thus sever crucial moral connections between the present and the past.

PLUS ÇA CHANGE . . . : THE MYTHS OF MORAL INVENTION AND DISCOVERY

Williams is decidedly reluctant to accept those versions of the relativism of distance which unreflectively sever moral links with the past. In *Ethics and the Limits of Philosophy*, for instance, he warns of the dangers of too glibly positing the moral boundedness of historical epochs. These dangers are most acute, he suggests, in regard to practices that involved the arbitrary, and often violent, domination of one group by another. Simply to accept the terms under which a dominant group may have sought to legitimate their practices of domination in the past, he cautions, could encourage a dangerous self-deception in contemporary moral reflection on existing social practices (Williams 1985, 165–166). Williams extends this concern in *Shame and Necessity*, in an inquiry into Greek attitudes about slavery. That work explores what he believes to be the "special relation" between historical study of the Greeks and the self-understanding of modern societies. In order to make sense of that relation, he begins by rejecting "anthropological" approaches, which in his view emphasize the alienness of the practices they study. He also rejects "progressivist" accounts of history (like Slote's, and possibly Sturgeon's), because they so widen the moral gap between ancients and moderns that it is difficult to see how study of the ancients might enhance or enlarge the content of modern self-understanding. Yet Williams remains convinced that some sort of relativist suspension of judgment is the only appropriate response to ancient Greek slavery. It is important to consider the sources of that conviction.

Williams remains committed to a fundamental but deeply problematic assumption underwriting most relativist arguments. He assumes that moral convictions are "intrinsically action-guiding": that, in general, if a person can appreciate the importance of a particular moral consideration, she will in fact act on it. Thus he contends that, for most Greeks, slavery "was not just, but necessary," and that "because it was necessary it was not, as an institution, seen as unjust either: to say that it was unjust would imply that ideally, at least, it should cease to exist, and few, if any, could see how that might be" (Williams 1993, 117). "Ideally," he suggests, those who believe an institution to be unjust will seek to end it. Yet even "ideally" it is far from self-evident that one who accepts a moral conviction will act on it. It is entirely possible—and in my view quite likely—that people do not always act in accordance with their settled moral convictions. It is equally possible that the failure to act on stable moral convictions could become a morally widespread phenomenon. Familiar facts of experience suggest that the notion of the "intrinsic prescriptive force" of moral judgments—of the necessary "action-guiding" character of moral considerations—is nothing more than a philosophical invention. Ironically, one philosopher commonly thought to have participated in its invention—David Hume—quite vividly reminds us how empirically unreliable the notion really is: "My sympathy with another may give me the sentiment of pain and disapprobation, when any object is presented, that has a tendency to give him uneasiness; tho I may not be willing to sacrifice anything of my own interest, or cross any of my passions, for his satisfaction" (Hume [1739] 1978, 586). To assume that moral considerations are more reliably action-guiding than they really are forces one to provide some explanation of why people sometimes fail to act on moral considerations that appear to have been "accessible" to them. Implicit in the views defended by Slote, Rorty, and (as I showed in Chapter 1) Harman is the cultural determinist notion that one's commitment to a particular way of life renders moral considerations that are not part of that life in some respect inaccessible. But these questions take on special urgency in *Shame and Necessity*, for, as I have noted, Williams also assumes that moral considerations against slavery were accessible to the Greeks. He contends, for instance, that "being captured into slavery was a paradigm of disaster, of which any rational person would complain; and . . . they [the Greeks] recognised the complaints as indeed complaints, objections made by rational people" (Williams 1993, 116–117).

I have claimed that the best explanation for the persistence of slavery in such circumstances will appeal to some form of affected ignorance. In this instance it is reasonable to posit that people who benefit from a social practice can effectively ignore those features of the practice—such as the rational complaints of those most severely harmed by it—that might prove morally unsettling. But some of Williams's critics will prefer a different tack. They will simply deny that the moral materials sufficient to underwrite a condemnation of slavery were in principle accessible to the Greeks. Theorists who believe that the history of moral thinking is a history of progress driven by the invention of new moral ideas, as well as moral realists who believe that moral thinking advances by the discovery of moral facts, will want to argue that Williams's account is incomplete. Yet many influential moral thinkers would deny that serious moral reflection—including philosophical moral inquiry—ever really tells its audience anything new. They would deny, that is, that moral reflection advances by means of invention or discovery. In the *Critique of Practical Reason*, for instance, Kant relished the "objection" that his *Groundwork of the Metaphysic of Morals* failed to provide any new moral knowledge. Mill claimed for utilitarianism (much as Kant had claimed for the categorical imperative) that it provided a richer understanding of the Christian injunction to love thy neighbor as thyself than any alternative modern conception. Even Bentham insisted that utilitarianism was already implicit in conventional justifications of moral practices, though he was deeply critical of the conventional tendency to resist the doctrine's implications for social reform. Walzer has suggested that all the moralities that we "discover and invent" turn out to be remarkably similar "to the morality we already have" (Walzer 1987, 20–21). I think that the suggestion is apt, and I will develop its implications in Chapter 4. For the time being, I will simply reiterate the point that Walzer himself makes: prophetic moral criticism that is most likely to underwrite genuine social change (including criticism of a socially sanctioned system of slavery) progresses not by moral invention or moral discovery but by reinterpretation of moral concepts and values already shared in the society under scrutiny.

It is beyond the scope of this project to trace the paths by which the reinterpretations embodied in the criticism of slavery actually took shape. Fruitful explorations would trace the means by which slave narratives and other testimonies of ex-slaves, along with anti-slavery tracts and novels by non-slaves, and the trans-Atlantic transfer of evangelical Protestant opposition to slavery, all worked to stimulate moral imagination. To be sure, ending slavery required far more than a rearrangement of the details of moral reflection. It is nonetheless important to understand that anti-slavery arguments embodied a fundamental reimagining and reinterpretation of the moral world. Interpretation, as I show in Chapter 4, is an inescapable component of moral argument and inquiry. The interpretive nature of moral inquiry underscores the central point of this chapter. The boundaries of any past era are always penetrable by moral reflection in the present, because anyone with a sufficient command of a natural language can reinterpret the moral language, beliefs, and sentiments of that era so as to become a serious, credentialed moral "insider." This ongoing reordering and reinterpreting of moral practices reminds us that what is new in moral reflection (in historical as well as cross-cultural reflection) is always in the details.

MORALITY AND ITS DISCONTENTS

> *Well, Euthyphro, the gods will quarrel over these things, if they quarrel at all, will they not?*
>
> *Plato,* Euthyphro

ON THE SUPPOSED INEVITABILITY OF RATIONALLY IRRESOLVABLE MORAL CONFLICT

Many contemporary theorists—even if they would reject any kind of meta-ethical relativism—will object that my argument so far does not undermine the real truth in relativism. These critics will argue that relativism simply recognizes the limited power of rational argument, as Geertz expresses it, to bring others around to new moral "seeings and doings." The limits of rational argument remain important, my critics will urge, even if relativists such as Harman can be shown to misconstrue their implications. Appreciating these limits, they will continue, demands skepticism about the possibility of rationally (and thus objectively) justifying the claims that underwrite serious moral disagreements—and hence skepticism about the possibility of rationally resolving them. What relativism *best* shows, on these accounts, is that rationally irresolvable disagreement is an unavoidable feature of moral experience. But, on these views, we need not search for conflicts between cultures; irresolvable disagreement may begin close to home. In familiar disagreements about abortion, or the moral status of animals, or the responsibilities of the affluent toward the poor, these critics contend, there is no rational, objectively valid way of settling disputes between the underlying moral claims. On these terms, moreover, the thesis that rationally irresolvable moral disagreement is unavoidable—the alleged truth in relativism—has become a fundamental presupposition of much recent, even vehemently non-relativist, moral philosophy. The thesis has had its critics, most notably Alasdair MacIntyre in *After Virtue*. Most contemporary moral thinkers, however, would probably second Charles

Larmore's claim that a "mature" view of morality must acknowledge rationally unsettlable moral disagreements as a permanent feature of moral experience (Larmore 1987, 38).

In this chapter I challenge such claims, along with several assumptions about morality, moral argument, and moral maturity that underwrite them. The persistence of serious and unresolved moral disagreement simply does not license the conclusion that some moral disagreements are intrinsically irresolvable; indeed, that conclusion is radically underdetermined by the facts of human experience. Of course, a powerful discontent about the persistence of serious moral disagreement leads many theorists to claim otherwise. If moral argument and inquiry were rational, they assume, moral inquiry would be heading toward "convergence" on some one way of life as morally best, or some one principle (or some one set of principles) as the appropriate arbiter of moral disagreements. The persistence of serious moral conflicts, they urge, displays the methodological infirmity and rational insufficiency of moral argument and inquiry. In this chapter, however, I maintain that such discontent rests on serious misconceptions about rationality in moral argument, the nature of moral inquiry, and the relation between moral inquiry and experience. I show that these misconceptions create an argumentative impasse between emotivism and influential critics of emotivism such as MacIntyre, and that they artificially limit the terms of debate about the vigor of the methods of moral inquiry.

Some theorists who defend the inescapability of irresolvable moral conflict may contend that they do so not out of discontent with moral disagreement but instead because they take that disagreement seriously. According to Isaiah Berlin, for instance, the political liberty that guarantees freedom of choice is objectively valuable largely because human beings cannot avoid having to choose between intrinsically conflicting ends and values (Berlin 1969). But such appeals to the inescapability of irresolvable moral conflict embody another kind of discontent about morality: an impatience with the complex processes of moral argument and inquiry which are most likely to make the resolution of serious moral conflicts possible. Even the moral pluralist has no access to a standpoint independent of human experience from which to declare any moral conflict intrinsically irresolvable. The future of humankind, moreover, may depend on a widespread willingness to trust that methods of moral argument and inquiry sometimes do allow us to resolve even the most serious and persistent disputes. Moral maturity, as I argue, thus demands that we reject the thesis that rationally irresolvable moral conflict is inescapable.

The most fundamental problem with that thesis is the lack of clarity of its central claims. What does it really mean, for instance, to assert that some moral disagreements are not simply rationally *unsettled* but rationally *unsettlable?* Experience consistently generates circumstances that give rise to moral conflicts. But from what humanly attainable vantage point might one justifiably declare any such conflict rationally irresolvable? Stuart Hampshire argues, for instance, that there must always be moral conflicts which cannot be resolved by any "constant and generally acknowledged" method of reasoning (Hampshire 1983, 152). Yet it is not clear why the absence of such a method could establish any dispute as in principle rationally irresolvable. Nor is it plausible that moral argument and inquiry might be distinctive in giving rise to disputes that outstrip the disputants' capacities to resolve them by means of generally acknowledged methods. Indeed, in some disciplines such disputes are an important engine of change, possibly even revolutionary change, in standards of argument and justification. In the case of moral inquiry—where, of course, in my view revolutionary change does not occur—it may always be possible to reinterpret and reorder moral notions accepted by the parties to a current dispute so as to devise a new method for resolving even the most serious current disagreement. To be sure, serious moral disagreements occur, and some of these disagreements conform to a familiar, sometimes troubling pattern of failure to end in agreement that some one course of action or state of affairs is correct. It is, doubtless, just this pattern that Plato's Socrates has in mind in this striking exchange with Euthyphro:

Socr.	Then what is the question which would make us angry and enemies if we disagreed about it, and could not come to a settlement? . . . Is it not the question of the just and unjust, of the honorable and the dishonorable, of the good and the bad? Is it not questions about these matters which make you and me and everyone else quarrel, when we do quarrel . . . if we can reach no satisfactory agreement?
Euth.	Yes, Socrates, it is disagreements about these matters.
Socr.	Well, Euthyphro, the gods will quarrel over these things, if they quarrel at all, will they not? (Plato, 1956, 8)

But why should the persistence with which disagreements conform to familiar patterns be thought to support the inference that rationally irresolvable disagreements must be a permanent feature of moral experience? In part, this inference presupposes a distinctive conception of rationality, which, adopting a notion of Robert Nozick's, I describe as the "coercive" conception.[1] On the coercive conception, rationally settling a dispute between competing claims involves formulating an argument for one of those claims which any sane person who understands the language, accepts the laws of logic and basic rules of inference, and makes no errors in reasoning would be compelled to accept. Establishing that any sane, logically acute person must accept a particular conclusion is, on this view, a matter of demonstrating the *superiority* of that conclusion over all competing solutions. Of course, as Stanley Cavell cautions in *The Claim of Reason*, this kind of conception always involves a normative ideal (Cavell 1979, 254). To say, for instance, that someone *must* accept the conclusion that "Socrates is mortal"—given the premises that "all human beings are mortal" and "Socrates is a human being"—does not mean that no human being will in fact fail to accept it. But the theorist of coercive rationality will have an important rejoinder. It will be urged that while there are uncontroversial grounds for questioning the reasoning abilities, linguistic skills, or even the sanity of one who denies that Socrates is mortal, there are no such grounds when someone denies that capital punishment, for instance, is morally acceptable. The theorist of coercive rationality insists, then, that there is an important asymmetry between argument in moral matters and much (if not all) argument in non-moral matters. This asymmetry is said to support the idea that rationally irresolvable moral disagreements are unavoidable.

But I want to challenge the conception of moral disagreements that underwrites such claims. To begin with, there are many different contexts in which a moral disagreement might fail to converge on a conclusion about one morally correct way to proceed. In some circumstances, in fact, a rational resolution of moral disagreement is attained by an agreement to disagree. Some of these resolutions are simply implicit agreements not to seek joint acceptance of a unique moral "solution," while others are positive affirmations of the value of tolerance. Consider the predicament of a young Islamic woman attending a secular college in a largely non-Islamic country, who wishes to affirm her commitment to the moral demands of her faith. Most of her non-Islamic classmates (and perhaps some of her Islamic classmates) will not share her conviction, for instance, that it is immoral for women to appear in public unveiled. But she achieves a rational resolution of disagreement with her peers simply by continuing to wear a veil— whether or not she also believes that any of her female classmates ought to do so as well. Rational resolution is not always a matter of bringing others around to one's own moral convictions; it is sometimes a matter of agreeing to disagree. But consider still another case of two friends whose professional lives take very different paths, with one friend pursuing a career that to the other embodies bad moral judgment. A rational resolution here would be an agreement to disagree about the boundaries of morally acceptable professions; indeed, this kind of agreement may sometimes be the only terms on which two people can continue a friendship. Such friends will be fortunate if they never confront circumstances in which the morally disapproving friend must choose between objecting to the other's profession and continuing the friendship. If so, an agreement to disagree can provide a stable resolution of their disagreement for a very long time. In both examples, agreements to disagree are sometimes the only way to achieve a rational settlement of serious disagreement. A genuine understanding of moral argument, as Cavell also urges, must allow that there can sometimes be rational *disagreement* about a moral conclusion (Cavell 1979, 254). Any conception of rationality which cannot allow for the rationality of agreements to disagree—especially, but not only, in moral matters—is profoundly suspect.

There is a second important difficulty, however, with inferring the unavoidability of rationally irresolvable disagreement merely from the failure of some moral disagreements to end in convergence on a unique solution. That inference rests on the assumption that the purpose of moral disagreement and debate is always, and only, to achieve convergence on a unique solution (cf. Cavell 1979, 255–256). Yet a very common purpose of moral argument—perhaps so common that it regularly escapes the notice of moral theorists—is simply to gain increased understanding of the person with whom, or the position with which, one disagrees. Moral argument for this purpose will be especially important to the foreign traveler, or the college student encountering unfamiliar habits and practices, or even to recent immigrants seeking to negotiate the terms under which they might fit at least some of their familiar practices into a new way of life. Of course, moral debate with those whose moral conclusions one rejects will sometimes yield as great a gain in self-understanding as in understanding of the other. On still other occasions, it may even generate a richer appreciation of the commitments and implications of one's own moral convictions than of anyone else's. But this, too, can be an appropriate and rational outcome—as well as a guiding purpose—of moral disagreement and debate. Periodic, serious scrutiny of one's settled convictions is, in fact, far more central to developing a sophisticated moral understanding and extending moral concern than contemporary moral theorists typically acknowledge. J. S. Mill's defense in *On Liberty* of the liberty of thought and discussion richly reinterprets this Socratic conception of moral thinking for a political context. Yet where the purpose of moral argument is not to achieve convergence on a determination of one morally best way to proceed, the failure to achieve convergence is not a failure of rational resolution. Recent philosophical discussion of moral disagreement has been dominated by reflection on matters where convergence is an urgent concern—particularly controversy about questions of public policy and the urgencies of decision making in medical ethics. But moral argument often takes place in contexts where a failure of convergence is quite irrelevant to the rationality of the result.

At this point, of course, the proponent of the idea that rationally irresolvable disagreements are permanent fixtures of the moral landscape may claim that only certain kinds of disagreement provide appropriate support for that idea—and that only disagreements about matters such as public policy and medical ethics can actually show how. Consider, for instance, a disagreement in a critical care unit about whether to prolong a patient's treatment, or a public confrontation about acceptable legal policy on abortion. As Martin Benjamin has suggested, such disagreements have at least two distinctive characteristics (Benjamin 1990, 30–31). First, in both cases the parties to the disagreement hope (or possibly even need) to continue in some cooperative social endeavor. Indeed, in both cases the very existence of the endeavor benefits substantial numbers of people beyond the disputing parties, and this places even greater burdens on the parties to the dispute. But, second, the parties in both cases disagree about some matter that requires a joint, and effectively non-deferrable, decision—which will have serious consequences not merely for the parties to the dispute but for one or more additional parties (Benjamin 1990, 30–31).[2] Failure to reach agreement on a joint decision about how to proceed may generate anger, resentment, or even moral indignation. Such cases may thus seem to be instances of rationally irresolvable disagreement: they seem to lack any means of settling on a unique result that would compel the assent of every rational person.

Yet while these disagreements are quite obviously rationally *unsettled*, it is not clear how one might justify the inference that they are rationally *unsettlable*. For much of the twentieth century, of course, it has been thought that emotivist conceptions of moral language and moral argument—if true, or even simply plausible—might make clear the grounds of such an inference. Emotivists claim to show that fundamental moral judgments are, ultimately, just non-rational preferences. They will assert, with A. J. Ayer, that it is impossible to provide any arguments that might show a fundamental moral value, or a set of such values, to be "superior" to any other (Ayer 1971, 147). Any claim about the superiority of one value over another, the emotivist continues, would itself be another judgment of value, and therefore not a *reason* that might figure in an argument for one's position. Such claims, if true, would surely support the claim that some serious moral disagreements are rationally irresolvable.

On closer scrutiny, however, emotivist accounts can be shown to imply that serious moral disagreement never really occurs. Ayer made this quite clear in the first edition of *Language, Truth, and Logic* (1936). His bold initial defense of emotivism contains the "at first sight . . . very paradoxical assertion" that "one never really does dispute about questions of value" (Ayer 1971, 146). Indeed, he continues, it is "because arguments fail us when we come to deal with pure questions of value, as distinct from questions of fact, that we finally resort to mere abuse" (Ayer 1971, 149). "Mere abuse" may seem too temperate a description of the occasionally deadly force that displaces discussion on issues such as abortion. In such cases the bitterness and rancor that distort the public expression of moral conflict work to extend the cultural half-life of emotivism. But even Ayer was aware of the difficulties with that "at first sight ... paradoxical" denial of the reality of serious moral disagreement. At the heart of those difficulties, I argue, is the assumption that serious moral disagreements are rationally irresolvable.

In the introduction to the second edition of *Language, Truth, and Logic* (1946), and in later treatments of these topics in *Freedom and Morality and Other Essays* (Ayer 1984), Ayer attempted to address the concern that emotivism denies important facts about moral experience, and thereby encourages moral nihilism. He never relinquished noncognitivist skepticism about morality and moral argument. He continued to claim that "pure" judgments of moral value have no cognitive content and cannot be true or false—on the grounds, roughly speaking, that there is no moral reality with respect to which they might be true or false. Moreover, he never retreated from the emotivist analysis of moral language: a pure judgment of moral value, he maintains, simply vents feelings and asserts no "genuine proposition." In his famous example, one who says "stealing is wrong" is really saying no more than "Stealing, boo!" But Ayer did revise his original thesis about disagreement. On this revision, a dispute about pure judgments of value is claimed to be a real disagreement, although a "disagreement without formal contradiction" (Ayer 1971, 28). The expression of conflicting feelings, he later wrote, "should not be confused with the making of incompatible statements" (Ayer 1984, 27–30). Further, the revised view allows that it may be possible to "alter another man's opinions" by a suitable choice of emotive language—even where it is impossible to contradict anything that he asserts. Ayer thus gives the impression of taking the existence of moral disagreement more seriously. But if the disagreement between a view that abortion is always morally impermissible and a view that it is not is at bottom a disagreement without formal contradiction, it is difficult to see how concepts such as "morally permissible" and "morally impermissible" could have any meaningful content. Ayer may well have been unperturbed by this result, but it fails to acknowledge that people who dispute the moral acceptability of abortion have any real disagreement at all.

C. L. Stevenson sought to free emotivism from what he described as the "seeming cynicism" about moral disagreement that many critics associated with the work of early logical positivists such as Ayer and

Carnap (Stevenson 1944, 267). He begins this effort by distinguishing two different kinds of disagreement: disagreements in "science, history, and their counterparts in everyday life," which involve primarily the opposition of beliefs, and disagreements in ethics, which involve primarily an "opposition of attitudes" (Stevenson 1944, 2–8; 72–73). He allows that some ethical disputes might be principally disagreements about beliefs—especially causal beliefs. Moreover, since he thinks it possible to adduce reasons to revise offending causal beliefs, he contends that ethical disputes principally concerning such beliefs might be susceptible of resolution by means of reasoning and inquiry. He claims, further, that debate about "controversial" moral issues almost inevitably involves both disagreement in belief and disagreement in non-rational "attitudes" (Stevenson 1944, 11–12). But Stevenson insists that some element in any moral judgment always goes "beyond cognition" to the "conative-affective natures" of human beings (Stevenson 1944, 13). On his view, this means that serious moral disagreements always involve some opposition of attitudes—opposition which can be resolved, if at all, only by "non-rational methods" such as persuasion, exhortation, and public demonstration (Stevenson 1944, 138–151). He thus reasserts the non-cognitivist conception of moral judgment and disagreement.

Even more important, when Stevenson finally explains what he understands by the expression "opposition of attitudes," the old emotivist cynicism about moral disagreement resurfaces. His analysis purports to show—if "only in an imperfect way"—how an opposition of attitudes is a genuine disagreement (Stevenson, 1944, 22–23). On his analysis, however, the exchange between two people engaged in a moral disagreement is translated, roughly, as:

A: I approve of this; do so as well.

B: No, I disapprove of it; do so as well.

But this is not a moral disagreement. It is a pair of successive, self-contained assertions expressing personal approval and disapproval (along with those curious commands to "do so as well"). Genuine moral disagreement presupposes the possibility of real dialogue and exchange, even about fundamental moral judgments. Typically, disputants not only attempt to offer a basis for their judgment, but also attempt to incorporate considerations raised by other parties to the disagreement. Stevenson's account leaves no place for any such exchange. In fact, there is no substantial difference between the emotivist reductions of Ayer and Stevenson, especially given Ayer's recognition that expressions such as "Stealing, boo!" or "Stealing, hooray!" might spur others on to action, and that some moral disputes might also be linked to disputes about "matters of fact" (Ayer 1971). Emotivism is thus incapable of licensing the inference that some moral disagreements are rationally irresolvable. The effort to understand moral argument by presuming that some moral disagreements are rationally irresolvable appears to be incompatible with believing that serious moral disagreement ever really occurs.

There is thus an instructive, if unfortunate, irony in David Wong's efforts to link his recent relativist analysis of moral language and moral argument to a presumed "truth in noncognitivism." That truth is that "many moral disagreements are irresolvable and that there is no single true morality" (Wong 1986, 95). Wong contends, moreover, that his analysis can capture this truth without attempting to reduce moral judgments to expressions of emotion or reports of subjective states or imperatives. On his view, "the moral reality with which moral statements correspond" is always dependent on human conceptual schemes (Wong 1986, 101). He proposes, further, to explain the (presumed) existence of irresolvable moral disagreements with the claim that, in general, the moral judgments that underwrite such disagreements are true only relative to a particular "morality" (Wong 1984, 151; 188). But, as I have argued, relativist attempts to confine moral judgments to a single culture, subculture, or epoch succeed only in explaining away genuine moral disagreement. Genuine moral disagreements are possible because the moral claims that underwrite them are intended, and assumed, by parties to the disagreement to transcend boundaries around cultures, subcultures, and the like. Relativist attempts to treat the moral judgments at the heart of a serious disagreement as true relative to a particular "morality" simply do not contain the conceptual resources to take moral disagreement seriously. Once again, the idea that some moral disagreements are rationally irresolvable—whether in its relativist or non-cognitivist incarnation—emerges as an implicit denial of the reality of serious moral disagreements.

My criticisms of this idea are different in important ways from the position developed and defended by Alasdair MacIntyre in *After Virtue*. While I contend that the very idea of rationally unsettlable disagreements implicitly denies that there are serious moral disagreements, MacIntyre argues that rationally irresolvable disputes occur—but only because *contemporary* moral practices represent a disastrous falling away from a "lost morality of the past" (MacIntyre 1981, 21). Contemporary moral arguments, he contends, appeal to diverse, and often incommensurable, moral concepts that have been torn from the "totalities of theory and practice" in which they once had a clear place. These arguments will therefore degenerate into disputes in which "we possess no rational way of weighing" the claims that underlie them (MacIntyre 1981, 10; 8). The most striking feature of contemporary moral language, according to MacIntyre, "is that so much of it is used to express disagreements; and the most striking feature of the debates in which these disagreements are expressed is their interminable character ... There seems to be no rational way of securing agreement in our culture" (MacIntyre 1981, 6). Emotivist accounts of moral language seem plausible, and rationally irresolvable disputes seem unavoidable, he continues, only because of the drastic disarray of modern moral language and practice. The catastrophic processes by which that disarray occurred are what MacIntyre claims to unmask. In more recent developments of this view, he seeks to recover what he considers a "lost" conception of moral argument and justification on which the rational justification of moral claims is embedded within culturally and historically specific traditions which are partly constituted by a generally unchallenged understanding of what rationality requires (MacIntyre 1988).

But this analysis rests on some implausible, and empirically indefensible, assumptions about the nature of contemporary moral disagreement. MacIntyre's example of "contemporary moral debate" about abortion illustrates this failing. For MacIntyre's account of "debate" about abortion is ultimately nothing more than a brief rehearsal of three different, and essentially self-contained, "rival moral arguments" that, he believes, have been influential in a variety of contemporary arenas (MacIntyre 1981, 6–7). The first of these self-contained arguments bases a conclusion that abortion is morally permissible on an appeal to a woman's right to determine the disposition of her own body.

The second (somewhat less familiar) argument bases the conclusion that abortion is morally impermissible on an appeal to the Golden Rule. On this appeal, a person who claims a right to life in his own case (and hence who "cannot will" that his mother should have had an abortion when pregnant with him) cannot, in accord with the Golden Rule, deny others an equal claim to the right to life. The third and final argument rejects abortion as immoral on the grounds that it is murder (MacIntyre 1981, 6–7). (Oddly, MacIntyre's account of this position never even mentions the idea of a fetal right to life, which has been the central element of the charge that abortion is murder.)

To be sure, all three arguments have some intrinsic interest: for the most part they do appeal to familiar features of the contemporary moral landscape. But after presenting these separate positions on abortion, MacIntyre's discussion of the debate about abortion abruptly ends. There is no suggestion about how, if at all, a proponent of any one of the three positions might attempt to respond to either of the others. In real debates there is always some effort to challenge other parties to the dispute on their own terms; an empirically plausible account would therefore attempt to show how parties to a *real* debate about abortion might actually try to engage one another in a discussion. Yet MacIntyre describes no such engagement. He is equally abrupt, moreover, in discussing his two other principal examples of contemporary moral debate—the question whether a modern war can be a just war, and debate concerning the rights and responsibilities of citizenship. After simply listing separate, self-contained positions on each topic, he immediately turns to philosophical analysis of the supposed conceptual incommensurability of the rival arguments in each debate and the varied historical origins of the "incommensurable" premises deployed (MacIntyre 1981, 9–10). But the abruptness of the transition to these general assertions rests on an implausible assumption: that an empirically adequate characterization of *real* debate about serious moral issues might do nothing more than list a series of separate, self-contained arguments.

Even more important, this account is conceptually inadequate on MacIntyre's own terms. One of the most famous elements of *After Virtue* is its attack on efforts to characterize human action atomistically (MacIntyre, 1981, 190). In a richly drawn picture of the assumptions needed to make human action and conversation intelligible, MacIntyre insists that "in successfully identifying and understanding what some-one else is doing we always move towards placing a particular episode in the context of a set of narrative histories, histories both of the indi-viduals concerned and of the settings in which they act and suffer ... [W]e render the actions of others intelligible in this way because action itself has a basically historical character" (MacIntyre 1981, 197). He is adamant that conversations, in particular, are always "enacted narra-tives" (MacIntyre 1981, 197). Why, then, does he never attempt to construct a narrative that might have given content to the idea of moral debate about abortion (or just wars, or the rights and responsibilities of citizenship)? Like the emotivist reductions offered by Ayer and Steven-son (albeit with a bit more internal tension), MacIntyre's analysis ig-nores the importance of the enacted narrative to making sense of moral conversation, and reduces contemporary moral debate to the mere rec-itation of disjunctive monologues.

Of course, MacIntyre seeks to account for the content of these monologues by appeal to the notion of rival, often incommmensurable moral concepts. But his attempts to develop this view repeat the rela-tivist mistake of ignoring the conditions under which genuine moral disagreement is possible. In the cross-cultural cases, as I have stressed, there must be some moral common ground shared by diverse cultures in order for there even to be a genuine moral disagreement. Thus, for instance, only when Herskovits notes cross-cultural agreement on the moral value of caring for children does his discussion of disagreement about polygamy reveal a genuine cross-cultural *moral* disagreement. Abortion debates within a single culture must, similarly, articulate a ground of moral agreement in order to allow the expression of moral disagreement. Contemporary debates about abortion bear out this ob-servation. In the United States, for instance, the language of rights—in claims about fetal rights to life, women's rights over their bodies, even citizens' rights not to have public monies used for purposes that violate particular religious beliefs—has long been the moral common ground in public controversy about abortion. These debates thus vividly refute MacIntyre's contention that contemporary moral debates are little more than contests between rival or incommensurable moral conceptions.

At this point, however, an astute defender of the doctrine of ration-ally irresolvable disagreement may think that I have conceded too much. Whatever the plausibility of MacIntyre's claims about rival moral concepts catastrophically torn from lost totalities of theories and practice, it may seem that real abortion debates do in fact produce circumstances in which there is no rational way of weighing the underlying moral claims. Particularly in the American context, it will be noted, debate about abortion often degenerates into a moral (and sometimes a legal) tug-of-war between defenders of fetal rights and defenders of abortion rights. But this result, I contend, is a function of deficiencies in the moral language of rights—not in moral argument as a whole, or even contemporary moral language as a whole. The language of rights pits the claims and interests of pregnant women against the claims and interests of unborn fetuses. This language thus embodies an inadequate, and socially dangerous, misinterpretation of the physiological and moral complexities of reproduction, and of the social relationships that may grow up around it. Parties to abortion debates framed in the language of rights therefore become unwitting co-conspirators in a morally distracting and socially destructive process. One unfortunate result of this process, increasingly prominent in the 1980s and 1990s, is a curious "family policy" that uses public monies and public power to prosecute pregnant women for harmful prenatal conduct, rather than providing the kind of social support—including affordable prenatal care and drug-abuse treatment programs open to pregnant women—that might prevent irreparable harm before it ever occurs.[3]

Rational resolution of public controversy on such matters will demand imaginative reinterpretations of the moral dimensions of the human capacity to reproduce (and of the claims and responsibilities of *all* those involved in, or substantially affected by, its exercise). This process of imaginative reinterpretation will require all the parties to contemporary disputes about abortion, in particular, to engage in the kind of scrutiny of settled convictions that few, so far, have been willing to make. To be sure, the demands of formulating public policy on disputed issues may initially place constraints on the public conduct of such scrutiny. For this reason a willingness to consider a compromise position that temporarily "splits the difference" between opposing positions, as Benjamin expresses it, may turn out to be an important moral virtue (Benjamin 1990). There is, moreover, room for debate on the question whether *Roe v. Wade* is a successful effort, in the legal domain, to achieve such a compromise. But the potential instability of any temporary resolution that remains rooted in serious moral disagreement foregrounds the need to intensify public efforts to seek a more robust resolution of the disputed issues. Such efforts will require a sincere and responsible public endeavor to reinterpret imaginatively the moral issues at stake.[4] Efforts to consign conflict about abortion to a realm of rationally irresolvable disagreement simply allow the parties to the conflict to evade their responsibilities for moral self-scrutiny. But so too do efforts to recover elements of an allegedly lost conception of moral argument and justification.

MacIntyre defines his view in terms of a "confrontation" with emotivism (MacIntyre 1981, 21). Yet in relying on a picture of contemporary moral disagreement as a static succession of essentially self-contained monologues, he fights largely on the emotivist's terms. Of course, he departs from emotivist individualism in claiming to root those monologues in concepts that were once integral components of rival totalities of moral theory and practice. But this effort is hampered by the familiar relativist confusions. MacIntyre presupposes the existence (in the past) of integrated, fully individuated, and self-contained moral wholes—something that the complexities of human history render improbable at best.[5] He then supposes that genuine moral disagreement might be possible without substantial moral agreement on fundamental notions. Finally, he assumes a great gulf between contemporary moral language and practice and the moral language and practice of the past with regard to the frequency and vehemence of moral disagreement. But Socrates' exchange with Euthyphro—stressing the inescapably quotidian character of serious moral disagreement—underscores the implausibility of this assumption.

PLURALISM, CONFLICT, AND CHOICE

Emotivism and relativism (and various confrontations with these views) do not exhaust commitment to the idea that rationally irresolvable disagreement is a permanent feature of moral experience. Many influential defenses of the idea presuppose pluralist conceptions of value that are typically neither emotivist nor relativist. Isaiah Berlin defends such a view in "Two Concepts of Liberty" (1958): "The world that we encounter in ordinary experience is one in which we are faced with choices between ends equally ultimate, and claims equally absolute, the realization of some of which must inevitably involve the sacrifice of others" (Berlin 1969, 168). According to Berlin, "Not all good things are compatible, still less all the ideals of mankind." The heterogeneity of ultimate ends means that "the possibility of conflict—and of tragedy—can never wholly be eliminated from human life, either personal or social" (Berlin 1969, 168; 169). This account is part of Berlin's extended criticisms of "positive" conceptions of liberty, which seek to impose constraints on individuals in the name of some allegedly a priori assurance about how to achieve a total harmony of values. He urges that the necessity of choosing between absolute but incompatible ends is what gives value to political freedom, conceived as "negative" freedom from any constraints that might be implied by particular accounts of positive liberty. The ineliminability of irresolvable moral conflict, he insists, gives value to political freedom "as an end in itself, and not as a temporary need" (Berlin 1969, 169). Sympathetic critics are likely to interpret such claims as evidence that Berlin takes moral disagreement seriously, while still defending the notion that rationally irresolvable moral disagreements are an unavoidable feature of the human condition.

Yet aspects of Berlin's response to potential critics should puzzle even a sympathetic reader, and raise new doubts about the view that rationally irresolvable moral conflict is a permanent fixture of experience. There is nothing particularly puzzling, of course, about Berlin's attacks on philosophical attempts to argue for some ultimate unity or harmony among the various ends that human beings can rightly pursue. Berlin cautions—echoing Heine—that concepts nurtured in the quiet of a philosopher's study might destroy a civilization, and he convincingly recounts historical movements that confirm Heine's point (Berlin 1969, 119). Such claims do not advance the case for value pluralism, but that is not their point. Rather, they simply express a liberal theorist's readiness to resist potential threats to political liberty. Their plausibility can be assessed in accordance with the value one assigns to liberty and the confidence one places in philosophical attempts to shape political processes.

More problematic are Berlin's criticisms of the private person who, with no grand political or philosophical designs, rejects value plural-ism—and, as a result, claims to experience none of the interminable moral conflict that Berlin believes to be an unavoidable component of any human life. In an account of the circumstances of human choice, Berlin contends that

> we are doomed to choose, and every choice may entail an irreparable loss. Happy are those who live under a discipline which they accept without question, who freely obey the orders of leaders, spiritual or temporal, whose word is fully accepted as unbreakable law; or those who have, by their own methods, arrived at clear and unshakeable convictions about what to do and what to be that brook no possible doubt . . . [T]hose who rest on such comfortable beds of dogma are victims of self-induced myo-pia, blinkers that may make for contentment, but not for understanding of what it is to be human. (Berlin 1991, 13–14)

What began as a compelling argument to resist the dangers of philo-sophically inspired political movements that might prove inimical to liberty here gives way to an unexplained insistence that to have moral convictions that one is unwilling to relinquish is somehow to fail to appreciate what it means to be fully human. This insistence echoes the closing lines of "Two Concepts of Liberty," in which Berlin affirms Schumpeter's view that to accept "the relative validity of one's convic-tions" and yet "stand for them unflinchingly" distinguishes the "civi-lised" person from the "barbarian." Resistance to this position, Berlin continues, signals a "dangerous moral and political immaturity" (Berlin 1969, 172). In later essays he retreats from the language of "relative validity," yet he never relinquishes the notion that to be morally and politically "mature" one must treat even one's deepest moral convic-tions as always open to revision (Berlin 1991, 10–14).

Yet why does maturity of any sort demand that none of one's deepest convictions can be immune from revision? There are some convictions that one cannot relinquish without endangering one's ca-pacity to be a moral person: the conviction, for instance, that anyone capable of moral concern and moral understanding is worthy of the respect due to all beings so capable. Because this conviction may be crucial to grounding the self-respect that is a fundamental prerequisite of moral agency, to relinquish it would undermine claims to moral maturity. This is one of the most compelling implications of Kant's insistence, in the *Lectures on Ethics*, that due regard to one's worth as a person may be a condition of one's capacity to observe one's duties to others. Equally important, why should political maturity require that all of one's deepest convictions be deemed potentially revisable? What of the person whose very status *as* a person worthy of respect is denied by those whose values she (wisely) chooses to reject? In particular, if one is—or is likely to become—the victim of some violent or coercive manifestation of prejudice, a failure to reject the claims on which that prejudice is based would be political (and possibly physical) suicide. More generally, it is a fact of political life that if some moral convictions are not generally deemed uncontestable, then no convictions can be contested at all. The institutions that protect the rights of the liberal pluralist publicly to describe the non-pluralist as benighted and misguided will survive only as long as most people place the value of those institutions beyond dispute. Liberal pluralists like Berlin may thus find unexpected value in the old political slogan, first proffered in a very different context, that "extremism in the defense of liberty is no vice."[6]

But what of Berlin's remaining charge that the person who experiences no interminable conflicts, whose values are unified by "unshakeable convictions," is in some way deficient or self-deceived? Berlin is not alone in making such a charge. John Rawls, for instance, similarly views the possibility of a "dominant-end" conception of human flourishing, which claims that there is a single dominant end to which all other ends one might pursue are subordinate. Rawls argues that such a conception does not violate principles of rational choice, yet he contends that it is "inhuman" and "strikes us as irrational or more likely as mad" (Rawls 1971, 552–554). Stuart Hampshire similarly urges that "even persons exclusively committed to one clearly delineated way of life, which they are sure is the only right one, ought to admit, if they reflect, that the virtues that they cultivate, and the moral claims that they act on, both entail a cost; even though they are sure that the cost ought to be paid" (Hampshire 1983, 159). Yet someone who understands his life as an effort to answer a calling or to pursue a vocation—whether in the religious sense or in its secular analogues—may find that alternative values and ways of life simply cease to be compelling alternatives for him.

To be sure, acting on a sense of vocation will not always eliminate internal conflict. Weber's famous account, in "Science as a Vocation," provides a particularly apt reminder of this fact. It is precisely because the academic life demands special sacrifices, Weber argues, that only those answering an "inward calling"—and who are therefore driven by a "strange intoxication, ridiculed by every outsider"—should consider it (Weber 1946, 134–135). But a person might well find that in her pursuit of a way of life for which she believes she has an inward calling, values and goods along the road not taken simply become external to her conception of human flourishing, and hence produce no moral conflict. There is nothing irrational or inhuman in this, unless she also attempts to coerce others into sharing her unshakeable convictions. Nor is a person who genuinely and freely chooses devotion to such convictions necessarily self-deceived. The capacities to live such a life are admittedly rare; they may even be the stuff of which saints—secular or religious—are made. Such dedication undoubtedly contains an element of mystery; contemporary charges of irrationality, madness, and self-deception may thus be attempts to fathom how a human being might fail to experience interminable conflict. Nietzsche's virtually lifelong efforts to demystify the "divine naïveté and sureness" of the Platonic Socrates—first detailed in *The Birth of Tragedy*—provide compelling evidence of how unsettling such an unflagging equanimity can be (Nietzsche 1967, 88–89). But surely a mature understanding of morality can resist the naive assumption that any human inquiry might provide the key to all mysteries.

The theorist of value pluralism may still wish to claim that ordinary human beings are susceptible to rationally irresolvable moral conflict. One faces such a conflict, she will argue, when one possesses no common standard for choosing between two equally commendable and important ends that cannot be pursued at the same time—especially, though not only, when choosing either alternative will entail an irreparable loss. Moreover, these observations call to mind familiar examples, such as Sartre's case of the young man who must choose between fighting with the Free French forces and staying home to tend to his devoted mother (Sartre 1965). Yet such cases do not establish the existence of rationally irresolvable conflicts. Instead they show that human beings must sometimes act in circumstances in which any choice that they make will give them, morally speaking, cause for regret. In many such circumstances, in fact, morality *demands* some degree of regret. Theorists of irresolvable conflict have ignored the importance of regret as a moral-reactive sentiment which, unlike remorse, is often appropriate—and sometimes required—when one has done no moral wrong. But as Michael Stocker has argued, it is sometimes rational to regret doing something that, morally speaking, ought to be done (Stocker 1990, 110–123). Part of what is required to enable the rational resolution of serious moral conflicts, especially in first-person cases, is thus an appropriate recognition of the moral importance of regret. Moral rationality here requires one not to perform two actions which it is impossible to do at the same time, but to perform one action and to feel regret that the required action had some undesirable consequences (Stocker 1990, 110–123).

It may still be objected that one faces rationally irresolvable conflict not because some circumstances of choice create reason for regret, but because morality sometimes fails to provide the agent with a common measure of value that would enable a rational choice between two equally compelling alternatives. Varied formulations of this objection have generated an extraordinary volume of philosophical literature about moral dilemmas and tragic choices. Critics charge that morality fails to be "practical," or that it is somehow incomplete, because it fails in such settings to tell one what to do. But what do these objections really mean? What does it mean, that is, to claim that morality—or even an attempt at a theoretical articulation of what morality requires— fails to provide a criterion for the rational resolution of serious moral conflict? For even in the least conflict-ridden cases, the most carefully articulated claim about what morality requires could never "tell" one what to do. No procedure or rule or "common measure" is ever self-interpreting. Nor can any moral standard exhaustively determine all the instances of its application. In a striking instance of this phenomenon, readers of Kant's *Groundwork* often complain (rightly) that nothing about the categorical imperative itself dictates precisely how one should formulate the maxim of a proposed action in order to determine whether the maxim conforms to the demands of duty.[7] Even a carefully articulated account of what morality requires does not free an agent from responsibility for the exercise of judgment.

A developed judgment shaped by extensive experience is an essential requirement for informed moral choice. But the exercise and development of the judgment required for moral reasoning is complicated by difficulties that affect practical reasoning in general. Moreover, these difficulties can be discerned in domains as varied as clinical medicine and legal reasoning, as well as in moral reasoning. One common difficulty is a function of what H. L. A. Hart once called the "open texture" of general rules. As Hart notes, even a very simple rule may generate complexities in application when one turns to consider marginal or ambiguous instances of the rules (Hart 1961, 124–132). Consider a law that prohibits vehicles in city parks. Should a disabled person's wheelchair be prohibited under the rule? Such situations demand an ability to recognize important similarities and differences between the types of things that the law was meant to prevent. An understanding of the rule is no substitute for the exercise of judgment. In clinical medicine, to take a different sort of case, the most precise textbook account of a familiar disease—even supplemented by sophisticated medical testing—cannot obviate the need for experience in detecting and diagnosing different manifestations of the disease in actual patients. Some diseases are harder to diagnose, in this respect, than others: to recognize autoimmune diseases such as multiple sclerosis or rheumatoid arthritis, for instance, requires an extraordinary body of tacit knowledge that no textbook definition can provide. No decision-procedure account of reasoning in clinical medicine is capable of capturing all of the necessary components of clinical skill. But it is equally inappropriate as an account of moral reasoning. For moral reasoning also requires the ability to recognize important similarities and differences between different moral situations, and the knowledge needed to develop this ability cannot be exhaustively articulated by a single rule or any finite set of rules. Albert Jonsen and Stephen Toulmin justly insist that honing one's capacities for moral judgment may require a far greater respect for the taxonomic skills of the casuist than contemporary philosophers have so far been willing to admit (Jonsen and Toulmin 1988).

But no single taxonomy of different types of cases could exhaustively determine all the relevant concerns that may confront moral agents in complex cases. In the law, for instance, the efforts of legal scholars to catalogue and analyze the appropriate precedents carefully and to describe the relevant "legislative intentions" do not eliminate the need for jurists to exercise what Hart calls "discretion"—especially in the hard cases (Hart 1961). Analogously, no taxonomy of appropriate moral precedents can relieve moral agents of the need to exercise judgment. Still further, no particular taxonomic resource could ever provide a *final* statement of the most reasonable ways of dividing up a field of experience for the purposes of practical reasoning. As James suggests in "The Moral Philosopher and the Moral Life," particular hypotheses about what the moral life requires, and actions performed in accordance with those hypotheses, subtly (and sometimes drastically) change the data of moral experience (James [1891] 1974). It is simply impossible to characterize exhaustively and finally the knowledge and the abilities required for the moral life, and this simply becomes most obvious in those situations of serious moral conflict that trouble theorists such as Berlin. But, finally, moral reasoning presents one quite distinctive problem. For an insincere moral agent may expand or contract what Joel Feinberg has called the "accordion" of description so as to thwart the realization of moral ends. The "accordion effect," Feinberg argues, is a familiar feature of language whereby an action or event can be described "almost as narrowly or as broadly as one pleases": like an accordion, an action can be stretched out or squeezed to a minimum in accordance with a variety of purposes (Feinberg 1970, 134–135). Sincerity (including an absence of self-deception) is thus a fundamental prerequisite of the moral life. Indeed, in some respects sincerity in the exercise of the elemental capacity to *describe* a moral problem may be even more important to moral choice than the possession of a developed judgment. But, more generally, in practical reasoning—from clinical medicine to morality—theories do not resolve conflicts, people do. They generally do so more adequately, of course, with the help of practical theories intended to help map out the terrain of the conflict.

Finally, the fact that there is—or at least seems to be—no available common measure to allow for the exercise of judgment in cases like that described by Sartre does not show that these cases are rationally irresolvable dilemmas. Nor does it show that they require a "criterionless choice," as Sartre famously tried to establish (Sartre 1965). In fact, the more intense the distress about the conflict in such a case, the more likely it is that *seemingly* incommensurable ends are actually rooted in some deeply held (if complex) commitment—a commitment that, once articulated, would provide a "common" measure of value.[8] For this reason, serious moral conflict in these first-person cases is the least likely kind of conflict to be even a plausible candidate for the label "rationally irresolvable." A concerted effort at self-reflection—a kind of first-person moral ethnography—might be required to reveal the deep-rooted common measure.[9] But recall that an ethnographer trying to display a cross-cultural disagreement as a genuine moral disagreement must eventually articulate the moral common ground between the cultures in disagreement. Moreover, this kind of articulation is always an interpretation; in the most difficult cases this process of interpretation may even require the ethnographer to scrutinize and reimagine her own settled convictions about the practices or institutions under consideration. Similarly, an agent's self-scrutiny in the face of a serious first-person moral conflict must seek to articulate the common value from which the conflicting commitments flow. This articulation may require similar reinterpretation and reimagination of settled convictions.

To be sure, self-reflective moral ethnography is not precisely like an ethnographic interpretation of cross-cultural disagreement. Self-reflection is far more complex than this analogy can suggest. In particular, as I maintained in Chapter 2, self-reflection is especially difficult when the ends under scrutiny are in some way constitutive of the self-conception under scrutiny. One need make no Freudian assumptions, for example, to understand that a young man's settled convictions about his relationship with his mother might prove particularly resistant to scrutiny. Even the most outwardly untroubled relationships between parents and children may be rooted in volatile emotions. Yet even limited self-scrutiny might allow the young man in Sartre's example to articulate previously unarticulated commitments—and in the process to generate reinterpretations and rearrangements of prior commitments so as to produce new ways of thinking about them (Taylor 1976). An agent confronted with a serious conflict may well find it difficult to engage in even a limited form of self-reflective moral ethnography. Such a person may well act on a criterionless choice: as

Charles Taylor has suggested, a person might just "throw" himself in one way rather than another (Taylor 1976). But this does not mean that there is no other option. In some cases concern about the costs of delaying a decision may limit the time available for self-reflective moral ethnography. But even limited self-scrutiny can provide the agent confronting serious moral conflict with some access to a "criterion" of choice—a criterion more robust than the equivalent of a coin toss. Of course, rational resolution of the conflict will still require the exercise of judgment, and the readiness to regret any costs resulting from its exercise. For this reason, an a priori commitment to the notion that some first-person conflicts "must" inevitably be rationally irresolvable may undermine any possibility of the very self-scrutiny that is most likely to make a rational resolution possible.

ON THE ALLEGED METHODOLOGICAL INFIRMITY OF MORAL INQUIRY

The doctrine that rationally irresolvable moral disagreement is ineliminable, I have argued, rests on seriously mistaken views about moral experience and moral rationality. Why, then, has it remained so compelling to so many contemporary theorists? Much of its continued appeal can be traced to influential attempts to denigrate the methods of moral inquiry in contrast with the methods of science. Theorists who make such attempts assume that moral inquiry can be a genuine aid in the moral life only if the theory resulting from such inquiry rationally selects some action or policy as the unique solution to particular cases of disagreement—and, more generally, selects some morally best way of life. Moral theory cannot do this, these critics charge, because there is no reliable, objective method for testing the claims of moral theories. According to W. V. O. Quine, for instance, "The empirical foothold of scientific theory is in the predicted observable event; that of a moral code is in the observable moral act. But whereas we can test a prediction against the independent course of observable nature, we can judge the morality of an act only by our moral standards themselves. Science, thanks to its links with observation, retains some title to a correspondence theory of truth; but a coherence theory is evidently the lot of ethics" (Quine 1981, 63). When moral disagreement occurs, Quine contends, "one regrets the methodological infirmity of ethics as compared with science." Should that disagreement extend "irreducibly to ultimate ends," one can only hope, with Stevenson, that moral language may work its "emotive weal" (Quine 1981, 63; 64–65).[10]

But the charge that the methods of moral inquiry are methodologically infirm rests on serious misconceptions about the nature and function of moral inquiry and about the connection between moral inquiry and experience. To be sure, there have been efforts to defend moral inquiry against the charge of methodological infirmity by showing that at least some standards of argument and "testability" in science can be applied to evaluate its results (Held 1982; Flanagan 1982). Owen Flanagan, for instance, has argued that normative ethics might conform to the epistemological demands set by argument and inquiry in science by relying on one, or both, of two methods (Flanagan 1982). The first method would involve empirical studies of the moral practices of actual social groups in order to test the success of various "moral strategies." The second method would involve appeal to the "imaginary practice" of sophisticated moral theory: comparing and contrasting the efforts of moral theorists who construct imaginary possible worlds in which different moral conceptions help determine the character of social life (Flanagan, 1982; 1988). Yet a critic is likely to object—along with Quine—that true, or reliable, prediction is an unassailable criterion of success in science, while there is no uncontroversial criterion of success to which normative moral theory might appeal.[11] The shortcomings of Flanagan's first method will be particularly striking in this regard. Consider, for instance, the disagreement between a theorist for whom the unfettered operation of a market economy provides a normative ideal and a theorist who thinks, with Proudhon, that "property is theft." What constitutes success on one theory is anathema on the other.

Flanagan's second proposal, appealing to the notion of "imaginary practice," more clearly reveals the complexity of criteria for theory selection in science. Moreover, it correctly emphasizes the way in which theory construction in science often relies on the testing of theories in imaginary possible worlds. Indeed, in some such cases it may be initially unclear what would suitably test the empirical significance of a theory, while in others it may not yet be possible to carry out the appropriate tests. It is thus that in physics, for instance, the strongest initial support for a theory will often appeal to a criterion such as mathematical consistency. But Flanagan notes that theory construction in science generally is constrained not by observational feedback alone but by observation conjoined with considerations such as consistency with, and conservation of, existing beliefs, as well as accuracy, simplicity, and scope of explanation (Flanagan 1988, 542–543). Still further, Flanagan might welcome Thomas Kuhn's contention that such criteria do not function as rules to determine theory choice, but instead serve as shared *values* used in judging theories (Kuhn 1977, 331; cf. 1970 184–185).[12] If Kuhn is right, these criteria will then "influence decision without specifying what those decisions must be" (Kuhn 1977, 330). On Kuhn's scheme, moreover, scientists will differ in their application of these criteria (Kuhn 1970, 185). This leads Kuhn to deny that one could ever construct a shared *algorithm* of theory choice. In his view, both the interpretation of criteria for theory choice as well as the relative weight assigned to those criteria tend to vary over time and according to the field in which the criteria are to be applied (Kuhn 1977, 326–335). Taken together, these considerations certainly point to the possibility of far more dispute about methods in science than conventional models of scientific inquiry have allowed. But should such claims be taken to narrow the gap between the methods of science and those of moral inquiry? For while Kuhn denies that values such as accuracy, consistency, and scope provide the grounds to construct an algorithm of theory choice, he nonetheless argues that they function at very early stages of theory choice in (normal) science to specify a great deal. They specify, for example, the kinds of considerations that may be relevant to theory choice, and especially the kinds of considerations a scientist will be expected to offer (to other scientists) in support of such a choice (Kuhn 1977, 331). On Kuhn's view, this helps explain why most newly suggested scientific theories do not survive (Kuhn 1977, 332).

Might there be any shared values governing theory choice in moral inquiry that function in a manner even roughly analogous to that of accuracy, consistency, and the rest in science? Careful scrutiny of the workings of moral inquiry suggests that there are no such values. To begin with, there is no consensus among philosophical practitioners of normative moral inquiry about the kinds of considerations that might even qualify as confirmational constraints on the claims of moral theory. Notions as varied as "the contents of conscience," "moral facts," "intuitions," and "moral experience" have been proposed as appropriate constraints. Further, even where there is some measure of agreement on what should count as an appropriate confirmational constraint, it is still unclear how any such constraint might function in a process of testing and rejecting "rival" or "competing" theories in order to select one of those rivals as the best theory (up to now). This is, roughly, the model of theory selection to which the methods of moral inquiry must conform if they are to meet standards set by argument and inquiry in science. But this is precisely the sort of characterization that moral inquiry always resists.

This difficulty is borne out by two of the most influential thought experiments in contemporary moral philosophy: those in Rawls's *Theory of Justice* (1971) and Nozick's *Anarchy, State, and Utopia* (1974). These theories might both be described as efforts to "capture," or give a theoretical account of, a familiar intuition: that it is wrong to treat persons merely as means to the promotion of some social purpose. Yet the resulting moral conceptions are, to put it mildly, quite different. In the just society described in *A Theory of Justice*, social institutions are arranged—subject to the priority of the principle of equal liberty and the fair equality of opportunity—so that inequalities in wealth and power benefit the least well-off representative person. On this conception, justice may require taxation to finance various transfer payments. The conception defended in *Anarchy, State, and Utopia* construes the only legitimate state as a "night watchman" writ large, protecting citizens against force, fraud, and theft, and ensuring the performance of contracts. On this conception, taxation to fund anything more than the minimal state violates the prohibition against treating persons merely as a means to some social purpose. How might the initial intuition—or even any implicit goal of successfully "accounting for" that intuition—provide a test that allows the community of moral inquirers to reject one of these theories as less "successful" than the other? Even on a conception of confirmation in science (like Kuhn's) that resists appeals to the idea of testing predictions against what Quine calls the "independent course of observable nature," it is difficult to find support for the notion that the methods of moral inquiry might be substantially similar to those of inquiry in (normal) science.

It is certainly true that debates in the history and philosophy of science, along with influential accounts in the sociology of knowledge, have focused attention on the actual practice of science in ways that undermine idealized characterizations of that practice. Even the National Academy of Sciences cautions beginning researchers in American graduate programs that scientific knowledge "emerges from a process that is intensely human . . . marked by its full share of human virtues and limitations" (National Academy of Sciences 1989, 1). While it may be an interesting philosophical question whether the results of this process somehow transcend the human virtues and limitations that shape it, no reasonable account of science can ignore the activities of the individuals, and especially the communities, engaged in scientific inquiry. For this reason, in many quarters the idealized search for a single "scientific method" has gradually given way to an examination of the methods of science: the techniques, principles, values, and tacit assumptions embodied in the practices of the communities within which science is carried out (National Academy of Sciences 1989). This reference to communities is important: like all serious human inquiry, scientific inquiry is conducted in and by communities of inquirers. In this respect, moral inquiry is no different from scientific inquiry. Yet, seconding a set of concerns first defended by thinkers as diverse as Michael Polanyi and Robert Merton, Kuhn makes some important observations about the special features of scientific communities—especially in the natural sciences—that help account for their ability to achieve consensus on the problems and procedures that shape successful inquiry.[13] Even theorists who might reject Kuhn's conception of confirmation in science can glean important lessons from these claims. But the lessons may be most instructive for those who share Kuhn's conception of confirmation in science and mistakenly expect that it might make moral inquiry look more like scientific inquiry.

Two characteristics of mature communities in the natural sciences are most important to understanding their success. Kuhn argues, first, that these communities are governed by clearly defined and efficiently administered terms for membership: terms that operate, for instance, in the educational institutions and professional associations and journals in which scientists conduct and evaluate their research (Kuhn 1970, 163–164). Second, Kuhn believes that mature communities in the natural sciences typically achieve an "unparalleled" insulation from the demands of "the laity and of everyday life" (Kuhn 1970 164–165). This second claim may seem problematic to thinkers concerned to stress that scientific activity always takes place in a specific social, historical, and especially economic context. Some critics will object that the values and preoccupations of "everyday life" often find their way into the workings of natural science by the most unexpected routes. Yet Kuhn's point is that the problems that communities of natural scientists pursue—not just the methods and procedures they rely on to solve them—are typically defined by those communities themselves. Kuhn urges, further, that in this respect there is an important contrast between the natural sciences and most social sciences—where research problems are often defended in terms of the social importance of the solution, and thus partly defined by concerns of the "laity and everyday life" (Kuhn 1970, 164–165). The processes by which natural science communities control their membership, as well the problem-defining processes that shape their research activities, are central to creating contexts in which the natural sciences—unlike the social sciences—produce their characteristic results. These processes are crucial components of the mechanisms by which the natural sciences develop those shared "paradigms" which define procedures and problems. One need not accept Kuhn's claims that failures in the problem-solving ability of "normal science" lead to revolutionary paradigm shifts, nor need one sanction his stance on attempts to distinguish between the context of discovery and the context of justification in order to agree that he identifies important features of the social structure of natural science. But, most important, these observations implicitly point to facts about moral inquiry—and about the community of moral inquirers—that help explain why moral inquiry cannot possibly conform to standards of argument and inquiry in the natural sciences.

To begin with, the community of moral inquirers simply lacks those characteristics that help ensure the ability of natural scientists to define the terms of their inquiries. Membership in the community of moral inquirers is not—and in principle could not be—limited to a specially trained group of researchers. One needs no special credentials or special training to extend everyday moral concern into critical reflection. Non-philosophers may assume that this belabors an obvious point, but it has often been overlooked by philosophers. Those concerned to make moral inquiry more like science, as much as those who denigrate it because it is not, have been particularly unable to appreciate the philosophical implications of facts about the community of moral inquirers. That community extends, in principle, to include any human being capable of reflection (even though in practice linguistic, religious, and cultural boundaries may limit the influence of any particular instance of moral inquiry). This means that even the most sophisticated normative moral theory, insofar as it is genuine moral inquiry, can never be more than a species of a familiar genus: the critical, sometimes unsystematic reflection that lived human experience constantly renders unavoidable. Admittedly, philosophy typically transforms the everyday concerns that give rise to moral inquiry—sometimes in quite extraordinary ways, and sometimes in ways that engender suspicion and mistrust of those concerns. In one of philosophy's most extraordinary episodes, for instance, logical positivist suspicions of everyday moral language and argument eventually led thinkers such as Ayer to deny the meaningfulness of everyday moral concerns. But philosophical suspicions may sometimes provide an important stimulus for critical moral thinking; Plato's image of Socrates as a gadfly on the neck of Athens is a vivid reminder of this fact.

I argue, further, that the philosopher's special training can allow philosophical moral inquiry to make valuable and much-needed contributions to the ongoing task of moral inquiry in general. Yet when philosophers seek to define the problems that moral inquiry should pursue by first denigrating everyday moral concerns—or when they attempt to turn moral problems into philosophical puzzles—they may sever the crucial link with the concerns that give particular problems their distinctive character as *moral* problems. The results may make good or even great philosophy, but they will prove unsatisfactory as a form of moral inquiry. As Hilary Putnam observes, having a moral problem "solved" by philosophy is sometimes like asking for a subway token and getting a ticket for a ride on an interplanetary spaceship (Putnam 1990, 179).

I have claimed that philosophical transformations of everyday concerns sometimes provide the only adequate stimulus for appropriately critical thought. But in attempting to effect such transformations, one must be mindful of the ways in which philosophical suspicions can be dangerously misplaced. A striking example of the failure to do so appears in David Brink's defense of philosophical moral realism. Brink laments the failure of moral theory to free itself, like science, from religious influences that "infect" moral thought and "artificially restrict" people's moral imaginations (Brink 1989, 206). He also decries the fact that "most lay persons, even those with strong moral sensibilities, seem largely unaware of, or uninterested in, even the outlines of theoretical work in ethics" (Brink 1989, 207). Yet he never stops to consider that a theory premised on the notion that religious beliefs simply "infect" and "restrict" moral thinking and imagination might be part of the problem. Just a few paragraphs later, for instance, Brink claims to find evidence for "moral progress" on the grounds, among other things, that "most people" no longer think slavery or racial discrimination to be acceptable (Brink 1989, 207–208). But he seems unaware that abolitionist movements in nineteenth-century England and America were largely expressions of evangelical religious convictions, or that many of the men and women who fought racial discrimination in twentieth-century America derived their inspiration from religious faith. Nor does he mention the ways in which Locke's seventeenth-century support for slavery, and Hume's eighteenth-century support of racism, for generations continued to fuel defenses of these practices throughout the English-speaking world.[14] To be sure, philosophical moral inquiry sometimes found its way into arguments against slavery and discrimination, and defenders of such practices have often claimed to find support for their convictions in religion. Yet there is little reason to believe, as Brink contends, that "systematic" moral inquiry would be more likely to promote, say, increased opposition to discrimination were it completely free of the influence of religious beliefs. Hume's well-known antipathy toward religious "prejudices" was combined with a vehement refusal, in the essay "Of National Characters," to scrutinize his acceptance of racial prejudice (Hume [1777] 1964a). C. D. Broad once argued that even the best moral theories cannot contain the "whole truth, and nothing but the truth" (Broad 1979, 1). For the nineteenth-century abolitionist and the twentieth-century supporter of civil rights, Broad's observation would have been an understatement at best.

But what might it mean for moral philosophy to embrace actively the link between philosophical moral inquiry and non-philosophical reflection about the moral life? In one of the more striking answers to this question, Kant argued that his account of the categorical imperative, in the *Groundwork*, revealed the ideally rational and objectively valid structure of the ordinary moral consciousness. He insisted that, like Socrates, he was making human reason "attend to its own principle." Accordingly, he relished one critic's observation that the *Groundwork* had told the reader "nothing new" about morality (Kant [1785] 1964).[15] Such claims embody a distinctive construal of the link between moral philosophy and the wider community of moral inquirers, but in so doing they make an important point—to adopt a phrase of Quine's—about the real empirical foothold of moral theory. Moral theory certainly has a foothold in experience, but it is not Quine's "observable act," nor Flanagan's ongoing practice of "moral strategies," nor even (except indirectly) the moral intuitions which might figure in the construction of moral thought experiments. Rather, the empirical foothold of moral theory, like that of all moral inquiry, is the self-understanding of the community of moral inquirers potentially addressed by the inquiry. Any moral stance—whether a sophisticated philosophical construction, a loosely connected set of prereflective intuitions, or an incoherent jumble of judgments and attitudes—will be bound up with particular visions of the sorts of persons who accept or reject such positions or intuitions, or who make such judgments and hold such attitudes. The empirical foothold of a moral argument or a philosophical moral theory is in the complex self-conceptions of those embroiled in the debate or addressed by the theory.

I intend the expressions "self-understanding" and "self-conception," which I treat as roughly synonymous, to have a much broader sense than usual. First, one's self-understanding includes beliefs not only about oneself but also about one's place in the natural (and possibly supernatural) world, and about one's relationships to other selves—about one's place in the social world. Further, the vocabulary in which one learns to give expression to one's self-conception, and the concepts that initially shape a self-conception, are products of the linguistic conventions of a given community. These conventions embody, among other things, complex and culturally influenced patterns of normative expectations about emotion, thought, and action that initially help determine the content of a self-conception. This means that a substantial portion of anyone's self-conception is powerfully influenced by social and cultural experience. But any culture that fails to encourage some degree of creativity in the exercise of judgment would create the conditions for its own demise. This means that the revisability of self-conceptions is a condition of cultural survival. It is thus, for instance (as I mentioned in Chapter 2) that the Appalachian women who sought to break with cultural prohibitions against work outside their homes gradually came to see themselves and their place in the world in dramatically new and different terms.[16] The revisability of self-conceptions is a condition of the possibility of moral inquiry, and indeed an important feature of moral theory is inextricably bound up with this fact. A central task of moral inquiry is to encourage the sort of self-scrutiny which may lead one to see oneself, one's relations to others, and one's place in the world (broadly understood) in a different way. Plato's early dialogues provide important examples of this task. When the reader wishes, for instance, that Euthyphro would stay with Socrates to renew his discussion of piety, the dialogue reveals one of the essential characteristics of moral inquiry. Although the aim of moral inquiry will sometimes be to effect a change in practice as well as in self-understandings, moral reflection can generate reform in practice only if it first encourages self-scrutiny. And this view, finally, requires no metaphysics of the self. There may be no knowable entity over and above the various self-conceptions to which any given person would assent over a lifetime, nor need there be an effort to posit such an entity in order to do moral theory. It is necessary to show only that persons are capable of assenting to, or dissenting from, a self-conception, and that they are capable of revising such conceptions.

The fact that moral theories must be addressed to beings capable of revising a self-conception does not mean that the content of moral theories can rightly exclude beings not so capable. Nor does it mean that the content of a moral theory is properly determined by the content of the self-conceptions of those to whom they are addressed. But a moral theory is pointless unless it is addressed to beings whose conduct and character might be influenced by its deliverances. This helps explain familiar methodological devices (rightly) employed by moral theorists. For the self-conceptions of those to whom moral theory is addressed will be "accessible" only by means of the pre-theoretical, or pre-reflective, intuitions to which they would assent at any given point in time. Contemporary theorists who announce their intentions to begin with intuitions simply do explicitly what moral theorists—such as Kant, for instance—have always done. In fact they are doing what adequate moral inquiry of any kind must do. Moral theory must start from the "inside": from the pre-theoretical deliverances of the moral consciousness of those to whom the theory is addressed. Adequate moral inquiry is therefore always a species of self-reflection. Much twentieth-century Anglo-American moral philosophy—especially that preoccupied with demonstrating that everyday moral concerns are in some way suspicious or in error—has ignored this fact. But this conviction that adequate moral inquiry is always a species of self-reflection has influenced much of the most compelling moral philosophy at least since Plato reported Athenian resistance to the Socratic contention that the unexamined life is not worth living. Attempts to revive this conception, moreover, have produced some of the most important moral theory of the twentieth century. For instance, in a seldom noticed passage in *A Theory of Justice*, Rawls insists that moral philosophy is the study of "principles which govern actions shaped by self-examination." "Moral philosophy is Socratic," he continues, and "we may want to change our present considered judgments once their regulative principles are brought to light" (Rawls 1971, 48–49).

But once the connection between moral inquiry and self-examination is restored to its rightful place at the center of moral philosophy, it should become clear that demands that moral inquiry be more like scientific inquiry are fundamentally misconceived. Critics who overlook the central role which self-scrutiny plays in moral inquiry are bound to misunderstand moral argument and normative moral theory. The most common misunderstanding is embodied in the expectation that a moral theory's foothold in experience should be capable of "confirming" or "disconfirming" that theory. For the relation between moral theory and experience makes any such expectation unintelligible. In some instances, of course, the aim of moral theory (or moral inquiry in general) is to effect a substantial change in the structure or content of its empirical foothold in self-understandings. Rawls's claims about the Socratic nature of moral philosophy provide a much needed reminder of the importance of this aim. The process of contemplating a moral theory does not always bring about substantial change in self-conceptions; nor is there reason to think that a moral theory has failed when it does not. Yet any reflective confrontation with a moral theory will inevitably reorder the settled convictions that one brings to its contemplation; in so doing, it will effect at least some change in the structure and content of self-understandings. Something quite similar happens, moreover, in a serious moral debate. It is thus, for instance, that when an opponent of abortion and a supporter of abortion rights come to see each other as human beings who differ about a moral stance—not as demons of one sort or another—they learn to see their opponents, and hence themselves, in a new way. This process often produces a profound revision in self-conceptions of the sort that may make constructive moral discussion possible for the first time. Taken together, these considerations also confirm that self-conceptions determine the content of those complex patterns of belief that Duncker described as the situational meanings of actions. Thus, for example, a person who believes that a fertilized human ovum is infused with an immortal soul at the very moment of conception will most likely disagree about the moral status of abortion with one who does not understand the world in this way. The failure to reach agreement in such cases does not show the non-rationality of moral discourse, or even the rationally irresolvable nature of disagreement about abortion. It shows, rather, how difficult it is to persuade another to see the world, and her place in it, in a new way. This is the unexpected kernel of truth in Ayer's sardonic comment about the resort to "mere abuse."

The difficulty of convincing another to see differently the world and one's place in it is equally evident in the more rarified disputes of moral philosophy. The Rawlsian democratic egalitarian fails to persuade the Nozickean libertarian that the part of Rawls's conception requiring the financing of transfer payments—the difference principle portion of Rawls's second principle of justice—is defensible. But the difference principle is addressed to persons who can accept a very distinctive vision of themselves. Rawls must be able to convince them both that they do not in a moral sense deserve their fortunes in the "natural lottery," and that any gain arising out of their arbitrary good fortune must be compatible with an institutional expression of concern for the expectations of those who have arbitrarily lost out (Rawls 1971, 100–108). The libertarian may concede the first revision in his self-conception, but he will surely insist that concern for the expectations of others cannot be institutionalized as Rawls's theory requires without violating the prohibition—expressed by the "intuition" which both views seek to capture—against treating persons merely as means. Yet the failure of Rawls's theory to convince the libertarian is not evidence of a rationally irresolvable conflict. Rather the democratic egalitarian fails to persuade the libertarian to revise his self-conception in a manner required to secure agreement that the difference principle is part of a defensible conception of justice. The failure to convince is not unique to moral disagreement: for instance, the disagreement between Cardinal Bellarmino and Galileo, and the dispute embodied in Einstein's resistance to quantum mechanics, were surely as serious as any dispute between libertarians and democratic egalitarians.

DOES PESSIMISM ABOUT MORAL CONFLICT REST ON A MISTAKE?

I have suggested that at least two forms of adjudication may be available in moral disputes (between two or more parties) where no currently available method of reasoning and argument has enabled rational resolution. In some disputes, opposing parties may seek—in Benjamin's phrase—temporarily to split the difference between opposing positions; that is, they may seek a temporary compromise. In other cases they may seek to carry out some mutually self-scrutinizing moral ethnography in the hope of generating a new ground of agreement as an outcome of careful articulation and reinterpretation of fundamental convictions. For a variety of reasons, however, these methods may fail. Agreement in these cases may be possible, if at all, only as the outcome of a kind of persuasion or conversion; on this Stevenson is surely right. But moral argument is no different in this regard from any other form of argument. Any dispute may outstrip the disputants' capacity to solve it by means of currently available standards of argument and justification. Reasons run out, so to speak, even in science. In a striking reminder of this fact, Wittgenstein imagines a man "who had grown up in quite special circumstances and been taught that the earth came into being 50 years ago, and therefore believed this. We might instruct him: the earth has long ... etc.—We should be trying to give him our picture of the world. This would happen through a kind of *persuasion*" (Wittgenstein 1979, sec. 262). There are many areas of human concern in which the effective working of a discursive reason-giving practice may be inseparable from some associated reimagining of the world. Finally, to give new life to an old saw, there are contexts in which a picture is worth more than a thousand discursive reasons.

These considerations do not show that moral theory might be just like scientific theory—but that is not my aim. Unalterable facts about the community of moral inquirers, the means by which moral problems emerge, and the distinctive connection between moral theory and its foothold in experience render all such efforts futile. But there is no reason to lament this fact, or to assume that moral inquiry has somehow failed to conform to standards of rationality in argument. Indeed, it is important to resist any effort to consign to the sphere of the non-rational realms of argument and inquiry such as ethics, which afford opportunities and stimuli for self-scrutiny. The capacity to treat our self-conceptions as revisable is an essential component of rationality. The willingness to exercise this capacity, moreover, is a condition of peaceful coexistence with others, and is the only attitude capable of ensuring that the structure of moral experience might fit comfortably with changes in the texture of non-moral experience wrought by continual social and scientific change. Moral inquiry is valuable not merely in spite of but *because* of the fact that many of the methods on which it relies are appropriate to its subject matter and to the character of the community of moral inquirers.

There is no reason to expect that moral disagreement might come to an end. Indeed, there is no reason to think that the process of moral inquiry might eventually result in "convergence" on some one theory as the only appropriate arbiter of moral disputes or the only adequate account of the morally best way of life. Disagreement, even serious disagreement, is endemic to moral experience. It is likely that on some matters—for instance, practices surrounding human reproduction, and the intentional killing of living beings (human and non-humans)—resolving a serious moral conflict at one point in time does not guarantee that the disputed issue will not reemerge as the subject of some future rational disagreement. As Putnam has suggested, the very idea that a dispute about abortion might be "solved"—once and for all—rests on a misconception of how moral argument and moral reasoning, especially on serious matters, properly work. In Putnam's view, "The very words *solution* and *problem* may be leading us astray—ethical 'problems' are not like scientific problems, and they often do not have 'solutions' in the sense that scientific problems do" (Putnam 1990, 180–181). Putnam wisely suggests relinquishing the problem/solution metaphor in favor of a metaphor drawn from the law—the metaphor of adjudication (Putnam 1990, 181). This metaphor offers a particularly rich understanding of the varieties of moral resolution. It also serves as an important reminder that disputes about serious moral issues often reemerge in new circumstances where they demand rethinking and reimagining of the moral complexities involved. But this is surely to be expected, since decisions taken now on the basis of some current resolution of a moral disagreement—about abortion or euthanasia, for instance—necessarily alter the world in which moral reflection can be done in the future. In fact, decisions taken now effectively alter the data of moral experience. For this reason, certain moral disputes may demand readjudication in the future, when the new data of moral experience reveal the insufficiency of the early resolution. Many serious moral issues will indeed demand repeated readjudication—and an associated reimagining and reinterpretation of the moral complexities of the situation—with every new generation that confronts the problem.

The failure to understand this fact, moreover, has distorted everyday moral inquiry just as much as philosophical moral reflection. The complexity of moral experience makes such difficult demands on human beings that the persistence of disagreement and conflict—and, especially, the need it generates to reexamine settled convictions—is an essential component of the rationality of moral reasoning and moral choice. Thus, not only is there no reason to think that serious disagreement will come to an end, but also there is little reason to hope that it will. Discontent about the persistence of moral disagreement simply rests on a misconception about the role and importance of moral disagreement. Of course, if there is no general agreement on the terms under which every potential moral inquirer might contribute to moral debate, no disagreement would be possible at all. Yet the persistence of moral disagreement—within a framework of fundamental agreement on the moral importance of allowing human beings to take part in that disagreement—is a central element of moral rationality. As Socrates cautions Euthyphro, even the gods—if they quarrel at all—would quarrel about the good, the honorable, and the just.

4 | MORAL INQUIRY AND THE MORAL LIFE

Who would want to introduce a new principle of morality and, as it were, be its inventor, as if the world had hitherto been ignorant of what duty is or had been thoroughly wrong about it?

Immanuel Kant, Critique of Practical Reason

Insofar as we can recognize moral progress, it has less to do with the discovery or invention of new principles than with the inclusion under the old principles of previously excluded men and women. And that is more a matter of (workmanlike) social criticism and political struggle than of (paradigm-shattering) philosophical speculation.

Michael Walzer, Interpretation and Social Criticism

MORAL INQUIRY AS AN INTERPRETIVE ENTERPRISE

The world in which ordinary women and men must attempt to realize central elements of the moral life is unavoidably complex. One need not accept a pluralist understanding of the moral domain, however compelling, in order to appreciate this fact. Moral complexity is often simply a function of complexity in the situational meanings of actions—those culturally shaped structures of signification on which, as Karl Duncker rightly argues, moral valuations depend. Of course, Duncker relies on the concept of situational meaning principally to counter descriptive cultural relativism. He argues that the "ethical essence" of particular actions depends on the concrete patterns of situational meanings with which they are associated, and that the situational meanings which undergird moral practices vary widely from one culture to another. But within any given culture, the situational meaning of an action or practice will be an intricate construction. Thus, for instance, evaluative positions on abortion will be rooted in a complicated pattern of beliefs about the nature and purpose of sexuality, the appropriate structure of families, and the rules that ought to govern relations between men and women—in addition to beliefs about the nature of personhood and the sanctity of human life. Such a complex structure of belief, along with any of its constituent elements, can be subject to quite varied interpretations. Disagreement about how to interpret such a structure—and thus about how to understand the practice framed by that structure—may create substantial moral disagreement concerning any given practice. It is thus, for example, that someone who understands capital punishment as an expression of a vengeful, pre-moral instinct will judge the practice quite differently from someone for whom it is an expression of a society's willingness to give certain criminals their "due." More generally, varied interpretations of practices which are taken to be central—or in some way seriously detrimental—to a shared way of life can generate substantial moral complexity within any culture.

This link between variation in the interpretation of situational meanings and the proliferation of moral disagreement has important implications. First, it supports Michael Walzer's view, developed in *Interpretation and Social Criticism*, that everyday moral argument is interpretive in character (Walzer 1987, 21). It also shows that Walzer is right to identify the "real subject" of everyday moral argument as "the meaning of the particular moral life shared by the protagonists" (Walzer 1987, 23). Familiar moral arguments—about capital punishment, abortion, welfare, the moral standing of animals—are rooted in disagreements about how to interpret important ingredients of a shared life. Imagination plays a fundamental role in everyday moral argument because securing agreement on the substance of shared moral life may require quite strenuous efforts to reinterpret that life imaginatively. But imagination plays an important role in moral reasoning generally: as Mark Johnson has argued, many of the concepts that are central to moral thinking are principally governed by imaginative structures—by metaphor and narrative, for instance (Johnson 1993, 33).[1]

Yet many contemporary philosophical accounts of moral reasoning and argument are unable to acknowledge the interpretive character of moral argument. On these accounts, moral reasoning is rooted primarily—if not entirely—in the capacity to understand and apply some principle, or some finite set of principles, that yields an (allegedly) context-free decision procedure for churning out solutions to easily characterizable moral problems. Yet context-free decision procedures are of little use in the efforts at imaginative reinterpretation that are central to the resolution of serious moral disputes. It may be possible to describe and classify some of the imaginative processes that allow the successful resolution of such disputes. And it certainly is possible to suggest ways in which one imaginative structure might be more likely than another to yield a constructive moral resolution. I have argued elsewhere, for instance, that constructive moral reflection about the practice of commercial surrogacy should take seriously some implications of the metaphor of a child as a gift (Moody-Adams, 1991a). But it is not possible to construct some algorithm that could exhaustively characterize those processes of creative imagination that are most relevant to the resolution of serious moral disagreements. This is why contemporary moral philosophers are so often unable to recognize how such disagreements might be rationally resolved. Finally, even articulating the issues at stake in a serious moral disagreement, and thereby framing the problem to be discussed, may itself be a difficult exercise in interpretation. Continued conflict about how to describe the principal antagonists on abortion—"pro-life" versus "anti-abortion"; "pro-choice" versus "pro-abortion"—provides a striking example of how difficult this process can be. Reasonably adjudicating such disputes (as well as the moral problems with which they are linked) may require reliance on processes of the imagination to settle on a shared interpretation of the problem to be discussed. Walzer's characterization of everyday moral argument as interpretive thus helps to clarify crucial features of everyday moral thinking and argument.

I suggest in this chapter that these links between interpretation and moral argument are of signal importance for thinking about moral inquiry in general. Indeed, I show that adequate accounts of moral inquiry—including philosophical moral inquiry—and of the moral domain itself require a careful understanding of the connections between interpretation and moral argument. Everyday moral argument and philosophical moral inquiry are species of the same genus, and there are good reasons to conclude that interpretation is a fundamental characteristic of the genus. The link between moral philosophy and self-scrutiny provides an especially compelling reason for thinking that interpretation is an important ingredient of philosophical moral inquiry. It is possible to scrutinize a self-conception, after all, only if central features of that conception have been clearly articulated; but articulation of a self-conception is always a complex exercise in interpretation. An unexpectedly wide variety of twentieth-century philosophers have embraced, or implicitly presupposed, the link between interpretation, self-scrutiny, and philosophical moral inquiry. Discerning that commitment may, however, require looking beyond a philosopher's explicit claims to supply "soberly logical" theses about moral judgments and concepts. R. M. Hare, for example, claims that his universal prescriptivism seeks to preserve the non-descriptive "insights" of emotivism, while rejecting its essentially "irrationalist" elements, solely by appeal to "the logic of the moral concepts" (Hare 1991, 455; 460; cf. 1963). Yet he has defined ethical theory as, primarily, an account of what "we mean by the words or the sentences that we use in moral discourse." Any such account, he adds, will have "implications" for epistemological concerns about how, if at all, it is possible to engage in "rational discussion" of moral questions (Hare 1991, 451). Philosophical reflection on such concerns will clearly reach beyond interpretation. Yet Hare's claims about the prescriptivity and universalizability of moral judgments surely constitute an interpretation—an articulation of the structure presumably implicit in what "we" already do. Hare once described his philosophical method as a "demythologised version of Plato's doctrine of *anamnesis*" (Hare 1967, 208). His subsequent writings on moral theory bear out that characterization.

Of course, twentieth-century analytic philosophy has sometimes taken the meaning, as well as the mythology, out of its accounts of moral language: in his later works A. J. Ayer defended his contention that moral concepts are "pseudo-concepts" as "a theory of what we are doing when we make ethical judgments" (Ayer 1984, 18). Describing such a position as an interpretation of moral practices may involve a questionable application of the concept; perhaps a view which denies the reality of central features of moral experience is not, in fact, a species of genuine moral inquiry. In any case, recent responses to noncognitivism's excesses—from views as varied as relativism and realism—

more genuinely aspire to interpret what "we" do in everyday moral practice. Thus, according to Nicholas Sturgeon, moral realism is the view that

> our moral terms typically refer to real properties; that moral statements typically express propositions capable of truth and falsity; and that our ordinary methods of arriving at moral judgments provide us with at least some approximate knowledge of moral truths. I suspect that, in addition, we ought not to count a view realist unless it holds that these moral truths are in some interesting sense *independent* of the subjective indicators—our moral beliefs and moral feelings, as well as moral conventions . . . that we take as guides to them. (Sturgeon 1986, 116–117)

David Brink likewise insists that moral realism is "presupposed by common normative practices of moral judgment, argument, and deliberation" (Brink 1989, 25). He also maintains that central features of common practices are "hard to understand" without an acceptance of realism, and that moral realism "could still be false" if moral inquiry and thought turned out to be "confused or misguided in some fundamental way" (Brink 1989, 24). Even relativist critics of realist interpretations—defending moderate as well as extreme forms of relativism—have claimed to make sense of "our" intuitions about the proper scope of moral concepts and judgments (Harman 1975, 8; Wong 1984, 24–25).

Of course, a philosophical account of normative moral theory often embodies an effort to systematize some interpreted structure of belief or judgment—principally in order to extend the application of that structure in new, or sometimes simply more orderly, ways. It is in this spirit that Kant, for example, insists that the categorical imperative is a new "formula" for determining duties rather than a "new principle" of morality. But the categorical imperative embodies Kant's account of the rational structure that underlies "ordinary" moral consciousness, and that account is the outcome of a complex exercise in interpretation. Of course one can dispute the success of Kant's efforts: critics may reject what they view as the reductivist tendencies of moral theories such as Kant's, or they may find his theory inattentive to the (purportedly) irreducibly cultural and historical dimensions of livable moral practices. But a disputed interpretation is still an interpretation. Indeed, Kant's writings are full of potentially problematic interpretations. At one point, for instance, he claims that the conception of moral worth bound up with the categorical imperative provides the most plausible interpretation of "passages from Scripture in which we are commanded to love our neighbour and even our enemy. For love out of inclination cannot be commanded; but kindness done from duty—although no inclination impels us, and even although natural and unconquerable disinclination stands in our way, is *practical* ... residing in the will and not in the propensions of feeling, in principles of action and not of melting compassion" (Kant [1785] 1964, 13). But whatever its idiosyncracies as an account of New Testament doctrine, this passage richly displays Kant's commitment to the importance of interpretation in philosophical moral inquiry. Such efforts lend powerful support to the claim that moral philosophy is fundamentally—though, of course, not exclusively—an interpretive enterprise.

Yet what is it that moral philosophy aims to interpret? In one respect the answer is quite simple: the structure of moral experience. The object of interpretation in moral philosophy is the complex web of belief, judgment, sentiment, and action that constitutes the structure of moral experience.[2] It is only through trying to understand this complex structure that one is able to make sense of the moral domain—regardless of whether, as realists seem to believe, this structure reliably points to anything independent of itself. This structure, moreover, is not in principle limited by any particular social or cultural boundaries. Thus, the object of philosophical interpretation is potentially much larger than the culturally and historically specific life that, as Walzer rightly notes, is often at issue in everyday moral disputes. To be sure, culturally and historically influenced norms about emotion, thought, and action eventually find expression in the situational meanings of actions and practices. For this reason, philosophical reflection about some kinds of moral issues must attend to the particulars of concrete cultural and historical experience. Yet the boundaries of cultures and historical epochs are not impenetrable walls, particularly on matters of moral significance; there is no antecedently given fact of the matter about the most appropriate way, morally speaking, to draw boundaries between cultures. As I have shown in Chapter 1, the idea that the moral practices of particular cultures or groups constitute fully individuable, integrated "moralities" or "moral systems" which it is the task of sophisticated moral inquiry to describe and analyze embodies a powerful misconception of the nature of cultural boundaries and of their link to diversity in moral practices. Moral philosophy may legitimately seek to identify, interpret, and analyze elements of the structure of moral experience that are not, and cannot be, confined to a single culturally or historically bounded place.[3]

The interpretive tasks of moral philosophy are complicated by the fact that the structure of moral experience is accessible only through particular *interpretations* of that structure. Moral philosophy is "doubly hermeneutic"—to adapt a phrase—in that it is the interpretation of interpretations (Hiley, Bohman, and Shusterman 1991, 5). Moreover, any particular interpretation of the structure of moral experience will be at least partly a product of self-understandings—which are in turn partly shaped (though not exhaustively defined) by the collective self-understanding of a particular social group. Thus, although the community of moral inquirers extends, in principle, to include any human being capable of reflection, the interpretations which are the object of moral philosophy are initially accessible only by means of acquaintance with the practices of a specific group. For this reason, any particular attempt to isolate and interpret the structure of moral experience will always presuppose a kind of moral anthropology, despite the likelihood that careful anthropology would eventually reveal that there is vast overlap and continuity in the moral practices of different groups. Even that moral philosophy which seeks primarily to systematize and extend some interpreted structure of belief and judgment (in the form of a normative moral theory) presupposes a moral anthropology. It is thus beside the point—as some critics of Rawls's methods in *A Theory of Justice* fail to see—to object to a normative moral theory simply because it makes clear the connection between moral theory and moral anthropology.[4]

Moral philosophy's interpretive tasks are further complicated by the fact that the structure of moral experience (in any of its interpreted versions) is accessible only through various kinds of linguistic and non-linguistic behavior. The starting point for philosophical reflection about morality must be what people do, and what they say about what they do. The moral philosopher can only hope that she correctly recognizes those aspects of behavior that are likely to reveal the structure of moral experience. Moral philosophy will therefore be generally affected by the radical underdetermination of hypotheses about the data of human behavior that, as I noted in Chapter 1, created such difficulties for the cross-cultural descriptive efforts of Richard Brandt and John Ladd. The problem of underdetermination may in fact help explain moral philosophy's own "Rashomon Effect": the great variety of occasionally competing philosophical conceptions claiming to make sense of the structure of moral experience. Alasdair MacIntyre has charged that the diversity of moral conceptions defended by contemporary moral philosophers is somehow a sign of the failure of contemporary moral philosophy (MacIntyre 1981, 20). But given the circumstances under which philosophical moral inquiry must begin, disagreement among philosophical conceptions (and not just in the contemporary philosophical world) is surely to be expected. Indeed, if James is right, as I think he is, this kind of disagreement and diversity in philosophical moral conceptions is to be welcomed. There can be no "final truth" in moral philosophy until the last human being has had her experience and said her say. Equally important, there cannot be even a partial truth in any moral philosophy that seeks—as so many contemporary accounts do—to sever links with the ongoing moral inquiry that is generated by the complexities of everyday life.

Surprisingly, Walzer expressly rejects the general characterization of moral philosophy defended here, despite his convictions concerning the interpretive character of everyday moral argument. He does accept that some moral philosophy is properly construed as interpretive. In fact, he claims to have developed such a conception in his *Spheres of Justice*, where he argues that moral philosophy should be an effort "to interpret to one's fellow citizens the world of meanings that we share" (Walzer 1983, xiv). But most moral philosophy, in his view, confirms Wittgenstein's arresting observation that the philosopher qua philosopher is "not a citizen of any community of ideas" (Walzer 1981).[5] As a consequence, Walzer believes, moral philosophy typically produces "philosophical artifacts" that have no special claims—if any claims at all—on the attention of human beings in their concrete social existence (Walzer 1983, xiv). He insists, by contrast, that the vision of an egalitarian society that he defends in *Spheres of Justice* is not a philosophical artifact; rather, it simply "picks out those deeper understandings of social goods" that are not evident in the everyday practice of American liberal democracy (Walzer 1983, 26). Walzer claims simply to bring to the surface what is "already here—hidden, as it were, in our concepts and categories" (Walzer 1983, xiv). At one point he considers whether all moral philosophy might be an intrinsically interpretive enterprise. But he eventually rejects this possibility as incompatible with the "sincere ambition" and, in some cases, the "dangerous presumption" of philosophers who—in his view—claim to discover or invent new moral conceptions (Walzer 1987, 21).

Yet to what extent does moral philosophy really emanate from the sort of ambitions (of discovery or invention) that Walzer supposes? Utilitarianism, on his view, provides the clearest example of a doctrine that embodies just such ambitions, though he seems undecided whether to view the doctrine as an effort of discovery or one of invention. In some passages of *Interpretation and Social Criticism*, for example, Walzer claims that Bentham took himself to have "discovered" the objective foundation of morality (Walzer 1987, 7n). Elsewhere he claims that utilitarianism is best construed as the result of philosophical invention (Walzer 1987, 21). Yet Bentham never claimed to have discovered the principle of utility; in fact, he attributed his initial conviction of its importance to his reading of Hume's *Enquiry*. Still further, in its most influential formulations the principle of utility is always defended as an interpretation of central elements of the ordinary moral consciousness. Bentham, for instance, claimed that the principle was part of the "natural constitution of the human frame," and that everyone at some point appeals to utility (however reluctantly) to make moral decisions, or to evaluate past actions and policies (Bentham [1789] 1948, 4). Bentham undoubtedly recognized that his efforts to systematize and extend what he took to be utilitarian convictions could generate unfamiliar, and sometimes controversial, moral conclusions. But this simply strengthened his confidence in the reformative powers of the doctrine—much as it heightened his disappointment at the conservative "ipsedixitism" he eventually came to find in Hume (Bentham 1983, 24). Three quarters of a century later, in an effort to reiterate the link between utilitarianism and everyday moral convictions, John Stuart Mill even asserted a connection between utilitarianism and basic elements of the Judeo-Christian tradition. " 'To do as you would be done by,' and 'to love your neighbor as yourself,'" Mill argues, "constitute the ideal perfection of utilitarian morality" (Mill [1861] 1979, 17). Mill was not simply making an effort to mollify critics for whom utilitarianism was a "godless doctrine"; he was trying to establish that utilitarianism clarifies and refines important elements of established moral convictions.

But Walzer offers one further example of a philosophical conception that, in his view, results from invention: the difference principle formulated by Rawls in *A Theory of Justice*. According to the difference principle, once social institutions guarantee equal basic liberties and fair equality of opportunity, the better life prospects of the most advantaged members of society can be just if and only if they are part of a total scheme which ultimately improves the life prospects of the least advantaged members (Rawls 1971, 75). Walzer is simply unwilling to accept that this part of Rawls's conception is the outcome of interpretation. In fact, he initially contends that the difference principle has "something of the novelty and specificity of revelation." Eventually, however, he settles on the claim that the difference principle is the result of an elaborate process of invention. Thus, according to Walzer, "as divine law derives its force from its creator, so the difference principle derives its force from the process by which it was created. If we accept it, it is because we have participated, or can imagine ourselves having participated, in its invention" (Walzer 1987, 12–13). Yet this allusion to the methodology of Rawls's hypothetical contractarian argument for the principles of justice also embodies some serious misunderstandings.

In particular, Walzer confuses Rawls's argument *for* the principles of justice with the interpretive efforts that shaped their content, and he ignores important passages in which Rawls expressly discusses the convictions which the difference principle seeks to interpret.[6] Rawls expressly contends, for instance, that the difference principle "provides an interpretation" of the principle of fraternity—a principle that he believes to have an important place in democratic theory, if not quite the importance of principles concerning liberty and equality (Rawls 1971, 105). The difference principle expresses a "natural meaning" of fraternity, he continues, by relying on the kind of reasoning to which members of a family appeal when they express reluctance to gain, unless they can advance the interests of the family at the same time. Rawls contends, further, that the difference principle "expresses a conception of reciprocity. It is a principle of mutual benefit" (Rawls 1971, 102). The reasoning underlying this last claim is complex. Rawls maintains that those who are most fortunate in the "natural lottery" (and who would thus possess the resources and capacities to derive substantial benefits from social cooperation) would have a difficult time persuading the less fortunate to collaborate with them in a scheme of social cooperation, except on terms provided by the difference principle (Rawls 1971, 103). However asymmetrical the benefits of the principle may seem, Rawls suggests, the principle embodies a reasonable interpretation of *mutual* benefit because it simply seeks to correct an asymmetry of benefits that would follow from unregulated social cooperation.

To be sure, the reasoning embodied in the difference principle has been widely challenged. The most controversial (and misunderstood) component of that reasoning is Rawls's claim that the difference principle best captures one of the "fixed points" of "our" considered convictions: that no one deserves her place in the distribution of natural endowments and talents (Rawls 1971, 102). Even those who accept that this is in fact a fixed point of moral reflection may dispute Rawls's understanding of its relevance to a conception seeking to determine the just distribution of social benefits and burdens.[7] Yet (once again) a disputed interpretation is still an interpretation. Indeed, the nature and extent of disagreement generated by the difference principle suggests that the process by which that principle was formulated is, in many ways, a model of moral inquiry as an interpretive enterprise.

If pressed, Walzer would surely acknowledge the interpretive dimensions of both the difference principle and utilitarianism.[8] Yet it is unlikely that this would lead him to relinquish his antagonism toward moral philosophy as generally practiced, because that antagonism is rooted in his objections to features of philosophical practice that he believes go *beyond* interpretation in seriously problematic ways. Walzer believes that philosophical efforts to systematize and extend the application of some (interpreted) element of ordinary moral concern—primarily in the form of a normative moral theory—typically ignore the particulars of moral experience and the complexity of the world in which actual moral thinking and argument take place. The moral world, in Walzer's view, "lends itself less to abstract modeling than to thick description" (Walzer 1987, 20). "Thick description" alludes to a notion first discussed by Ryle, and later developed by Clifford Geertz, in an attempt to show that only certain kinds of description and analysis can adequately account for the complexities of meaningful behavior (Ryle 1971; cf. Geertz 1973). In a typical example Ryle considers what would be required to capture the differences between rapidly contracting an eyelid in an involuntary nervous tic, rapidly contracting an eyelid in an intentional wink (perhaps to communicate quietly some conspiratorial plans), and rapidly contracting an eyelid in a parody of a wink (perhaps to elicit public laughter at the failure of another's efforts at a wink). Ryle suggests that a "thin" description—one focusing principally on the physical contracting of eyelids—cannot produce a plausible rendering of the differences among these cases. In Geertz's development of Ryle's view, it is possible to recognize and adequately recount the differences between a tic, a wink, and a parody of a wink only if one is attentive to the multilayered structures of "inference and implication" within which such differences become intelligible (Geertz 1973, 7). Thick description involves interpreting intentions and expectations, and especially the intricate public structures of meaning within which it is possible to form intentions and act on complex expectations. Thick description is thus *interpretation* of those structures that constitute the complex contexts within which meaningful actions—winking, or betting on a cockfight in Bali, or writing an indignant letter to the *New York Times*—become possible. It is interpretation, one might say, of the structure of some realm of complex human experience.

Geertz goes on to argue that the principal tasks of ethnography should be defined by reference to just such interpretive efforts; he defends a "semiotic" conception of culture as a collection of "socially established structures of meaning" (Geertz 1973, 12). Ethnography, in his view, is an interpretive science "in search of meaning"—an enterprise in which progress is "marked less by a perfection of consensus than a refinement of debate" (Geertz 1973, 5; 29). Geertz has urged, further, that ethnography is more akin to literary criticism than to a search for lawlike generalizations or formulations of abstract models of interpreted structures (Geertz 1973, 9). The culture of a people, he maintains, is "an ensemble of texts . . . which the anthropologist strains to read over the shoulders of those to whom they properly belong" (Geertz 1973, 452). For Walzer, by contrast, a defensible moral philosophy is a search for meaning in that ensemble of familiar moral "texts" that one shares with one's fellow citizens. Moreover, while Walzer expressly sanctions the search for "hidden meanings" in familiar places, he might well be reluctant to claim access to hidden meanings in an unfamiliar culture. Like many contemporary ethnographers, Geertz is adamant about the importance of trying to make sense of the "native's point of view" on an unfamiliar culture (Geertz 1983, 55–70; cf. 1973). But, as Jeffrey Stout has noted, Walzer's allusions to the method of thick description do suggest a commitment to the view that a defensible moral philosophy will draw on the methods and presuppositions of interpretive ethnography (Stout 1988, 228). Walzer seems to think, that is, that a plausible moral philosophy is ultimately a special kind of interpretive ethnography.

Now, I do not mean to suggest that the tasks of moral philosophy might be exhausted by an interpretive ethnography of familiar moral practices. A vast array of activities can qualify as moral philosophy— including the efforts of normative moral theorists to interpret the structure of moral experience succinctly so as to encourage a rethinking of the moral domain. Walzer's claims to find hidden meanings in familiar practices are no less (albeit certainly no more) problematic than the normative moral theorist's claims to reconstruct rationally some element of the beliefs and judgments underlying those practices. Yet Walzer's criticisms provide a much needed impetus to reflect on the connections between ethnography and moral philosophy. A central aim of this book, in fact, is to show just how important those connections really are. I have argued, for instance, that undertaking the task of self-reflection, especially in a serious first-person moral conflict, bears important similarities to ethnographic reflection. I have claimed, further, that reflection on successful ethnographic methods might provide important lessons for philosophers seeking to understand and articulate the details (and the difficulties) of serious moral disputes—even disputes between people within the same culture. Still further, on the model of philosophical moral inquiry that I defend, it is impossible to get at the truth in ethics without an appreciation for what people from diverse cultures have had to "say"—even though what they in fact have to say often turns out to have a far more familiar ring than relativists are wont to admit. Just as Carol Gilligan's work in empirical psychology has directed philosophical attention to the question of whether women speak about morality in "a different voice," ethnographic studies reveal the need for moral philosophy to listen more intently to the voices of those in diverse cultures.[9]

Thus, I welcome Geertz's contention that the task of making these voices audible in new places is part of the essential vocation of interpretive ethnography (Geertz 1973, 30). Careful consideration of ethnographic methods might also have a salutary effect in challenging the glibness of the vast majority of contemporary moral philosophers who claim to interpret—and sometimes even to justify—what "we" think and do in everyday moral practice. Most such claims proceed with no accounting of who might be included in that "we," and how philosophers can plausibly claim to know what "we" think. As I showed in discussing the flaws of the relativism of distance in Chapter 2, philosophers often need to scrutinize and explain the assumptions on which their fieldwork depends. Ironically, anti-theory critics who reject normative moral theory for its alleged insensitivity to the "particular" are often the most inattentive to the particularity of "us." Their demands to confine philosophical moral inquiry to the description of "shared" moral understandings, that is, too often ignore the existence of those who are unwillingly excluded from the scope of such understandings.

Yet Walzer's efforts to link moral philosophy and ethnography also serve as a necessary reminder that moral inquiry is not exhausted by the activities of philosophers engaged in normative moral theory and those who take part in serious moral disputes. For it is possible to conduct sophisticated moral inquiry while engaged in the practice—as well as the theory—of a variety of fields of study: particularly in the social sciences, in history, and in literature. Thus, Geertz rightly urges that an ethnographic account of a Balinese cremation ritual, for instance, can be an exercise in "the social history of the moral imagination" (Geertz 1983, 40). In a different way historical debate about the problem of slavery in Western culture can be an exercise in moral inquiry. David Brion Davis's influential studies of slavery initially took shape, in his words, out of concern about "a problem of moral perception" (Davis 1966, vii). Moreover, as I noted in Chapter 2, the debate sparked by Davis's arguments—especially in the work of Thomas Haskell and his critics—raises concerns about relativism and objectivity in a manner that closely parallels important debates in moral philosophy. And of course a great novelist may be centrally engaged in moral inquiry. Ryle makes a compelling case, for instance, for viewing Jane Austen as a moralist in the "thick" sense: as a novelist who wrote partly from a serious interest in general—even theoretical—questions about human nature and conduct (Ryle 1971, 1; 276). Lionel Trilling similarly speaks for many readers of *Huckleberry Finn* when he argues that "no one who reads thoughtfully the dialectic of Huck's great moral crisis will ever again be wholly able to accept without some question and some irony the assumptions of the respectable morality by which he lives, nor . . . be certain that what he considers the clear dictates of moral reason are not merely the ingrained customary beliefs of his time and place" (Trilling 1970, 121).

Trilling's discussion of Huck's moral crisis, in *The Liberal Imagination*, makes the kind of contribution to moral inquiry that only someone trained to attend to irony and satire (unlike some philosophers) can successfully make.[10] Geertz convincingly argues, moreover, that much of Trilling's literary criticism—like much of Geertz's interpretive ethnography—should be construed as a contribution to the social history of the moral imagination.[11] But more generally, all such inquiries are indispensable aids to reflection about the moral life, by virtue of the interpretive dimensions of the relevant results.

THE INTERPRETIVE TURN AND THE CHALLENGE OF "ANTI-THEORY"

Walzer's preference for thick description over "abstract modeling" does more than emphasize the richness and complexity of moral inquiry and the important links between ethnography and moral philosophy. His view is one of a soaring chorus of attacks on the philosophical discussion, production, and refinement of normative moral theory. On these views, any effort to systematize and extend the (interpreted) beliefs or sentiments underlying everyday moral concerns will simply be too general, too abstract, or too reductive to be of use in concrete moral reflection. Most of these critics also argue that philosophers should relinquish moral theory altogether, usually in favor of some enterprise more akin to description. Walzer, of course, recommends thick description of the world "of meanings that we share." According to Bernard

Williams, the only legitimate role for philosophy in a plausible "reflective criticism" is a "phenomenology of the ethical life," which reflects on "the ways in which we experience our ethical life" (Williams 1985, 93). Cheryl Noble urges moral philosophers to search for "wise or otherwise valid moral generalizations" based on inquiries into "social questions, human nature," and "awareness of the sources and conditions of our common sense moral judgments" (Noble 1989, 62). Annette Baier is similarly convinced that moral philosophy should rely more heavily on empirical inquiry, but she is more hopeful than Walzer, Williams, or Noble that a plausible model of such a philosophical conception already exists. She contends that Hume's descriptive moral philosophy provides the most helpful model for understanding "modes of individual and social moral reflection as they actually exist now." A concerted reliance on Humean methods, she continues, is most likely to ground philosophical moral inquiry in "the economic, historical, and psychological facts" (Baier 1985, 237; cf. 244). But in the most anti-theoretical contribution to this chorus of attacks, Richard Rorty simply declares that "we already have as much theory as we need" (Rorty 1990, 642). Instead of supporting the rise of that "edifying discourse" which he once hoped would fill the cultural space left by the "demise" of epistemology, Rorty has recommended that moral and political philosophers simply give up their theorizing and devote more attention to the "sordid details" of experience as described by poets, journalists, and anthropologists, among others (Rorty 1990, 642).[12]

But the anti-theorists' discontent with normative moral theory is rooted in a simplistic and ahistorical conception of the "facts" to be described. The ahistoricity of these views is particularly surprising in light of the widespread influence, in anti-theorist circles, of Berlin's arguments for value pluralism. Berlin's view, as I noted in Chapter 3, is centrally concerned with the dangers in the philosophical tendency to ignore the social and political influence of philosophical activity. But there are less ominous reasons to attend to the influence of philosophy. To adapt James's notion, philosophy has historically generated some of the most influential "hypotheses"—I call them interpretations—shaping the conditions within which it is possible to contribute to moral experience. Indeed, in many respects contemporary moral debates have expanded and intensified the influence of philosophical interpretations of moral experience. Disputes over social welfare in contemporary liberal democracies, for example, typically turn on a language of property and property rights that has been shaped in large part by complex philosophical reflection on normative moral theory. Indeed, moral thinking in general is more saturated than ever before with normative theories, and not just in those cultures in which the theories originated. Thus, for example, an array of groups throughout the world press for moral (and legal) rights to keep or regain their "cultural property," and beleaguered indigenous peoples appeal to rights of cultural survival to challenge the environmental destruction that threatens their existence. Philosophical interpretations of the structure of moral experience are inescapably embedded in such claims, which is why the investigation, refinement, and development of normative moral theory is essential to helping make sense of them. Indeed, it would be a dangerous abnegation of intellectual responsibility to suggest that contemporary moral philosophers should play no role in sorting out the contributions of philosophers in shaping such claims. At the very least, moral philosophers have an important role to play because the institutional mechanisms that preserve moral philosophy as a discipline (libraries, universities, professional associations, and learned journals) also preserve a valuable tradition of appreciating the complexities at issue.

Some anti-theory philosophers argue against normative moral theory by appealing to ostensibly empirical inquiries into the processes and practice by which morality is transmitted from one generation to another. In one such account Annette Baier argues that the average person's moral convictions are not acquired by the "self-conscious acceptance of a theory" because parents do not normally transform their moral beliefs into theories. Rather, she contends, parents typically "impart moral constraints by example and by reaction to behavior, not by handing on explicit verbal codes of general rules, let alone moral theories" (Baier 1985, 208). But Baier's view rests on an incomplete account of the transmission of morality. The important question often is not whether moral convictions are *acquired* by "self-conscious" acceptance of explicit rules or theories, but to what extent rules or theories might have shaped many of the convictions that parents seek to impart. In many societies some of the most important "examples" and "reactions" by which parents impart moral convictions and constraints are inextricably bound up with social practices that are governed by many *explicit* as well as implicit rules and theories. In those societies, moreover, the situational meaning of central social practices has been powerfully influenced by the spread of normative theories articulated by philosophers. In a contemporary liberal democracy, for instance, it is impossible to teach moral constraints surrounding the institution of property without presupposing explicit rules, and usually also some particular theory of property.

Few parents initially teach moral constraints by explicit reference to moral rules and underlying theories—which, after all, very young children are not equipped to understand. Moral training usually begins by appeal to specific constraints on behavior in particular situations. But general rules, and even an underlying theory, can become important in moral training, especially if a child refuses to be satisfied with the response "because I said so" when she asks why she should abide by her parents' prescriptions. Consider the child who has learned convictions and constraints associated with respecting property but wonders why some people are homeless or go hungry. There are few parents who would not be both willing and able to produce some explicit rule or rules—and probably even a theory, or a substantial portion of a theory—to answer such a query. Admittedly some of the background theories to which people are likely to appeal in such settings may have little to do with philosophy. Thus, for instance, some parents may appeal to their religious convictions. Others, especially the parents of a child who is herself homeless or hungry, may appeal to less hopeful convictions; they may even condemn a social system that they believe excludes them. But the theory or rule appealed to in such circumstances will often be one that has been articulated and reshaped by philosophical activity. This is particularly likely to be so in liberal democratic societies, where debates about issues such as hunger and homelessness are almost always shaped by philosophical theories about liberty and equality. Philosophy can also have a role to play in helping to make explicit those features of social practices which are bound up with philosophical conceptions. After all, even Walzer will allow that an interpretation (as thick description) may reveal heretofore hidden meanings. Yet there is no single path by which philosophical theories have become important components of the cultural conditions of emotion, thought, and action.

This means that intellectual historians, literary critics, and interpretive ethnographers, as well as philosophers, will have an important role to play in helping trace the paths of particular theories.

But the philosophical articulation and refinement of the theories at issue will sometimes be indispensable to constructive moral reflection in such settings. Consider a dispute about the welfare system of a contemporary liberal democracy. It is a dispute about how—given what Rorty would call the "sordid details" of economic life—political life ought to proceed. Any policy that advances the dispute beyond the familiar impasse will embody a complex theory of the "proper" balance between liberty and equality. Although I reject claims about the rationally authoritative status of the methods and inquiries of philosophers, I contend that moral philosophy is likely to make important contributions to such debates for two important (if mundane) reasons. First, the discipline of philosophy inculcates special appreciation of (and usually special commitment to) standards of reasonableness in argument. Second, the moral philosopher's knowledge of alternative ways of interpreting moral experience may sometimes enable her to produce the kind of thought experiments which can stimulate moral imagination—but which, unlike real experiments, need not sacrifice real human beings.

A careful account of moral training would no doubt need to distinguish between different kinds of moral constraints. One of the most important differences—suggested by Hume's distinction between natural and artificial virtues—is the difference between moral constraints associated with institutions which are principally a product of the gradual development of social conventions (such as property) and moral constraints associated with institutions and practices less dependent (if at all) on social conventions (such as a family). The process of teaching a child some of the moral constraints associated with membership in an institution such as the family, for instance, may be very similar to the process envisioned by Baier: a matter of teaching almost entirely by "examples" and "reactions," without need for explicit rules or theories. But even Hume readily acknowledges that family life is thoroughly structured by social artifices: not only the "rules of justice" that govern property, promises, and contracts, but also regulations defining and prohibiting incest, as well as requirements concerning "chastity and modesty in women" (Hume [1739] 1978, 484–526). If the bonds uniting families are governed by social artifice as well as by "nature," a parent might sometimes need to rely on an explicit rule, or even a theory, to explain the importance of constraints thought to follow from such bonds. Further, in some instances the social influence of these rules and theories might well be traceable to the influence of a philosophical conception. It cannot be denied that philosophy sometimes will have had little direct influence on a way of life indigenous to some traditional societies. As I have suggested, however, few traditional societies escape being directly affected by societies in which philosophy has played a powerful cultural role.

Anti-theory arguments are problematic not only for the facts they misdescribe but also for those that they simply ignore. As I argue in Chapter 2, virtually every society confines some persons to its margins, economically, politically, or culturally, and often altogether. Those "commonsense" moral judgments which critics such as Noble expect to produce "wise or otherwise valid" generalizations are often inextricably bound up with cementing the boundaries within which some marginalized group is confined; as Trilling argues, this is one of the most powerful lessons of *Huckleberry Finn.* Of course, philosophy is sometimes less successful than other forms of moral inquiry—particularly that contained in literature—in helping to reveal the shortcomings of "common sense." Further, recent social history provides compelling support for Walzer's insistence on the "workmanlike" character of the social change that is likely to remedy these shortcomings. The American civil rights movement, for instance, was at least half a century in the making, and it depended on the extraordinary courage and conviction of thousands of people inspired by a complex amalgamation of philosophical theory, theology from various religious traditions, and the social criticism of great literary figures (Morris 1984). Still further, Walzer plausibly denies a socially influential role to "paradigm-shattering" philosophical speculation. But, as I have argued, moral inquiry *never* shatters paradigms—not even in its most sophisticated philosophical forms. Normative moral theory will not teach anything wholly new about morality because genuine moral inquiry, including the most "abstract" normative moral theory, is always an exercise in interpretation. It is noteworthy that philosophical reflection about the

equal worth of persons, along with philosophical defenses of civil disobedience and a vehemently Socratic conception of the moral importance of serious self-examination, played a key role in shoring up the
courage of those who risked—and sometimes lost—their lives in support of civil rights. The anti-theorist's insistence that "we" do not need
moral theory would surely ring hollow for those—such as defenders of
civil rights in the American South or, more recently, student leaders in
Tiananmen Square—who risk their lives in the hope of generating
reflection on the failings of "commonsense" judgments that deny their
freedom, and sometimes their very humanity. Philosophical moral theory is sometimes most important for the effect it has on those who
simply seek to encourage others to reinterpret central elements of the
moral world.

To be sure, my efforts to establish the fundamentally interpretive
character of moral philosophy cast doubt on the notion that moral
philosophy might have some special authority to "validate" the claims
of one moral conception over another. But in my view, Walzer rightly
challenges the authority of "philosophical artifacts" in the real moral
world. Fully acknowledging the interpretive character of philosophical
moral inquiry, as I argue, requires relinquishing some of the epistemological preoccupations that have dominated Anglo-American moral philosophy for much of the twentieth century. Moral philosophers who
expect that moral argument would become more rational and orderly if
only moral philosophy could produce more and better systematic moral
theories have simply misunderstood the nature and possibilities of
philosophical moral inquiry. Even the most systematic moral theories
do not solve moral problems; people do. Moreover, the kind of moral
reasoning demanded by serious moral disputes always requires the sincere exercise of judgment formed by experience, occasionally freed up
by moral imagination. Yet moral theories are not therefore dispensable;
they may sometimes be the most efficient and reasonable means for
inspiring the kind of self-scrutiny needed to encourage imaginative
reinterpretations of everyday moral practices. To be sure, an ethnographer's thick description, a novelist's vision, or a sense of religious
vocation will sometimes succeed where philosophy fails. But to recognize this simply shows what a mistake it would be to try to exile the
ethnographer, the novelist, or the religious thinker—or, indeed, any

non-philosopher engaged in genuine moral inquiry—from the community of moral inquirers.

These considerations concerning the interpretive dimensions of philosophical moral inquiry provide a compelling rejoinder to an anti-theorist objection concerning the "peculiarity" of normative moral theories in comparison to scientific theories. In one version of this charge, Noble insists that while a respectable scientific theory always has a genuine epistemological "task" to perform, normative moral theories do not. She claims that genetic theory, for instance, has an essential role to play in answering otherwise unanswerable questions about heredity; no matter how much practical knowledge it might be possible to acquire (about animal breeding, say) without genetic theory, for those who lack an understanding of it, there will always be "limits to their expertise and certain matters of which they must remain ignorant" (Noble 1989, 56). Normative moral theories, in Noble's view, are very different: "Any question that a moral theory can answer can be answered without a moral theory" (Noble 1989, 57). A normative moral theory, she maintains, is a superfluous "pseudo-theory" that philosophers can only try in vain to validate—always at the expense of attention to the nature and sources of genuine moral knowledge (Noble 1989, 56). Yet what Noble finds superfluous about normative moral theories is, as Kant insists, an important measure of their success. Like any interpretation, a moral theory may enrich and broaden one's appreciation of a familiar domain—sometimes, as Bentham recognized, in ways that lead to unfamiliar conclusions about elements of that domain. But it should come as no surprise that normative moral theories never reveal anything wholly new about the structure of moral experience. Noble—like many "anti-theory" critics, and many contemporary moral theorists as well—simply fails to appreciate the interpretive character of normative moral theory.

The view of moral theory defended here admittedly presupposes a conception of "theory" that does not conform to the conception associated with theories in the natural sciences. But, as I have argued all along, there is no reason to expect that moral theory should conform to standards of argument and inquiry appropriate in the natural sciences. On the view of moral philosophy that I defend, "theorizing" means something like "critical reflection."[13] When such reflection issues in an attempt—philosophical or otherwise—to simplify and systematize the structure of moral experience (or some aspect of it), it may then be said to produce a normative moral theory. But any such theory is always a species of that critical reflection on the beliefs, judgments, and sentiments underlying everyday moral practice that lived moral experience repeatedly encourages. Moreover, philosophical theorizing about morality can provide a particularly rich contribution to that body of reflection—partly, though not exclusively, by virtue of its capacity to stimulate reflection on some interpretation of the structure of moral experience that underlies everyday practice. Noble contends that moral theories make "no contribution" to the moral life (Noble 1989, 61). But she simply ignores the potentially beneficial influence of the interpretive efforts embodied in normative moral theory.

This oversight neglects basic facts about the development of moral capacities—in particular, that they must be developed and exercised in a culturally and historically specific way of life. From informal, largely anecdotal claims about the "feral" child phenomenon to more systematic inquiries in the social sciences, there is much evidence to suggest that being encultured is a condition of the possibility of responsible agency (Geertz 1973; Moody-Adams 1994a). Becoming capable of moral judgment and moral action requires learning a language along with the interpretation of moral experience embedded in that language; learning to exercise moral imagination in order to find one's way around in complex or unfamiliar aspects of the moral domain; and developing the cognitive and affective capacities that underwrite an ability and a willingness to develop moral concern. But precisely because it is difficult to develop such capacities independent of an upbringing in a particular way of life, the capacity to engage in critical reflection on familiar practices and institutions has special moral importance. The single most important piece of knowledge underlying the human capacity to be moral may well be the knowledge that any human practice or institution (however familiar) can always go wrong. There is even reason to suspect—though it cannot be proven—that this knowledge of human limitation and fallibility is *itself* a piece of moral knowledge.[14] But, whether or not knowledge of human fallibility is a piece of moral knowledge, one needs no systematic moral theory to obtain it. Noble thus reasonably doubts whether access to knowledge that is genuinely necessary for morality depends on success in providing a valid normative moral theory. But she goes wrong in failing to understand that even a cursory scrutiny of a normative theory may sometimes expose, and even discourage, some particular manifestation of the tendency to affect ignorance of human fallibility. Affected ignorance of human fallibility is such a common source of wrongdoing that its exposure may be one of the most valuable contributions for any theory—normative or otherwise—to make to moral life.

A PYRRHIC VICTORY?

It is important to retrace briefly the path by which I have arrived at this optimism about the importance of moral theory in everyday moral life. In Chapter 3 I challenged the claim that moral inquiry is methodologically infirm compared to science by denying that the methods of moral inquiry are properly compared to the methods of (natural) science. Genuine moral inquiry is a species of self-reflection, and philosophical theorizing about morality must start from the pre-theoretical moral consciousness of those capable of being addressed by the theory. But self-reflection that qualifies as moral inquiry first requires a careful articulation of the self-conception under scrutiny. And this articulation is an exercise in interpretation. In this chapter I have discussed the implications of the link between moral philosophy and self-scrutiny by means of the notion that moral philosophy—like all moral inquiry—is an interpretive enterprise. The pre-theoretical deliverances from which philosophical interpretation begins are accessible to the moral philosopher only by reflection on linguistic and non-linguistic behavior; moral philosophers must presume that it is possible to isolate and identify some portion of this behavior that may reveal the structure of moral experience. In this regard, then, moral philosophy always presupposes a kind of interpretive ethnography—although it usually involves fieldwork in familiar places.

Yet, as I argued in Chapters 1 and 2, it is not possible to determine in advance what the range of any "familiar" moral judgment really is; indeed, as I will show, the applicability of some moral judgments appears to be limited by no cultural boundaries whatsoever. Thus, moral philosophy can quite reasonably seek to interpret the structure of moral experience in general. This is why the philosophical interpretation of moral experience can include such a diverse body of critical reflection. Philosophical moral inquiry, after all, includes work as varied as Walzer's attempts to discern the (local) social meanings of various goods and practices, and Kant's attempts to reconstruct rationally what he took to be the objectively valid structure of human moral consciousness. Finally, no philosophical interpretation of the structure of moral experience—not even a systematic moral theory—can solve moral problems, but it can influence the decisions and actions of human beings who contemplate its implications, principally by virtue of its tendency to encourage self-scrutiny. Thus, not only does this conception of moral philosophy as an interpretive enterprise allow a robust defense of the integrity of normative moral theories *as* theories, but also it supports a reasonable (if cautious) optimism about the importance of such theories—and of philosophical moral inquiry generally—in everyday moral argument.

But does this account of moral philosophy, and especially its defense of moral theory, amount to a Pyrrhic victory? Many contemporary moral philosophers will certainly think so. They may charge that any effort to defend moral philosophy as an interpretive enterprise is a distraction from the epistemological projects in which moral philosophy, on their view, ought to be engaged. For most such thinkers, in fact, a final verdict on the rationality and validity of moral reasoning and argument must wait on philosophy to achieve substantive "results" in these areas. As Norman Daniels has expressed this conception, moral philosophy must face up to the task of "solving the problems of justification and theory acceptance in the moral domain" (Daniels 1980a, 21). Daniels rejects as "erroneous" any suggestion that there is an important link between the methods of philosophical moral inquiry and the methods of interpretive ethnography. Moreover, because he has sought to show how moral philosophy might "solve the problems" of justification by building on some of Rawls's early claims about the methods of philosophical moral inquiry, he has been especially critical of some of Rawls's suggestions that there might be a plausible link between moral philosophy and moral anthropology (Daniels 1980a, 22–23).[15] Daniels is critical, for instance, of Rawls's self-described "provisional" claims in *A Theory of Justice* that moral philosophy is "the attempt to describe our moral capacity," and that the theory of justice seeks to describe "our sense of justice" (Rawls 1971, 46–53). In Daniels's view such claims, however provisional, simply muddy the water; the main task of moral philosophy is to "increase our ability to choose among competing conceptions" (Daniels 1979, 237).[16]

Yet this project stands in a peculiar relation to Rawls's own work. Rawls has gradually moved away from the idea that justification of a moral conception might be *primarily* a task of the moral epistemologist. Indeed, Rawls has argued in his later works that the "real" task of justifying a conception of justice is not principally an epistemological matter but a "practical social task" (Rawls 1980, 517–519; cf. 1994).[17] Yet he does not relinquish the idea that philosophy has an indispensable role to play in helping carry out that task. The philosophical articulation of "our sense of justice," as Rawls conceives of it, will not merely articulate a structure that underlies *current* considered convictions. For, on his conception, philosophical moral inquiry may provide reason to think that a subset of current moral convictions fails to fit into a rationally coherent interpretation of the structure of moral experience. Such an inquiry would be incomplete without some argument to show how revising or relinquishing some considered conviction could secure a more coherent moral conception, and such argument will surely include an effort to *justify* the appropriate revision. Just such an effort is contained, for instance, in Rawls's argument that the interpretation embodied in the difference principle would regulate inequalities in a manner compatible with at least some democratic ideas. To understand why such efforts are crucial, it should be noted that central presuppositions of Rawls's argument for the difference principle challenge familiar democratic tolerance for the notion that "private vices" such as unfettered selfishness can always be "public virtues." The difference principle effectively revises and realigns central commitments of democracy. Rawls's arguments for these revisions and realignments—his justifications of them—do not authoritatively justify the entire conception of justice that contains them. Yet they are an indispensable element in the ultimate task of justifying that conception. Thus, Rawls's claim that his conception of justice as fairness is "political" not "metaphysical" is not a Rortean call to replace philosophy with some nonphilosophical successor.

To be sure, Rawls now maintains that justifying an entire conception of justice to regulate the basic social institutions of a democratic society is a task which cannot be completed by philosophy itself. He seems to imagine a division of justificatory labor between philosophers—who articulate, and argue for, potentially revisionary interpretations—and the community of moral inquirers, of which philosophers are merely one part. The community of inquirers (however these boundaries might be drawn for a particular purpose) must itself complete the task of justification, and the role of philosophy is to provide a conception which (in principle) could secure collective agreement. Rawls's conception of justification has thus become more explicitly Deweyan, subtly reaffirming Dewey's conception of moral philosophy as a contribution to the collective self-scrutiny of the culture from which it emerges, rather than the principal authoritative source of decisions about how, and whether, a moral conception is justified (Dewey 1994, 1–8). This Deweyan conception is an implicit rejection of the self-conception of much contemporary moral philosophy (in Daniels's account, as in many others) on which moral philosophers simply hand down the "results" of their inquiries to the non-philosophical public.

Of course, much of Rawls's more recent work addresses special concerns—much like those raised by Walzer—about the relation between philosophical reflection about social justice and the workings of an ongoing democratic polity (Walzer 1981; 1989; Rawls 1985; 1994). In these writings he considers the question of what authority moral and political philosophy might have in the public culture of a contemporary liberal democracy. But there is a more general problem about the authority of philosophical moral inquiry that philosophers must also address. After all, a form of inquiry is genuine moral inquiry only insofar as it preserves a link with the concerns of everyday moral inquirers. Philosophers who expect the deliverances of moral philosophy to "solve" problems of justification and theory acceptance in the real moral world must be able to say why they think the claims of philosophy are relevant to that world. Thus, the challenge to philosophical efforts at normative moral theorizing implicit in the criticisms of thinkers such as Walzer, Baier, Noble, and Rorty remains compelling. Why, these critics ask, should a philosophical claim about what justifies a moral conception, or about some specific conception that best satisfies allegedly relevant constraints on moral justification, be thought to have authority in the realm of everyday moral concerns? Contemporary moral philosophers have often chosen simply to ignore the challenge implicit in this question. But ignoring the challenge will not bring an end to the serious concerns that give rise to it.

As Noble rightly points out, any normative moral theory that a philosopher might endorse as justified will invariably raise questions about precisely what conclusions and actions the theory requires. Moreover, as I noted in Chapter 3, even a sympathetic reader will encounter great difficulties in trying to decide precisely what conclusions follow from the proper application of the most carefully articulated philosophical theories. Of course, in my view these difficulties are inevitable: they are a function of difficulties that beset moral reasoning and argument in general. Moral theories do not, indeed cannot, solve moral problems for the very simple reason that no principle or rule that might be intended to systematize moral reasoning can be self-interpreting. The task of interpreting and applying a moral rule or principle calls on skills that cannot themselves be formalized or systematized. Yet while these facts about moral reasoning are not intrinsically problematic, Noble rightly objects that they create a special problem for the "authoritative" view of moral philosophy, that is, for the view that moral philosophy is the principal source of arguments for establishing the validity of moral conceptions. If one must try to decide the correctness of any particular normative moral theory without knowing what actions the theory really enjoins, Noble reasonably contends, then normative moral theory has clearly failed to be authoritative in any meaningful sense of the word (Noble 1989, 57).

This objection may seem unfair. Some philosophers will urge that it is often possible to provide a rough but workable account of what kinds of actions a theory enjoins. Yet the existence of disagreement among philosophical theories of morality—what I have called the Rashomon Effect in moral theory—creates further difficulties for the authoritative view of moral philosophy. It is a good thing, in my view, that there are many different philosophical versions of the structure of moral experience. Like C. D. Broad, I consider it implausible that even the best moral theory could contain "the whole truth and nothing but the truth" about morality. To be sure, it may be possible to produce considerations that rule out some moral conceptions as generally unacceptable; I have even suggested what some of these considerations might be. Thus, in challenging Berlin's version of value pluralism (in Chapter 3) I argued that there are good grounds to reject any theory that requires one to accept a self-conception denying one's very status as a moral agent. Nonetheless, I doubt that one could show that any moral conception decisively defeats the claims of all "rival" theories to rational acceptability. It is simply highly unlikely that some one moral theory—even a "systematic" moral theory—could possibly capture all the richness and complexity of the structure of moral experience. But the persistence of unmitigated philosophical disagreement is disastrous for any attempt to defend the authoritative conception of moral theory, since it leaves the task of adjudicating between competing moral theories to the person contemplating them. It is simply unclear how defenders of the authoritative view might rebut Noble's criticisms of moral theory.

Some philosophers will insist that philosophy has just not made enough progress in this regard. In fact, much contemporary moral philosophy seems to be inspired by a vision of philosophical convergence on "the one true" normative moral theory. Thus, for instance, Peter Singer claims to believe that "the puzzle of ethics is starting to come together," and that moral theory has helped to lay out all the pieces of the puzzle (Singer 1991, 545). A more qualified expression of this kind of confidence is embodied in Brink's contention, discussed in Chapter 3, that "secular moral theory" is a "relatively underdeveloped" area of inquiry (Brink 1989, 206). Moral theorists will make progress toward a "convergence" of moral thinking, Brink believes, if moral theory is freed from what he views as the constraints of religious belief, and if there is a sufficient increase in the number of people "working full time" to produce systematic moral theories (Brink 1989, 207). Yet, ironically, Brink proclaims the importance of progress in moral theory while also maintaining that the considered moral convictions of "most people" already reveal significant "moral progress" (Brink 1989, 208). He claims, as I have noted, that most people "no longer think that slavery, racial discrimination, rape, or child abuse" is "acceptable," and that even those who "still engage in these activities typically pay lip service to the wrongness of these activities" (Brink 1989, 208). Still further, the changes in practice that Brink cites as evidence of "moral progress" have occurred despite the "underdeveloped" state of moral theory. They have sometimes occurred in spite of the explicit urgings of influential moral philosophy to the contrary—such as Locke's defense of New World slavery and Hume's defense of racism. Brink's account thus plays into the anti-theorist's hands: by allowing that it is often possible to know what is right and wrong independent of (and even in spite of) moral theory, he makes Noble's description of normative moral theory as "superfluous" seem all too apt.[18]

At one point Brink seems to recognize that his stance toward common moral convictions demands a special effort to establish that moral theory nonetheless makes a real contribution to moral life. To this end he attempts to defend the idea that moral philosophy, and especially the "systematic study of morality," will always produce at least some "moral experts." He even asserts that "moral philosophers (or at least some among them) must be *among* the moral experts." Since moral philosophy is "the systematic study of morality," he contends, moral philosophy will quite certainly produce at least some experts (Brink 1989, 96). Yet why should it be thought that a knowledge of moral conceptions, or any kind of study of moral philosophy, produces moral expertise? Evidence of moral expertise is displayed in reliably living a moral life, and there is absolutely no evidence that moral philosophers do this better than—or even as well as—non-philosophers. Moreover, though the origins of moral expertise no doubt include an ability to appreciate at least the rudiments of a systematic moral conception, the moral importance of personal qualities such as sincerity, self-awareness, and creative imagination makes it quite unlikely that *genuine* moral expertise could be exhausted by a knowledge even of all available moral conceptions. But there is a further difficulty with Brink's treatment of moral expertise in his claim that quite possibly everyone is "roughly equally knowledgeable about the moral facts" (Brink 1989, 96). How, then, critics such as Noble will ask, does moral theory make any contribution to moral knowledge at all? It is quite clear, they might argue, how scientific theories contribute to knowledge of natural facts: someone who has never studied physical theory, for instance, will not be able to say anything very knowledgeable about quarks. If it is possible to be as knowledgeable about moral facts without moral theory as it is with moral theory, then moral theory must be irrelevant to the moral life.

An effective challenge to this skepticism about the relevance of moral theory to moral life must begin by relinquishing the vain insistence on the authoritative status of philosophical moral inquiry—along with the implausible notion that moral philosophy produces moral expertise. There is a middle way between the skeptical anti-theorist view on which moral philosophy should be *replaced* by some other discipline—such as cultural anthropology, or experimental psychology, or literature, or some combination thereof—and the unsupportable view that moral philosophy is the final court of appeal on questions of moral justification. That middle way involves thinking of moral philosophy as a valuable and distinctive participant in the ongoing process of moral inquiry. What is valuable and distinctive about moral philosophy is not the extent to which it might contribute to the production of "moral experts." What is important, rather, is that the discipline of moral philosophy typically inculcates a special familiarity with (and sometimes a special commitment to) standards of reasonableness in argument, along with knowledge of the potential strengths and weaknesses of different interpretations of the structure of moral experience, and a special appreciation of canons for scrutinizing new interpretations. Of course, great moral philosophers may also possess special abilities to reinterpret imaginatively the structure of moral experience. Yet this further attribute is not necessary, in my view, to establish the importance of moral philosophy and moral philosophers. The distinctive ways in which moral philosophers evaluate, and sometimes even generate, interpretations that help make sense of moral experience can play an important role in influencing moral thought and action. Yet philosophy is only one contributor to the process of moral inquiry. Philosophy is not authoritative in moral argument; nor is it even *primus inter pares*. But philosophical interpretation of the structure of moral experience—in all its varied forms—can nonetheless make significant contributions to ongoing moral inquiry and the moral life.

For many moral philosophers, of course, such claims will seem a heretical disavowal of everything that is important to the enterprise of moral philosophy. In the preface to *Reason and Morality*, Alan Gewirth succinctly formulates the orthodoxy which my view seeks to challenge: "The most important and difficult problem of philosophical ethics is whether a substantial moral principle can be rationally justified. On the answer depends the possibility of construing the difference between moral right and wrong as objective and universal and hence as knowable by moral judgments on which all persons who use rational methods must agree" (Gewirth 1978, ix). On Gewirth's conception, moral philosophy is not just another contribution to ongoing moral inquiry, nor is philosophical disagreement about substantial moral principles just another species of moral disagreement. The philosophical problem of rationally justifying a supreme moral principle is "of first importance for the guidance of human life" (Gewirth 1978, ix). Implicit in his claim is the notion that the aim of moral inquiry—especially philosophical moral inquiry—should ultimately be to identify one moral conception, or one supreme moral principle, as best able to defeat the claims of all "rivals" to rational acceptability.

This assumption is an intriguing extension of the coercive conception of rationality that I described at the outset of Chapter 3. Gewirth insists that finding some one principle on which all rational persons "must agree" is a necessary requirement of the moral life. But, as I have shown, the coercive conception of rationality ultimately yields an inadequate understanding of moral inquiry and the moral life. Further, it encourages misunderstanding of the nature of interpretations of moral experience. To be sure, some interpretations are better than others. Yet no one moral interpretation can contain the whole truth and nothing but the truth about morality; there will generally be more than one good interpretation of the structure of moral experience. Nor is it a requirement of the moral life that moral inquiry ought to seek to justify rationally some one best moral conception.

OBJECTIVITY AND THE ASPIRATIONS OF MORAL INQUIRY

There is no reason to worry that this stance leaves unresolved what some philosophers might call the problem of moral objectivity. To begin with, many accounts of this problem—especially in attempts to respond to relativism—rest on the assumption that one can defend moral objectivity only by showing that there is some "single true morality" whose truth is guaranteed by a realm of "absolute moral values." But efforts to identify isolable moral "values" (including moral realist claims about "moral facts" and "moral properties") simply misunderstand the language and practice of moral inquiry. Such efforts detach moral concepts from the activities and practices in which they make sense. In so doing, they overlook the richness and complexity of ongoing moral inquiry—the myriad ways in which human beings articulate and interpret moral concepts, rules, and principles in action, as well as display moral sentiments and responses in emotions, attitudes, and actions.[19] A plausible conception of moral objectivity must resist the effort to reify moral "values" because questions of value cannot profitably, or plausibly, be reduced to questions about isolable entities or properties that might be identified, or even "exist," independent of ongoing moral inquiry.[20]

The belief that questions about moral objectivity must nonetheless be addressed in this way is rooted in a familiar widespread assumption about the concept of objectivity. It is commonly assumed that any plausible conception of objectivity must establish that there is a reliable connection between any inquiry described as objective and some realm that exists independent of that inquiry. Yet this assumption unwisely ignores the grammar, in the Wittgensteinian sense, of the concept of objectivity. For to assert the objectivity of any human inquiry is, first of all, to affirm the possibility that the results of that inquiry might transcend the "intensely human" limitations of its methods. Any claim that some inquiry is objective thus embodies an *aspiration* to the transcendent validity of the outcome of inquiry. Acknowledging this link between objectivity and human aspirations, moreover, helps illuminate familiar concerns about objectivity in everyday life. An interviewer who seeks objective assessments of applicants for a job, like judges in a piano competition who seek objective grounds for choosing a winner or a professor who seeks to assess student essays objectively, aspires to results which transcend the limitations of her preconceptions and unreflective preferences. In each case objectivity demands reliance on grounds of assessment that can be justified to any reasonable and qualified judge. Ideally, objectivity demands that methods of inquiry entirely eliminate the influence of the narrowly personal perspective of the inquiring subject—even though in most everyday inquiries objectivity is always a matter of degree, a function of the extent to which the methods of inquiry effectively *minimize* the perspective of the inquiring subject.

But the link between objectivity and aspirations is crucial even in contexts that seem to demand a more robust conception of objectivity than that appealed to in these everyday inquiries. To be sure, familiar philosophical defenses of the objectivity of science might suggest otherwise. Williams, for example, sometimes seeks to defend the objectivity of science, not with claims about human aspirations, but by appeal to the possibility that science will eventually converge on "the way the world really is" independent of human inquiry (Williams 1985, 133–156). Williams also insists, of course, that even when a culture's ethical language seems to "stretch beyond its boundaries," this can only be "a point about the . . . aspirations of ethical thought, not about its objectivity" (Williams 1985, 159). Yet no one—not even a philosopher—can stand completely beyond the bounds of human inquiry in order to compare any of its results with the way the world "really is." Williams's view contains a plausible claim only if he can establish that there is a fundamental difference between the *aspirations* of science and those of moral inquiry—some difference that makes it rational to aspire to the objectivity of science, and not to the objectivity of moral inquiry.

Yet before we turn to consider whether he can find such a difference, it is important to note a second crucial feature of the grammar of the concept of objectivity. For any claim that some inquiry is objective also implicitly asserts that it is possible to secure uncoerced agreement on at least some results of that inquiry. In fact, the occurrence of uncoerced agreement on some conclusion often serves—and I think reasonably—to bolster confidence in aspirations to transcendent validity, and hence in the objectivity of the inquiry in question. This is most obvious, perhaps, in the informal inquiries of everyday life. Thus, the professor whose colleagues without prompting second her assessment of an essay reasonably concludes that her assessment meets the demands of objectivity appropriate to the inquiry. But important defenses of the objectivity of science cite the regularity of uncoerced agreement in science as compelling evidence that science's aspirations to transcendent validity are rational. According to Williams, in fact, the objectivity of science is fundamentally linked with "the idea of a convergence that would be *uncoerced:* if it were not uncoerced, we could not describe it as a process that arrives at the truth" (Williams 1985, 171). Of course, the occurrence of uncoerced agreement on some conclusion is not sufficient to prove the objectivity of the inquiry which produced it; nor does Williams intend to make such a claim about science. Further, since accounts of the objectivity of science are so often associated with a coercive conception of rationality, it will be important to distinguish between the coercion associated with a rationally compelling argument and the coercion that involves the use of physical violence—or the threat of violence—as a means of compelling agreement. But if Williams is right, once this distinction is drawn, confidence in the objectivity of science is rational because of the regularity with which scientific inquiry achieves consensus without resort to violence or other forms of coercion.

But there is uncoerced moral agreement, and in my view it provides as defensible an anchor for moral inquiry's aspirations to transcendent validity as does uncoerced agreement in the case of science. Critics may insist that the persistence of serious moral disagreement helps establish the infirmity of moral inquiry. But, as I argued in Chapter 3, what the persistence of moral disagreement shows is simply that the background consensus that is needed to underwrite substantive moral agreement is sometimes bound by more narrowly social and cultural constraints than the analogous background consensus in science. Relativists, noncognitivists, and even less skeptical pluralists, claim to find rationally irresolvable, or "fundamental," disagreements in virtually every realm of the moral domain. Yet a careful scrutiny of moral disagreement—of the sort I have tried to offer in the first three chapters of this book—simply does not support these claims. To be sure, even within a single culture, sincere and well-placed observers who share a language, and who can agree about the truth of sentences concerning tables and chairs and rabbits—and possibly even about electrons and black holes—can disagree about the moral status of abortion, the moral acceptability of using violence to promote desirable ends, or the moral acceptability of consuming meat. But this simply shows that moral reflection structures experience in ways that are not coincident with reflection about rabbits, electrons, and black holes. Some philosophers will conclude that moral reflection and moral inquiry are thus concerned with data which have no place in a naturalized vision of the world. Yet it is at great cost that this vision is taken to be exhaustive—in Quine's famous phrase—of "what there is." Moral argument and moral inquiry are valuable not merely in spite of but because of the fact that they rely on methods appropriate to their subject matter—methods fundamentally different from the methods of science.

Critics of my claims may seek to denigrate uncoerced *moral* agreement in comparison with uncoerced agreement in science. This effort will usually begin with the claim that uncoerced moral agreement presupposes a complex "stage setting"—some substantial background agreement in belief and valuation—while science (allegedly) does not. Yet uncoerced agreement in science also presupposes an indispensable background of collective agreement. A substantial portion of this stage setting is, to be sure, deeply embedded in linguistic structures that are less likely to be bounded by culture than those that are essential to moral argument. But an important component of the background agreement that makes science possible depends on learned structures of reasoning and belief which are linked with membership in scientific communities, and especially with the training in problems and procedures accepted by those communities as appropriate to scientific inquiry. The agreement that arises out of membership in scientific communities is, moreover, remarkably complex, and it is constantly being renegotiated as new ways of interpreting the relationship between criteria of theory choice—such as simplicity, explanatory power, and the like—emerge over time. Even respected members of natural science communities risk marginalization should they fail to accept some widespread renegotiation, much as Einstein did for his resistance to quantum mechanics. In general, then, uncoerced agreement on scientific results is just as deeply rooted in a collective background agreement as is uncoerced moral agreement. However plausible (or implausible) the notion that science will one day converge on a conception of "the way the world really is," this possibility is not what sets the stage for uncoerced agreement on its results.

A final attempt to challenge my claims about moral objectivity may appeal to the idea that the grounds for assessment of scientific claims are fundamentally different from those in any other inquiry. It may be claimed that grounds for assessment in science (unlike those in any other inquiry) can always be defined with reference to aims that have unconditional value—value independent of human desires or aspirations. It may be urged, to adapt a phrase of Quine's, that grounds for assessment of scientific theories are defined by reference to the goal of determining a theory's "efficacy for truth or prediction" (Quine 1986, 664). Critics may claim, further, that even when the immediate goal of theory construction in science cannot be successful prediction, the ultimate goal is nonetheless compatibility with theories that do in fact maximize true predictions. Yet while there is certainly widespread general agreement—perhaps approaching unanimity—on the value of maximizing true predictions, it is not obvious that doing so has unconditional value. Hume once noted that human beings reasonably come to value theories which generate true predictions because of the role that such theories often play in helping to promote human aims and interests (Hume [1739] 1978, 448–454). But if so, then when true predictions fail to play this role, it is not unreasonable to question the value of theories from which they derive. It is thus, for instance, that one may reasonably wonder about the value of theories that generate reliable predictions about a person's chances of developing some dread incurable disease. There may even be circumstances in which it would be *unreasonable* not to question the value of maximizing true predictions. The aims that underwrite the grounds of assessment in science are no more "unconditional" than the aims associated with assessment in any other human inquiry.

But the general point of my claims about objectivity must be clear: I claim that the aspirations of moral inquiry are rational, and that morality is thus objective. Reasonable confidence in the aspirations of science is rightly rooted in the regularity of uncoerced agreement in science. But, as I will show in Chapter 5, an understanding of the processes by which noncoercive methods can be successful in moral argument reveals that the aspirations of moral inquiry are just as reasonable. Some critics may still object that uncoerced agreement in science is somehow superior to uncoerced agreement in moral inquiry, because moral inquiry does not appear to be converging on a single moral conception. Yet convergence on a unique "solution" is not an invariant requirement of objectivity. Achieving objectivity in human inquiry and argument does not always demand that one be able to select out one and only one path of action as an absolute, unquestioned ideal. Sometimes one achieves objectivity by generating a set of criteria that allows one to choose from a group of generally acceptable alternatives. At other times objectivity may also demand being able to rule out certain ways of thinking, or certain courses of action, as unacceptable. But the point of central importance is that objectivity does not always require uniqueness (Wolf 1992, 790–791).

In fact, uniqueness is not a central requirement of objectivity in a variety of non-moral domains of inquiry. Clinical medicine, once again, provides an instructive example. Clinicians who treat various auto-immune diseases (such as multiple sclerosis, lupus erythematosus, and rheumatoid arthritis), for instance, would point out that there is no absolute unquestioned "ideal" treatment for every patient with such diseases. As I noted in Chapter 3, attempts to control such diseases according to current theories of acceptable treatment alternatives are a lot like efforts to resolve certain moral conflicts (including debates about abortion or about affirmative action policies, for instance). Any decision taken now will alter the conditions which the clinician and the patient will face in the future, and sometimes it alters those future conditions dangerously and irrevocably. Finally, attempts to control such diseases require repeated renegotiation of the clinical domain, much as the resolution of complex moral issues will often require re-peated renegotiation as the moral data change. The complexity of the moral domain is not wholly unlike the complexity of the condition of a patient with a chronic illness: it simply will not support a conception on which objectivity requires absoluteness and uniqueness.

A plausible defense of moral objectivity should, of course, also point out that there is far more convergence on at least some moral matters than many critics of moral inquiry are willing to acknowledge. Consider the regularity with which certain moral ideas—such as the ideas embed-ded in what is commonly called the Golden Rule—appear in different cultures.[21] Some theorists have sought to explain such convergence by appeal to the notion that some rudimentary background agreement on the structure of moral experience is natural—that is, independent of hu-man cultural forms.[22] Yet while this claim makes sense of important fea-tures of moral life, it is important to avoid some familiar pitfalls in defending it. For even if it were possible to get completely "beneath" or "behind" the cultural constructions that constitute accessible *interpretations* of the structure of moral experience in order to provide some account of the natural dimensions of that structure, the complex demands of moral reflection in the lives of real persons would render any such account incomplete and unhelpful. In the complex moral world that human beings inhabit, moral reasoning demands judgment sharpened by experience, sincerity, and imagination. Any attempt to provide an account of an uninterpreted structure of moral experience would thus be of little help in advancing genuine moral understanding. Equally important, it is not clear how any human inquiry—whether in philosophy or in the natural or social sciences—could in fact get at the "bare" structure of moral experience, unaffected by central features of some particular interpretation of it. More plausible, and ultimately more useful in moral reflection, are efforts to articulate and evaluate some currently unarticulated interpretation of moral experience, or to subject some currently articulated interpretation to careful rational scrutiny.

Some critics will still protest that my claims about the objectivity of moral inquiry do not show why moral argument and inquiry are not incomplete without philosophical efforts to "validate" moral conceptions authoritatively. Philosophers, in particular, may assume that moral thinking and action will fail to be rational if it is not possible to provide a philosophically validated, systematic, and succinct account of what one needs to know in order to think and act morally. Yet, as I have shown in this and the previous chapter, some capacities central to moral reasoning—such as the creative imagination—are not subject to systematization. Further, some essential components of the moral life do not even involve knowledge at all: sincerity is not an epistemological problem. Still further, much of what one needs to know in order to be moral, such as that human beings are fallible and that human practices can always go wrong, requires no systematic formulation.

The notion that the proper task of moral philosophy is to validate systematic moral conceptions remains compelling to many contemporary philosophers because contemporary moral philosophy has artificially narrowed the moral domain. Normative moral theory has, for the most part, become an extended debate about how to provide the best accounts of "right action"—as though the range of moral concern and moral inquiry might be bounded by concern about the requirements of obligation and action. Despite renewed attention to the possibilities of virtue theory and to problems of moral character in general, contemporary moral theorizing often seems to be an endless tug-of-war between competing accounts of moral action. Many philosophers have thus become unable to appreciate the fact that a knowledge of principles or rules could not possibly be sufficient for the moral life, or to recognize the importance of non–action-guiding moral judgments—including those that sometimes demand moral reactive sentiments such as regret, forgiveness, guilt, or moral indignation. Yet historically the most illuminating moral theory has been enlightening and compelling less for the systematic character of its constructions than for its capacity to stimulate self-scrutiny by enriching the moral imagination. If contemporary moral philosophy is to recapture the attention of sincere, reflective people seeking new ways to make sense of moral experience, moral philosophers must seek a different conception of the subject.

The most suitable candidate for this task, in my view, is the Socratic model of moral inquiry. Although it has been richly reinterpreted in a variety of philosophical conceptions, it is in essence a model on which moral inquiry serves principally to stimulate reflection on the nature of the life worth living. On this conception, the notion that philosophy might validate moral conceptions—or, in more skeptical hands, demonstrate that no such conception can be validated—would be anathema. But it is difficult, if not impossible, for philosophical moral inquiry to stimulate self-scrutiny in an audience that philosophy typically chooses not to address. The empirical foothold of moral inquiry must always be the self-understanding of the moral inquirers addressed by it. But self-understandings are partly shaped by the regularities in belief and behavior associated with particular ways of life, particular cultures. Philosophical moral inquiry that might plausibly claim the attention of a community of moral inquirers must thus attempt to contribute to the collective self-scrutiny of the cultures which those inquirers accept. No such contribution will be compelling or defensible without a more subtle appreciation of the complexity of culture than that informing most contemporary philosophy, especially the implausible assumptions

of relativist understandings of culture. Equally important, moral philosophy can return to its Socratic roots only if it proceeds from a richer
understanding of the nature of moral inquiry itself, and of the complex
relation between culture and moral inquiry. Thus in Chapter 5 I turn
to more sustained reflection on the nature of moral inquiry and culture
and on the relation between them.

5 MORALITY AND CULTURE THROUGH THICK AND THIN

Human social groups tend to find their openness toward the future in the variety of their metaphors for what may be the good life and in the contest of their paradigms.

Victor Turner, Dramas, Fields, and Metaphors

THE NEED FOR THICK DESCRIPTIONS OF MORAL INQUIRY

Competing interpretations of the structure of moral experience unavoidably shape the moral world in which human beings must judge, choose, and act. But interpretations can shape the moral world only *in and through* moral inquiry. This means that discerning the truth about what the moral life both demands and makes possible—the truth, that is, about morality—will require understanding the inquiry that articulates those demands and possibilities. Moreover, as I show in this chapter, an understanding of moral inquiry is especially important in efforts to comprehend the relation between morality and culture and the varied claims that morality may make on human beings. Moral interpretations are often embodied in actions, and not clearly articulated by the agents who perform those actions. Some agents, moreover, may not fully appreciate the commitments embodied in their actions unless explicitly prompted to do so. But an action must always embody some humanly accessible interpretation of the structure of moral experience in order to count as moral action. Thus, a child whose actions reveal that he values kindness to others could, if prompted, articulate the moral importance of kindness—however simple that articulation might be. Even an agent who claims to act on divine commands, or divine inspiration, must interpret those commands, or the content of that inspiration, in order to be able to realize their aims in her actions. Any moral action taken now—whether a religious acolyte's attempt to realize divine commands or a child's simple expression of kindness toward others—helps shape the data of moral experience to be encountered in the future. In so doing, moral action contributes to ongoing moral inquiry and at the same time helps determine the demands and possibilities of morality. But this is merely one way in which the data of moral experience—along with the concepts, propositions, attitudes, and practices that constitute morality—are partly determined by the processes of moral inquiry. An adequate understanding of morality will therefore demand a careful account of the moral inquiry that helps to shape morality.

Let me clarify what I mean by claiming that an adequate account of moral inquiry is an essential prerequisite for understanding morality. Most important, I do not contend that an *exhaustive* understanding of morality could ever be provided by an understanding of moral inquiry alone, however comprehensive and richly textured that understanding might be. After all, I have argued (in Chapter 4) that aspirations for the transcendent validity of moral inquiry are reasonable, and that they are reasonable on the same grounds as are aspirations for the transcendent validity of scientific inquiry. In this chapter I argue that aspirations to the transcendent validity of moral inquiry are indispensable to the engaged moral inquiry of everyday life; theorists such as Rorty and Williams who disparage these aspirations simply fail to understand the conditions which make much important moral inquiry possible. Yet one cannot understand the whole truth about morality without understanding moral inquiry. The fact that philosophical analyses of morality so often begin by severing the link between morality and moral inquiry may well explain why those analyses so often misconstrue the notions they purport to clarify. Such accounts may begin, for instance, by examining the concept of obligation, or the concept of virtue, or even the concept of moral objectivity—as though such concepts might be understood independently of the contexts of inquiry in which they have a place. But recent developments in the study of science remind us (as I argued in Chapter 3) that even the complex claims and practices defensibly said to constitute science cannot be understood apart from the contexts of scientific inquiry. Since moral inquiry is at least as complex an activity as science, the claims and practices constitutive of morality cannot be understood apart from the contexts of moral inquiry.

But moral inquiry, I have argued, is far more complex than most contemporary conceptions allow. Thus, for instance, while it often takes place within specific cultures, the boundaries between those cultures are not morally impenetrable walls. Further, moral inquiry (unlike scientific inquiry) cannot in principle be confined to particular communities of officially credentialed participants. Some of the most important moral inquiry, I argue, takes place in the difficult contexts of everyday life. Understanding the contexts of moral inquiry—within as well as across cultures, and in familiar as well as unfamiliar contexts of everyday life—requires careful articulation of the attitudes, assumptions, and standards of argument at work in those contexts. It requires, that is, a kind of moral ethnography. More precisely, it demands thick descriptions of the contexts in and through which moral intention, expectation, and meaningful action take shape. Only thick description can yield a suitable appreciation of the contexts and processes of moral inquiry, and of the means by which moral inquiry helps shape the varied claims and practices claimed to constitute morality. Only thick description, that is, can ultimately yield an adequate understanding of morality.

Relativists in philosophy and the social sciences sometimes claim special understanding of such matters: human cultures, they argue, are the principal (for some the only) contexts in and through which moral inquiry takes place. Yet, ironically, although these relativists claim to deepen and enrich understanding of those contexts, the views they defend presuppose some of the thinnest imaginable accounts of moral language and moral inquiry. Many relativists construct moral barriers between cultures by claiming to find radical differences between one kind of moral concept or judgment that is accessible and intelligible across cultural boundaries and one kind that is not. Harman, for instance, believes that moral "ought" judgments are always relative to a group's implicit agreement to accept moral rules.[1] In a more recent example, Williams distinguishes between essentially "thick" and essentially "thin" ethical concepts. Every culture has some "thick" ethical concepts, which can be applied properly only if one understands complex facts about the local social world in which they are rooted (Williams 1985, 167; cf. 129; 140–141). Treachery, brutality, courage, and gratitude, he claims (without any real discussion of why he settles on just these concepts), are some thick ethical concepts familiar in "our own" culture. These concepts are to be distinguished from the "thin" concepts embodied in "abstract and general" reflection. But Williams offers very few examples of what qualifies as a thin ethical concept (his main examples are "good," "right," and "ought"), and no careful account of the characteristics by which such concepts might be identified. Still further, he proceeds to claim that some ethical concepts are by their nature so "thick" with cultural and historical tradition that no cultural "outsider" can fully understand or make adequate use of them. Once again, he offers an insufficient account of how one might distinguish these concepts from culturally "thinner" ones—though he does attempt to link his defense of this view to familiar debates about the relativist implications of Evans-Pritchard's anthropology. The concepts that no outsider can fully understand or adequately use, he suggests, are culturally thick in the same sense as concepts "relating to religion, for instance, or to witchcraft" (Williams 1985, 142).

Yet the attempt to identify moral concepts that only a cultural insider can fully grasp fails as an account of moral language. Of course, moral inquiry within specific cultures and historical periods often relies on concepts that are deeply rooted in culturally and historically specific traditions. But the possible and plausible uses of moral concepts cannot be fully determined or exhausted by the content of any one set of cultural or historical traditions, and this is what a thick description of moral inquiry reveals. As Michael Walzer has argued, it is always possible to give thin as well as thick accounts of any moral term. On Walzer's formulation, moral concepts *always* have both "minimal and maximal meanings" (Walzer 1994, 2–3). I would add, reiterating a conclusion of Chapter 1, that a concept is a moral concept *only* if it is possible to give both thin and thick accounts of it. Williams's effort to distinguish between intrinsically thick and thin moral concepts simply obscures important facts about the richness and complexity of moral inquiry.

Three central features of moral inquiry that relativism is unable even to recognize, let alone interpret, are explicable only by appeal to the fact that moral concepts are always susceptible of both thick and thin interpretations. To begin with, internal moral criticism in one culture can successfully appeal to moral concepts first articulated in another only because it is always possible to produce both thick and thin interpretations of moral concepts. Consider, for instance, the complex exchanges between the moral language of different cultures that are implicit in the links between Gandhi's development of the concept of "satyagraha" (firmness in the truth) and King's account of nonviolent civil disobedience (Gandhi 1957; King 1964). These exchanges provide powerful evidence that a concept which is "thickly" rooted in religious and cultural traditions distinctive to one society can be constructively and imaginatively applied in new cultural settings. Indeed, it has been argued that the principles embodied in the nonviolent struggle for the rights of AfricanAmericans constitute a very "significant development of Indian ethics in the twentieth century" (Bilimoria 1991, 55). Of course, on my view, significant moral criticism is always an effort to encourage reinterpretation of the structure of moral experience as a way of bringing about a change in practice. This means that internal moral criticism of a particular culture—even criticism of the sort plausibly described as "prophetic"—never involves the invention or application of radically new moral ideas. Accordingly, applying a concept first articulated in one culture in order to make sense of moral experience in a second is only one way to encourage a novel reordering of the second culture's more familiar moral ideas—in the hope of encouraging a reinterpretation of the structure of moral experience, and usually a corresponding change in practice. Novelty in morality and moral inquiry, as I have argued, never occurs in basic concepts but only in the reordering and reinterpretation of significant details.

The susceptibility of moral concepts to thick and thin interpretations also helps explain why internal moral criticism sometimes detaches culturally familiar moral terms from the traditions of the culture it seeks to criticize and then gradually links them to a new set of cultural understandings and forms. Perhaps the most vivid example of this phenomenon is the arduous process by which the American concept of freedom has been severed from traditions which once underwrote the acceptance of chattel slavery—and may one day be fully severed from the legacy of legally sanctioned discrimination on the basis of race and gender. To be sure, any reinterpretation of a culture's moral concepts eventually produces new "thick" uses and understandings of culturally central moral language. But the concepts themselves will continue to have what Walzer calls maximal and minimal meanings, and thus will continue to have an indefinitely large array of thick and thin uses. In fact, it is because moral language always has its thick and thin uses that moral criticism of so-called hegemonic cultural forms within culturally complex societies is possible.[2] It is important to avoid assuming that moral criticism in such circumstances is easy. It is equally naive to assume that a social movement or group which successfully articulates a moral criticism of some hegemonic cultural form will thereby necessarily accomplish all of its important practical aims—without at least some additional "extra-moral" struggles.[3] Yet any cultural form that purports to give moral legitimacy to some group's position of social dominance, no matter how oppressive the social and political institutions which underwrite that dominance, must always rely on concepts which can be reconfigured as part of some new moral interpretation. Under the appropriate circumstances, moreover, such an interpretation may sometimes be turned against the dominance of that very group.

Finally, it is because moral concepts always allow both thick and thin interpretations that they cannot be confined to a particular culture or historical period. Moral inquiry is capable of transcending the boundaries of culture and history because the complexity of moral concepts makes possible complex realignments and reinterpretations of the structure of moral experience. These processes were at work in Gandhi's extraordinary efforts to adapt moral notions first articulated by Tolstoy and Ruskin, and sometimes even in Christian theology, to new cultural contexts (Gandhi 1957). But it also explains why Jeffersonian notions of equality, for example, can be detached from the acceptance of chattel slavery. Equally important, it explains why it is neither anachronistic nor intellectually suspect to contend that Jefferson's decision to continue owning slaves—despite his express commitment to equality—can be recognized as a morally culpable instance of affected ignorance. No adequate account of moral language can license the relativism of historical distance that attempts to isolate Jefferson's slaveholding from contemporary moral scrutiny. Indeed, such attempts must eventually make it impossible to appreciate the notion of equality that Jefferson so eloquently articulated. It is possible to appreciate the moral eloquence of Jefferson's arguments for equality only because it is possible to subject the moral failings of some of his practices to critical scrutiny.

But an appropriately thick description of moral inquiry has implications beyond a richer understanding of the relation between moral language and culture. Such a description will also influence in important ways our understanding of the nature of membership in the community of moral inquirers. For example, a woman who appeals to an international women's group to protest a practice of female circumcision and infibulation in her own country—possibly even to seek protection from those who would perform the practice on her or her children—by virtue of her protest proclaims her membership in a cross-cultural community of moral inquirers. Relativists who defend the moral isolationist response to such circumstances effectively ignore this woman's claim to be heard in the moral debate that is likely to ensue. James's contention that there can be no final truth in ethics until the last person has had his experience and his "say" serves as an important reminder of the implausibility—and the potential injustice—of attempts to erect impenetrable cultural barriers between groups of moral inquirers.

Of course, such circumstances may present morally compelling reasons to refrain from "outside" interference with the practice as a whole. There is an important difference, for instance, between criticizing the coercive use of a practice against one person—and possibly even intervening to assist her—and criticizing that practice as a whole. There is an even more momentous difference between intervening on behalf of one person who seeks protection from the practice and attempting large-scale intervention in the regular daily workings of that practice, especially when such intervention may affect those who have expressed no dissatisfaction with the practice. But intervention on behalf of one internal critic, as well as external criticism of the practice, are both consistent with respect for the practice. External criticism, in particular, recognizes the importance of the human capacity to seek a reasonable defense of that practice and leaves room for participants to decide whether to defend the practice to outsiders. Large-scale intervention in a practice, by contrast, clearly embodies something less than respect for the practice. Yet, as I show in greater detail later in this chapter, the mere fact that some practice is part of a distinctive culture does not bestow on that practice an indisputable moral authority. Defenders of segregationist policies in the American South, for instance, long derided resistance to segregation as the work of "outside" agitators interfering with the southern way of life. Still further, any practice that can survive only by being shielded from external reflection and criticism should raise serious moral concern. Knowledge of one's human limitations and fallibility is indispensable to rational moral inquiry.

James's richly suggestive conception of membership in the community of moral inquirers poses a special challenge to societies in which the theoretical investigation of moral reflection and action has assumed the character of a professional discipline. For James's conception denies the coherence of projects that would erect barriers between theoretical investigations and the moral reflection of everyday life. Such projects are admittedly complex. They embody, on the one hand, the cult of expertise so deeply embedded in the culture of the technologically advanced nations that accommodate most professional moral philosophy. That dynamic clearly informs the efforts of some philosophers to identify special purposes—such as "validating" and justifying moral conceptions—for which the community of moral inquirers might be limited to a specially trained group of researchers. But philosophy has no special authority to "validate" or justify moral conceptions; that task, I have argued, cannot be completed without contributions from a more inclusive community of moral inquirers. The projects of anti-theory critics, however, too often ignore the role which moral theory, and moral philosophy in general, have played in shaping the contexts within which even everyday moral inquiry takes place. As James cautioned, "the hypotheses which we make" before the end of moral inquiry and "the acts to which they prompt us" are important ingredients of the conditions determining what any person's "say" about morality will be. Much of the moral language that helps shape the economic, social, and political dimensions of the contemporary world is a product of distinctively philosophical efforts to articulate interpretations of the structure of moral experience. Philosophical contributions to ongoing moral inquiry, therefore, cannot be irrelevant to making sense of the structure of moral experience. A thick description of moral inquiry must steer a middle path between the anti-theorist's fetishism of "everyday" moral thinking and argument and the systematic ethical theorist's fetishism of philosophical moral inquiry.

MORAL CONFLICT, MORAL CONFIDENCE, AND MORAL OPENNESS TOWARD THE FUTURE

An appropriately thick description of moral inquiry should also reveal the extraordinary variety of circumstances in which moral inquiry is actually carried out. That variety is not merely a function of the thick and thin uses of moral language. Equally important are the differences among points of view—within as well as across cultures and historical periods—from which moral inquiry may be carried out. Moral inquiry maybe carried out from the vantage of a relatively disengaged moral spectator: in the philosophical articulation and evaluation of normative moral theories, in the social scientist's attempt to describe moral practices, in literary representations of the moral imagination. But most moral inquirers cannot maintain a completely disengaged spectatorship for very long, if at all. In fact, most moral inquirers—including most moral philosophers, social scientists, writers, and literary scholars—will have their moral "say," and so contribute to the ongoing process of moral inquiry, primarily as actors, not as spectators. Moral inquiry, as I have already suggested, is often engaged inquiry carried out as action in the world. The final truth—or, better, the *whole* truth—about morality must somehow take account of this fact. A compelling and defensible understanding of the whole truth about morality will therefore demand a richer understanding of the conditions under which engaged moral inquiry takes place.

But what might it mean to provide an adequate account of the conditions of engaged moral inquiry? It would mean, first of all, recognizing the importance of conflict to the development of moral inquiry. Engaged moral inquiry most often develops by means of constructive reinterpretation and articulation of the structure of moral experience. Moreover, it develops primarily through moral disagreement and conflict. Of course, the persistence of moral conflict is commonly assumed to show that the methods of moral inquiry are infirm. It is often assumed, moreover, that moral inquiry fails to meet central requirements of objectivity because it appears unlikely that moral inquiry will ever yield convergence on a single moral conception. Yet, to adapt a notion defended by the anthropologist Victor Turner, human beings find their moral "openness toward the future" in the contest of competing moral interpretations, not in some imagined progress toward convergence on one interpretation of the structure of moral experience.

It is sometimes difficult to recognize the benefits of serious moral disputes, especially when some of these disputes (about abortion, for instance) seem to threaten the political stability of the societies in which they take place. Of course, some episodes of moral conflict come to unsatisfying and even dangerous conclusions. But, as I argued in Chapter 2, the most common deficiency in essential moral knowledge can be attributed to the phenomenon of affected ignorance, especially affected ignorance of the possibility that habitual and accepted practices might be wrong. This deficiency can affect human beings in any culture and at any point in history. Conflicts between competing moral interpretations, moreover, are sometimes the only effective means of rationally compelling both human cultures and individuals to confront the limited and fallible nature of the moral interpretations they have come to accept. It is precisely because human beings are limited and fallible, and eminently capable of affecting ignorance of their various limitations, that convergence on a single interpretation of the structure of moral experience (within or across cultures) would be morally quite dangerous, if not utterly disastrous. The critical reflection and self-scrutiny so often generated in response to moral disagreement are central components of the moral rationality of individuals, as I have shown. But moral disagreement and conflict are essential to the moral vitality of individual cultures, and ultimately to the moral openness of humanity to the future. Any effort to seek intercultural, or even intracultural, convergence on a single moral conception will be fundamentally incompatible with the wider requirements of rationality in moral inquiry. The notion of ultimate convergence on a single unified theory may be an appropriate ideal to guide explanation and description in science, but it constitutes a serious hindrance to the adequate development of moral inquiry.

One may wonder precisely *how* conflicts between competing moral interpretations underwrite the moral openness of human beings, and human cultures, to the future. This concern is important because many familiar accounts of moral conflict and disagreement—especially in emotivism and relativism—so thinly characterize those conflicts that they cannot illuminate the processes that lead to constructive moral disagreement. To be sure, relativism and emotivism have helpfully focused theoretical attention on some kinds of conflict that drive the development of engaged moral inquiry—from the garden-variety moral argument between individual parties to the large-scale disputes about conflicting moral evaluations that can sometimes powerfully divide nations. Yet relativist and emotivist claims that some of these disagreements are rationally irresolvable—or "fundamental"—misunderstand the nature of moral disagreement. Recent debates about moral dilemmas and tragic choices have focused attention on the first-person conflicts that reflect the complexity of the moral world, although efforts to understand these conflicts seriously misconstrue the circumstances that produce them. But there has been a remarkable lack of attention to a third type of moral conflict—one that is in many ways more instructive about how moral conflicts might underwrite moral openness to the future. Engaged moral inquiry also includes those conflicts that Walzer aptly describes as "workmanlike" social and political struggles: struggles carried out by excluded or oppressed persons and groups, who must sometimes risk their lives in the course of moral inquiry. No account of moral inquiry can be complete as long as there is insufficient appreciation of the conditions under which various kinds of engaged moral inquiry take place. It is important, in particular, that even *nonviolent* "public demonstration and display" (to borrow C. L. Stevenson's apt phrase) carried out in the hope of generating cultural self-scrutiny and change is moral inquiry of the most personally risky sort.

Perhaps the single most important fact about risky, workmanlike moral inquiries is that they presuppose the attitude I have described (in Chapter 1) as moral confidence. Moral confidence involves, first, a conviction of the worth of making judgments that purport to transcend historical and cultural boundaries, and second, a conviction that it is sometimes possible to justify such judgments (across various boundaries) without resort to threats or coercion, political oppression and domination, or physical violence. Moral confidence is essential to the continued development of engaged moral inquiry because it is an essential ingredient of the willingness to engage in noncoercive action in a morally complex world. Confidence in the possibility of an uncoerced moral consensus about abortion, for instance, is embodied in the efforts of those disputants who seek to avoid violent (and recently deadly) encounters which threaten the stability of the moral world. Of course, moral confidence is sometimes overwhelmed by other considerations. A group of people might believe, for instance, that to relinquish any element of their current moral interpretation would undermine the integrity of all the beliefs that constitute it—or sometimes even their own integrity as persons.[4] Still others may be reluctant to acknowledge the common humanity of the people with whom they disagree, and so they may refuse to appeal to the fundamental human capacity to reinterpret imaginatively the structure of moral experience. Some people may even confuse moral smugness with moral confidence: they may simply be unwilling, that is, to consider that they might be wrong. Yet unwillingness to recognize a common humanity is probably a more typical cause of the failure of moral disagreement to be resolved by noncoercive moral inquiry. Whatever the cause, when moral confidence is overwhelmed by any of these considerations, the results are typically disastrous.

In view of the ease with which moral confidence can be overwhelmed by other considerations, it is all the more remarkable that the efforts of those involved in some well-known "workmanlike" moral inquiries have been rooted in little *besides* moral confidence. Only moral confidence, as I have defined it, can explain the courage of the Freedom Riders in the American South in the early 1960s, or Chinese students in Tiananmen Square in the spring of 1989, who persevered in the conviction that—through uncoerced agreement—others might come to accept their efforts to revise some dominant interpretation of moral experience. Yet theorists who seek a truth in relativism are typically reluctant to defend this kind of moral confidence. According to Williams, for instance, to be "confident in trying to make sure that future generations shared our values, we would need, it seems to me, not only to be confident in those values—which, if we can achieve it, is a good thing to be—but also convinced that they were objective, which is a misguided thing to be" (Williams 1985, 172–173). Williams rightly suggests that the aspiration to a transcendent validity in moral inquiry—to the objectivity of morality—is essential to the moral confidence at work in the political struggles I have just described. He then predictably disparages any such aspiration as "misguided." But understanding the efforts of those who must risk their lives in order to defend contested values will ultimately yield a richer account of the reasonableness of aspirations to moral objectivity than could ever be dreamt of in Williams's philosophy.[5]

Consider, for instance, one of the most instructive ironies of the

American civil rights movement in the early 1960s: white citizens in southern states experiencing nonviolent protest of Jim Crow laws could sometimes be heard to describe *visibly nonviolent* demonstrations as, nonetheless, a kind of "violence."[6] Such descriptions bear an uncanny resemblance, of course, to the impatience of Plato's Euthyphro in response to Socrates' insistent questioning. Surely the "violence" which these citizens claimed to find in nonviolent protest was the experience of being rationally compelled to confront a moral failing. One principal aim of the nonviolent protests of the civil rights movement, in King's words, was precisely to create a "crisis," or a "tension in the mind," whereby supporters of segregation would be forced to confront the social reality of segregation (King 1964, 79). But the point of creating this tension was to produce circumstances in which at least some segregationists would eventually be *rationally compelled* to admit the inconsistency between democratic principles of equality and legally sanctioned discrimination on the basis of race. Stevenson predictably viewed such protests as large-scale models of non-rational persuasion (Stevenson 1944). But a procedure in which persons are rationally compelled to admit a moral failing quite clearly conforms to the ideal of rational argument embodied in the emotivist's commitment to the coercive conception of rationality. Indeed, a moral argument which progresses in this way powerfully challenges the familiar insistence that there really is an asymmetry between moral argument and argument in non-moral contexts.

Moral argument, as I acknowledged in Chapter 3, does not always persuade. Thus, many white southerners refused to relinquish their prejudice, even long after the offending laws were struck down. But relativists, emotivists, and moral subjectivists accord such refusals more significance than they deserve. Such refusals are analogous to Einstein's refusal to concede the explanatory force of quantum mechanics: that refusal is not evidence of the implausibility of the theory. Analogously, no refusal to relinquish racial prejudice could show that condemnation of such prejudice is not rationally required. What such refusals show—in science or in moral inquiry—is that new, possibly as yet undeveloped methods of argument and inquiry are required if we are to elicit uncoerced agreement. Some political struggles may frustrate reasonable expectations that we can develop new ways for eliciting uncoerced moral agreement. For many contemporary thinkers, the 1989 crackdown on students in Tiananmen Square provides a particularly troubling example.[7] Further, the pacifism implicit in political struggles designed to set forth moral arguments may have important moral limitations. Gandhi notoriously sought to apply the principles of "Satyagraha" in World War II, for instance, urging nonviolent Jewish resistance as a means of arousing the conscience of the world to Hitler's violence. George Orwell rightly worried that pacifism in response to the extreme cruelty and violence of totalitarianism might often be indistinguishable from a policy of appeasement (Orwell 1950). Yet this possibility cannot negate the moral successes of nonviolent political struggles. Such success, however provisional or limited, plausibly bolsters confidence in the rationality of aspirations to the transcendent validity of moral inquiry.

In this respect, as I have urged, moral inquiry is very much like scientific inquiry, where the success of uncoerced agreement likewise reasonably bolsters confidence in its objectivity. To be sure, regular uncoerced agreement cannot conclusively establish the transcendent validity of science. Indeed, according to Rorty, the regularity of uncoerced agreement in science has nothing to do with the rationality of aspirations to the transcendent validity of science. Uncoerced agreement is central to science, in Rorty's view, merely because of purely contingent facts about the kind of people who get elected to the Royal Society and the National Academy of Science. Natural scientists, he claims, have simply been "conspicuous exemplars" of "virtues" such as a preference for "persuasion rather than force, relative incorruptibility, patience and reasonableness" (Rorty 1991a, 61). But however plausible this explanation, it is nonetheless incomplete. A general preference for persuasion rather than force in any human inquiry must surely be rooted in *confidence* that methods of argument and inquiry will eventually produce agreement without violence or physical coercion. This confidence, even in the case of science, must in turn be rooted in aspirations to the transcendent validity of the results of inquiry. The "desire for objectivity," in other words, is essential to the confidence needed to support the scientist's preference for persuasion rather than force. Scientists— like human beings engaged in any human inquiry—can maintain their confidence that it is possible to justify results in science (without resort to violence) only by retaining the aspiration which Rorty so hastily dismisses.

Of course, Rorty has famously urged replacing the desire for objectivity—especially in political struggles—with a desire for something he calls "solidarity." According to Rorty, if "we could ever be moved solely by the desire for solidarity, setting aside the desire for objectivity altogether, then we should think of human progress as making it possible for human beings to do more interesting things, and be more interesting people, not as heading towards a place which has somehow been prepared for humanity in advance" (Rorty 1991a, 27–28). "Solidarity" for Rorty is a matter not of sharing a common truth or a common goal but of sharing a "common selfish hope" that one's world "will not be destroyed" (Rorty 1989, 92). Yet, as Hobbes tried to show, a "common selfish hope" is not sufficient to prevent life from being nasty, brutish, and all too short. Moreover, genuine solidarity must be rooted in a generalized social faith that it is sometimes possible to justify contested convictions without resort to physical coercion. Solidarity thus presupposes the existence of widespread aspirations to the transcendent validity of moral inquiry (broadly understood to include at least some political inquiry). It presupposes, that is, widespread social acceptance of the reasonableness of the desire for objectivity in moral inquiry. Solidarity in this sense is conspicuously lacking in social movements—including, sadly, some more radical elements of the anti-abortion movement—that turn to assassinations and terrorism in order to make themselves heard. By contrast, it was quite clearly embodied in the struggles of students in Beijing's Tiananmen Square. In one of the most memorable images from the spring of 1989, an unarmed student stood in the path of armored tanks seeking to suppress a movement for democratic reforms. That lone student's courage—like the efforts of the democracy movement he came to represent—was a powerful display of faith that the results of moral inquiry may have transcendent validity.[8] Such faith incorporates the belief that uncoerced moral agreement is always possible, in spite of the repeated frustration of expectations, and that belief, if I am right, must be rooted in aspirations to the transcendent validity of the results of human moral inquiry.[9] The disengaged moral inquirer—relativist, ethnocentrist, or otherwise—is free to renounce this moral faith, and the aspirations associated with it, only because most other human beings do not.

These considerations show that the whole truth about morality is likely to be extraordinarily complex. Indeed, it is reasonable to posit that when everyone has had her experience and her "say," the whole truth about morality will come down to some kind of pluralism about evaluative practices and standards. And on such a pluralism there is sometimes more than one rationally defensible solution to a moral problem, sometimes more than one morally worthy way of life, and no "supreme" principle or procedure to unify all moral considerations into some hierarchical ordering. On this view, still further, the whole truth about morality will mean that a morally defensible solution to some difficult problem, or even a morally acceptable way of life, *may* nonetheless generate cause for regret. If my speculations are plausible, the whole truth about morality will thus bear out the truth of what Thomas Nagel describes as the "fragmentation of value" (Nagel 1979, 128–141).[10]

Yet the limited pluralism that I expect to be the whole truth about morality must also be distinguished from Berlin's influential moral pluralism, discussed in Chapter 3. First, on the limited moral pluralism I describe, it will sometimes be neither irrational nor indefensible to embrace evaluative practices that one believes to eliminate moral conflict from the realm of personal decision and action—practices that are also thereby believed to limit circumstances in which moral choices inevitably occasion deep regret. Those who choose to adopt such practices may need to separate themselves from those who embrace the fragmentation of value. But some such efforts can be defended on the pluralism defined here. Just as there may be circumstances in which it would not be unreasonable to question the value of maximizing true predictions, there can be circumstances in which it is not unreasonable to choose to minimize the consequences of the fragmentation of value. Attempts to eliminate serious moral conflict from the realm of decision and action become problematic, on this conception, only if the ideals and principles embodied in one's practices entail an attempt to coerce others into an unquestioning acceptance of one's practices. The whole moral truth, however, is likely to be a pluralism that allows for the reasonableness of some lives that seek to reject it.

But this limited pluralism is a critical pluralism, a conception of the plurality of moral values that leaves room for the critical analysis and rejection of some ways of life and some practices as outside the range of moral acceptability. Thus, as I have claimed, a way of life that involves the use of violence or other non-argumentative efforts to coerce others' acceptance of it is outside the critical pluralist's understanding of acceptable ways of life. A critical pluralist may consistently claim, still further, that at least some moral convictions must be respected as uncontestable. Indeed, as I showed in Chapter 3, if at least some convictions are not deemed uncontestable, then no convictions can be contested at all. To provide a complete account of the specific convictions that a genuinely critical pluralism would show to be uncontestable, or to attempt to fit them into a defensible and richly textured interpretation of the structure of moral experience, would be beyond the scope of this inquiry. Yet—to reiterate a suggestion made in Chapter 3—political institutions compatible with the whole truth about morality would surely need to embody a conviction that everyone is entitled to an equal chance to participate in moral debate. Indeed, a limited critical pluralism grounds a more reliable defense of tolerance—and freedom of conscience and inquiry—than the generally uncritical pluralism defended by theorists such as Berlin.

Yet despite its apparent links with such values, critical pluralism is nonetheless compatible with the objectivity of morality. Moral objectivity is consistent, for instance, with an important consequence of the pluralism defended here: that rational resolution of a moral disagreement does not always require convergence on a single conclusion about how to proceed. As I have argued, the objectivity of morality is compatible with the fact that two people—or two cultures—may sometimes agree to disagree about the solution to some serious moral problem. Moral objectivity is also consistent with the fact that a rational resolution of first-person moral conflict may require that the agent nonetheless regret whatever choice she finally makes. Moral inquiry and the moral life do not require that it be possible to justify some one moral principle, or some one set of moral principles, as rationally superior to all others—or even to show that some one way of life is rationally required of all human beings. Indeed, the very idea that some one "supreme" principle or moral conception or particular way of life might adequately characterize all the considerations and demands to which the moral life gives rise simply ignores the complexity of moral experience, and of the moral expertise needed to make sense of it. Still further, these facts about the complexity of moral experience and moral expertise can now be understood as a function of what is most likely the whole truth about morality. I cannot claim to have proven the truth of the critical moral pluralism tentatively defended here; the development of moral inquiry could in principle show my speculations to have been wrong. Yet thick description of the contexts of moral inquiry, and of the methods and procedures to be found in those varied contexts, provides considerations "capable of determining the intellect" (in Mill's phrase) to accept the plausibility of a limited critical pluralism that is consistent with moral objectivity.

CRITICAL PLURALISM, CULTURAL DIFFERENCE, AND THE BOUNDARIES OF CROSS-CULTURAL RESPECT

The fragmentation of value, and the critical moral pluralism it appears to underwrite, are in part a function of the varied demands that experience may make on human beings. Many important differences in the experiences of human beings can in turn be attributed, at least in part, to collectively constituted differences in cultural traditions and practices. Thus, the moral pluralism provisionally defended here can take seriously the existence of cultures, and allow that the contest of moral interpretations is often most heated in conflicts among different cultural practices. Cross-cultural moral disagreement, indeed moral disagreement of any kind, will sometimes generate disputes that outstrip the disputants' capacity to resolve them by generally agreed-upon methods. But rational resolution of a moral dispute—even between cultures—is not always a matter of "bringing others around" to one's own moral convictions. To begin with, any adequate conception of rationality must allow for the rationality of agreements to disagree, as I argued in Chapter 3. Moreover, there will be occasions when the failure to secure agreement must be attributed to the inadequacy of one or both competing moral interpretations. Unfortunately there is no decision procedure for determining what constitutes such an occasion, or for discerning when either or both parties to some dispute should substantially reconsider their interpretations. But contemporary disagreements about abortion—particularly those disagreements framed in the language of rights—offer a perfect example of the sort of case in which at least some convictions of all parties are in need of imaginative rethinking and revision.

I have claimed that agreements to disagree often produce stable resolutions of moral disputes, but I have also noted that some kinds of circumstances are likely to undermine such agreements. When friends disagree about the boundaries of morally acceptable professions, for example, circumstances may arise in which one friend is unable to preserve the integrity of her moral ideals unless she severs the ties of friendship. An animal rights activist may simply become morally unable to ignore a friend's participation in research requiring experimentation on animals. Such disputes have an important bearing on cross-cultural disagreement: although it is misleading to assume that a culture is like an individual person, the *relationship* between cultures may sometimes bear an important analogy to relationships between persons. In particular, those who hope to preserve their culture from what they consider morally corrupting outside influences will need to limit relationships with other cultures, much as a person who wishes to preserve the integrity of her moral ideals may find that she needs to sever ties of friendship. Old Order Amish communities in the United States, for example, have long sought to preserve the integrity of their moral ideals in just this way. These communities interpret the biblical injunction from Paul's Epistle to the Romans—"Be not conformed to this world"—in such a way that preservation of their cultural traditions *requires* an emphatic rejection of most other American cultural forms. It should not be forgotten, however, that it is far more difficult for a culture to isolate itself from other cultures than it is to sever individual ties of friendship. Recent studies of contemporary Amish communities have detailed some of the difficult processes by which those communities must constantly renegotiate a cultural truce with the world around them. On matters of health care, education, and technological change, for instance, it is a difficult task—even for those most committed to separation from modern American culture—to accomplish that aim completely (Kraybill 1989; 1993).

But the modern world as a whole is becoming increasingly inhospitable to the kind of separation which the Amish work so hard to maintain. A vast array of economic, political, and social changes—many on a global scale—have made the complete separation of cultures more difficult than ever. The interconnection of cultures is not a new phenomenon: as I argue in Chapter 2, most cultures have long been the product of complex and sometimes quite heterogeneous influences. A complete understanding of the cultural "fall-out," in Victor Turner's phrase (Turner 1974), of wars, conquests, refugee movements, exploration, and trade would undermine most claims of cultural "purity" in beliefs, customs, and habits. Yet newly complex patterns of immigration and alien residency have created a previously unimaginable cultural complexity in many modern nation-states. Some commentators, such as Terence Turner, suggest that global economic changes have had even more far-reaching effects. Thus, the proliferation of multinational corporations, the accompanying growth in migratory or "transnational" labor, and the widening influence of international markets on the economy of individual nations may all be undermining the sovereign importance—and often the internal stability—of nation-states themselves (Turner 1993, 423). One consequence of these changes may be newly vehement assertions of cultural identities that ignore or cut across national boundaries, and the related phenomenon of multiculturalism—especially, but not only, in the Anglo-American context (Turner 1993, 423–424). Still further, even in relatively stable societies, global cultural diversity has taken on a special moral urgency because of growing economic and environmental interdependencies between large modern states, as well as between large modern states and smaller traditional societies. These interdependencies make it even more difficult to avoid serious cross-cultural conflicts of moral interpretations.

Some of the most serious conflicts are likely to arise from the difficult relations between highly industrialized, economically developed nations and those nations just beginning to confront the challenges and complexities of economic development and technological change. The potential conflicts in this area are of special interest in any consideration of the consequences of moral pluralism, since they raise difficult questions about the possibilities and requirements for respecting cultural differences. Some development economists, for example, posit that the well-being of developing nations will depend in part on their ability to increase the literacy rate among women, and on their readiness to accord women greater access to contraception as a means of family planning. But such theories, as might be expected, generate extraordinary controversy in societies where dominant cultural attitudes remain resistant to changing the social, economic, and political position of women. What kind of response to such cases might be licensed by a plausible pluralism? Susan Wolf contends that in some such conflicts it is difficult, if not impossible, for a pluralist to preserve respect for the plurality of values embodied in different cultures—and hence for the cultures themselves—unless she simply refrains from making any critical judgment at all (Wolf 1992). This seems to mean, however, that the respect for cultures implicit in pluralism is ultimately indistinguishable from those relativist calls for moral isolationism that I have so assiduously sought to reject. Are there in fact circumstances in which pluralism must collapse into a refusal to make a critical moral judgment?

The refusal to make critical moral judgments—whether or not it is recommended as a normative stance for others—is often treated as a morally neutral response to cross-cultural conflict. But this refusal has seemed to provide a neutral response only because it is so often defended in the context of disengaged moral inquiry. In discussions of the practice of female circumcision, for example, it is common to insist to an audience that does not have to live with the practice that female circumcision "must be understood in context as part of a cultural whole" (Marglin 1990, 12). But it is quite another thing to claim that one can plausibly remain "neutral" in the midst of immediate and direct conflicts about the practice of female circumcision. In some highly publicized cases in recent years, individual women have pleaded for political asylum so that they or their daughters would not be required to undergo the circumcision and infibulation practiced as part of the culture in which they themselves were raised. In a related development, the expansion of immigration from countries that practice ritual circumcision has led some of the countries in which these new immigrants have settled to consider legal regulation of the practice—but, it is important to note, only *within* the boundaries of the newly adopted country. In a few instances, immigrants who have continued the practice in spite of legal prohibitions have been convicted of violating the laws of their adopted countries.[11] In such situations a relativist effort to withhold judgment cannot be a morally neutral stance. Given the proximity of the disputed practice and the strength of the convictions held by parties to the disputes, "not to choose" is quite clearly *to choose*—and to choose in favor of continuing the practice. Disengaged relativists–cum–cultural pluralists will, of course, seek to defend the neutrality of their stance. They will object, first, that a cultural "outsider's" readiness to criticize or interfere with such a practice shows disrespect for the cultures that accept it. They will claim, second, that such efforts may even mask a malevolent wish to dominate, perhaps even to destroy, the culture whose practice is being criticized.

But what really fuels the first objection alleging disrespect? Its defenders are likely to begin by claiming that criticism of the practices of another culture may destabilize the mechanisms of belief and habit that support the practice. Defenders may further object that the practices of traditional societies are particularly fragile in this regard. Williams, for instance, insists on the excessively "unreflective" nature of traditional cultures (Williams 1985 162–163). But, as I have shown, the suggestion that traditional cultures are somehow less reflective than non-traditional cultures (or, *pace* Winch, that their practices might be more "integrated" than those of non-traditional cultures) is poorly substantiated. Traditional practices produce skeptics, even within traditional societies themselves. In this instance, moreover, that complex set of procedures known as female circumcision and infibulation has long been the subject of internal criticism. Some internal critics have questioned the acceptability of subjecting circumcised women to serious risks of infection and death, risks which in some societies continue throughout the entire period of a woman's childbearing years. Internal critics have, further, challenged the legitimacy of certain theological justifications of the practice.[12] Still other internal critics question the attitude toward women (and female sexuality) that they believe to be implicit in more extreme versions of the practice—for instance, those that require restitching of the remaining genitalia after a woman has given birth. To be sure, some elements of the debate about this question have appealed to concepts first articulated in non-traditional societies, in particular to the idea that autonomy in the disposition of one's body has genuine moral importance. But the use of a moral concept first articulated in one culture to carry out internal criticism of another is simply a reflection of the richness and complexity of moral language and the ultimate impossibility of erecting moral barriers between cultures. Since the concept of autonomy is in no sense the moral property of any single society, the criticism embedded in these debates is in no way culturally inauthentic.

Moreover, a practice that is too fragile to withstand external criticism would appear to be already in serious trouble from internal resistance. To be sure, it is far from clear that female circumcision is in such a precarious position in the cultures in which it is practiced. But even if it were, it would not be obvious that cultural outsiders are in any way obligated to refrain from criticism to ensure that their judgment does not hasten the disappearance of the practice. In America cultural acceptance of tolerance for free speech embodies a particularly delicate balance between internal acceptance and internal criticism. But that balance can be disturbed. Extreme violence in American television and films aimed at children, for instance, has generated unprecedented internal resistance to long-accepted attitudes about freedom of speech. The irresponsible exercise of First Amendment freedoms has given rise to increasingly vehement demands to regulate or restrict those freedoms in other areas as well. Criticism of pornography's effects on the social equality of women, for example, has even created unexpected political associations between feminist opponents of pornography and conservative critics of sexually frank expression. Yet on what basis would it be legitimate to suggest (or demand) that non-American critical pluralists should refrain from any criticisms that might increase internal dissatisfaction with the exercise of free speech? Internal irresponsibility has already undermined confidence in the institutions which protect free speech. Americans who would protect the cultural tradition of freedom of expression must address this internal threat, rather than expect the conflict to be resolved by attacking external criticism. The same holds true, I contend, for defenders of practices in traditional societies. Finally, relativists often forget that cultural survival is not a matter of the static preservation of every practice that has ever been part of a culture. Cultures change, and cultural survival depends on the ability to change—which in turn depends on the tendency of the culture to allow individual agents to develop the judgment and imagination needed to adapt to various stresses (internal and external) on the culture. I do not deny that the forced prohibition of a cultural practice by cultural outsiders is often (though not always) morally indefensible. But when external stresses on a practice come merely from criticism, and not from externally imposed prohibitions, respect for a culture requires that its inhabitants be allowed to make what *they* deem to be appropriate choices about the value of that practice to their culture. Anything else constitutes condescension, not respect.

Efforts to prohibit immigrants from engaging in some practice in their newly adopted home raise more complicated concerns. Here the relativist's concern about the "contexts" of particular practices yields unexpected insights. For instance, in most societies where female circumcision is practiced on a large scale, the practice is interwoven into a complex set of moral, social, and economic customs and beliefs. In such communities assumptions about the character of a woman who has not undergone the relevant procedures may affect her ability to obtain a suitable spouse, and ultimately her economic and social status. It is certainly likely that some members of immigrant communities will bring to their new homes substantial portions of this web of belief, custom, and habit, and these allegiances should not be taken lightly. But it is also true that the decision to adopt a new home—particularly one in which many of one's native rituals, habits, and beliefs are unfamiliar, or even prohibited—raises the question whether immigration is not sometimes, by its very nature, a tacit rejection of central cultural traditions of the home that one has left (Raz 1994, 69).

There can be no simple answer to this question. Immigrants who have moved to escape economic hardship or political persecution might sometimes argue that the greatest harm caused by hardship and persecution is the tacit, or even explicit, prohibition of the sincere expression and observance of their group's traditional values. Further, in some cases, especially where immigration involves a movement from former colonies to the home of former colonizers, there will be complicated moral, political, and economic questions about the causes leading to immigration in the first place. Even in such circumstances, however, those in the immigrants' newly adopted home are not entirely wrong to imagine that immigration is a tacit rejection of at least some traditions of the immigrants' former home. Of course, efforts to prohibit immigrant traditions may sometimes be rooted in hostility and prejudice toward immigrants themselves rather than in any principled objection that some practice is incompatible with constitutive convictions of the adopted country. But surely at least some practices may rightly be subject to principled objections. After all, even in the realm of "familiar" customs, the traditions of small social groups may be legitimately prohibited if they conflict with constitutive convictions of a larger political society. So in America, for example, fraternity "hazing" rituals have been widely outlawed.[13] It is hardly surprising, then, that some unfamiliar customs might be incompatible with the constitutive convictions of a newly adopted country.[14]

At this point a relativist may insist that a critical moral pluralist—merely *as* a pluralist—should be especially wary of external criticisms of another culture. The pluralist, it will be urged, should be disturbed by any external criticism that might contribute to the disappearance of a cultural practice, since the pluralist is centrally committed to the notion that many different ways of life, and practices internal to those ways of life, can have moral value. Pluralism might thus seem to require a presumption that the practices of every culture—and by extension every culture—should be treated as in principle valuable and worthy of non-interference. Here the astute relativist would surely be right. Having claimed that no one philosophical theory can contain the whole truth about morality, I also contend that no one way of life (even that embedded in the complex culture of a modern nation-state) could realize or contain the whole truth about morality. For this reason I presume that every culture is in principle valuable and worthy of non-interference, and I take this presumption to be central to a critical moral pluralism.

But I follow Charles Taylor in holding that this presumption is simply a "starting hypothesis" with which one must approach critical reflection on another culture and its practices (Taylor 1992, 66–67). Thus, the plausibility of the presumption, and its importance in a critical pluralism, does not conclusively establish the overriding worth of any particular practice or any particular culture. No practice, and indeed no culture, has overriding moral importance merely because it happens to exist. A critical pluralism leaves open the possibility that careful reflection on an unfamiliar practice or culture may reveal grounds for rejecting that practice or culture as in some way indefensible. Of course, critical pluralists are also committed to the possibility that careful reflection on a practice or a whole way of life—through study or travel or through serious engagement with someone who knowledgeably defends it—may yield compelling reasons to affirm its overriding moral importance, and hence a position of non-interference. The critical pluralist accepts Herskovits's claim that, when examined from the viewpoint of a knowledgeable insider or a knowledgeable participant-observer, a practice may be seen "to hold values that are not apparent from the outside" (Herskovits 1972, 14). But such an examination, as I showed in Chapter 2, is possible only if it is also possible to make an unfamiliar way of life intelligible to an outsider in familiar terms. Any relativist who concedes the possibility of such understanding has already conceded too much to the critical pluralist position.

The relativist who will not concede this point, however, is unable to advance beyond the initial premise of equal worth—and hence unable to say anything of substance when challenged to provide an intelligent defense of the value of the unfamiliar practice. As a result, when the practices of different cultures come into serious conflict (as they do in the examples I have given), unfamiliar cultures become little more than occasions for marveling at difference, and those who accept those cultures are reduced to exotic specimens of sheer "otherness" (Moody-Adams 1994a). But "post-Nietzschean" celebrations of astonishment at confrontations with diversity are incompatible with recognizing the humanity of those who accept, and may seek to preserve, another culture. What respect for culture, or for the people who accept a culture, can possibly reside in the relativist's conception of culture as principally a shield against criticism? To view those who accept another culture as so fundamentally "other" that they cannot engage in reasonable moral inquiry is to see them as less than fully human. In short, the notion that subjecting unfamiliar practices to external criticism fails to respect unfamiliar cultures simply will not stand up to careful scrutiny.

But what about the objection that external criticism of another culture's practices implicitly embodies a dominating "cultural imperialism"? It is tempting to dismiss this claim simply by insisting that there is an obvious difference between criticism and cultural imperialism. But there is an important kernel of truth in linking the criticism of other cultures with cultural imperialism. The attitude of the critical moral pluralist—who presumes the equal worth of cultures, though she is willing to criticize them and to engage those who accept them in debate—clearly embodies a preference for one particular *kind* of culture over others. I have suggested, for instance, that political institutions compatible with the whole truth about morality would have to treat as incontestable the notion that each person should be guaranteed equal opportunity to make a contribution to moral debate. If I am right, an acceptance of pluralism is thus inseparable from a commitment to values such as the tolerance of diversity and freedom of conscience and inquiry. Taylor has rightly argued that such values do not provide "a meeting ground for all cultures"; instead they are "the political expression of one range of cultures, and quite incompatible with other ranges" (Taylor 1992, 62). Yet a critical moral pluralism is not thereby *indistinguishable* from cultural imperialism. After all, the members of any cultures under scrutiny can simply reject the values linked with the acceptance of pluralism—and many cultures, in fact, do just this. This is what the Old Order Amish do, even from within the national boundaries of societies whose values they reject. This same rejection is differently embodied in the stance of those fundamentalist societies in which the separation of church and state is anathema. Perhaps the relativist also will want to join in rejecting the critical pluralist's presumption of the equal worth of cultures. This may well be the only way to accord overriding moral importance to the range of cultures which reject the presumption. Yet in so doing, the relativist would be opting for the lesser value of societies accepting pluralism, and thereby relinquishing a defining tenet of relativism.

The example of women who seek asylum to protect themselves or their daughters from a practice they reject raises a somewhat different set of concerns about moral judgment and culture. What does a plausible critical pluralism allow when such pleas seriously conflict with active moral defenses of the practice in question? It is worth noting, to begin with, that such conflict poses a particularly difficult challenge for the isolationism implicit in moral relativism. The plea for protection is, among other things, an impassioned request to relinquish the isolationist stance: to consider the practice not just as an unfamiliar cultural phenomenon which affects exotic, unidentified "others," but as a practice which has unwanted effects on the lives of real human beings. As I have suggested, the person who explicitly criticizes a tradition found in the culture in which she was raised is asking to be included in cross-cultural moral debate about that tradition. Of course, some relativists may respond that a person who criticizes one of her culture's practices in this way must be culturally "inauthentic," and that her comments should not be taken to constitute a reasonable or important objection. These relativists are implicitly claiming to know that some practices are the "authentic" practices of other cultures, and to be able to identify which parties internal to the culture might be reliable sources of critical reflection on the culture. Such claims are the natural companions, moreover, of isolationist efforts to silence the external critic because she has not been brought up in the culture whose practices she criticizes. Yet all such claims serve as a means of silencing debate, a tendency which the critical pluralist will quite obviously reject.

The attempt to distinguish between authentic and inauthentic voices of a culture is particularly problematic, and never more so than when it involves external efforts to silence members of a group who are too often silenced in internal moral debate. Of course some women defend female circumcision; but to claim that other women's criticisms must therefore be rejected as inauthentic embodies a dangerous interpretive arrogance. The concept of "tradition" has been used in many different cultural contexts to try to give moral legitimacy to a wide array of oppressive abuses of power.[15] Thus, whether or not justifications of female circumcision fit this description, there is even reason to be suspicious of attempts from "inside" a particular culture to dismiss internal critics as "inauthentic" and unreliable. One who claims special knowledge about the "authentic" traditions of a culture by relying on such claims (even as an ethnographic participant-observer) may be helping to cement the power of oppressive and abusive cultural elites. In many cases, in fact, a refusal to contemplate internal criticism of some cultural tradition will make one not a respecter of culture but simply an agent—however unwitting—of traditional oppression and abuse.

THE STRANGE CAREER OF "CULTURE"

Moral isolationism is not the only source of resistance to a critical pluralist's respect for cultural difference. One of the most powerful objections rests on an assumption that is in many ways independent of the relativism that underwrites moral isolationism. Indeed, in some of its manifestations this assumption is inconsistent with basic anthropological claims to which relativism ostensibly appeals. This is the assumption that in referring to a culture, one is implicitly referring to the collective identity of a group—a collective identity, moreover, that predictably (some would add *unavoidably*) determines the identity of individuals who accept (or are assumed to accept) the culture under discussion. On this conception, a culture is not simply the general way of life of a people; it is in some way constitutive of their identity (individually and collectively). But this conception must be conjoined with two additional assumptions in order to constitute a serious challenge to the critical pluralist's claim to respect cultural difference. First, it must be claimed that there is special moral value, even overriding moral importance, in simply being who one "really" or "essentially" is—in being "true" to oneself. This claim embodies what has been called the ideal of authenticity (Trilling 1972; cf. Taylor 1991; 1992). The second assumption is that there is an essential link between culture and authenticity. On this assumption, cultural practices can be authentic in the appropriate way because cultures are constitutive of *essential* identity. On the resulting conception, to criticize a cultural practice is not merely to challenge a particular set of habits, beliefs, and customary activities; it is to challenge the "essential" identity of particular persons and the group to which they belong—and thus (it is suggested) their very existence. Also on this view, the authenticity of essential identities should legitimately shield cultural practices from moral criticism.

Some of the most important objections to this conception will no doubt focus on the notion of authenticity. In particular, why should the mere fact that some practice expresses an (allegedly) essential identity make it intrinsically morally legitimate? After all, some of the most atrocious crimes in human history have been couched as expressions of some group's "essential" identity. Even if an ethics of authenticity could provide a plausible response to these objections, there would still be reason to object to any effort to link an ethics of authenticity with the concept of cultural difference.[16] First, such efforts are commonly associated with a tendency to treat cultures as though they were badges of group identity. This tendency, in turn, risks reifying cultures, as well as exaggerating their separateness and distinctness, and encouraging the fetishizing of cultures in ways that effectively put them beyond any effort at critical reflection (Turner 1993, 411–412). But second, the notion that culture constitutes essential identity too often makes the concept of culture interchangeable with quasi-biological and highly problematic concepts such as "ethnic group" and "race." Of course, many people continue to believe that these concepts reveal something important about the essential makeup of persons—from their character to their cognitive and creative abilities.[17] But popular mythology and bad science obstruct real cultural understanding.

These quasi-biological notions become even more problematic when they are assumed to be interchangeable with the concept of culture. Some who defend such views even insist that an identification of someone as a member of a particular racial or ethnic group is an implicit reference to a clearly identifiable culture—as if culture were somehow transmitted in the genes.[18] There is certainly room (and even a genuine need) for some plausible conception of collective cultural identity that might avoid the essentializing tendencies of such views. Defensible conceptions might be rooted, for instance, in reflectively scrutinized shared self-understandings. But the tendency of those conceptions which insist on linking culture with "race" is wholly to ignore self-understandings in favor of quasi-scientific claims about allegedly objective biological characteristics.

The reasons for the emergence of this tendency are admittedly complex. Surprisingly, in some contexts—especially in the United States—certain groups have been drawn to this stance as a means of expressing their own resistance to discrimination against them. Discrimination on the basis of race has so often been conjoined with efforts to devalue ways of life lived by those discriminated against that the linking of culture and racial or ethnic identity has sometimes seemed to be a gesture of liberation. But there is a powerful irony in such gestures. Developments which eventually led to the modern anthropological concept of culture involved an effort to resist confining—and unsupported—essentialisms, especially the essentialisms of the racial thought embedded in nineteenth-century anthropology (Stocking 1982, 217–233; cf. Rabinow 1983; Wolf 1994).[19] It is certainly a mark of the strange career of "culture" that it has come to be linked with some of the very ideas that it was developed to resist.

The attempt to link cultures with racial or ethnic identities is further problematic in suggesting that cultures are somehow the exclusive preserve of particular groups of people (Turner 1993). The origins of this tendency can be traced to counter-Enlightenment views of the eighteenth century, in particular to J. G. Herder's notion, in *Reflections on the Philosophy of the History of Mankind*, of "the genius of a people" (Herder [1784–1791] 1968). Herder claims that the development of any individual person is limited by, among other things, the "genius" of the group to which that person belongs. To be fair, in one sense this view simply anticipates some generally benign assumptions informing the twentieth-century anthropological notion of enculturation. The concept of culture eventually developed in the work of Franz Boas, a principal shaping force in American anthropology, has even been described as an attempt to define the "genius of a people" in terms other than those of racial heredity (Stocking 1982, 214). Yet Herder's account also displays the intrinsic ambiguity in some of the notions with which Boas began. For despite Herder's express resistance to the racial hierarchies of his day (even Kant, for instance, attributed different degrees of humanity to different races), his repeated concern that some circumstances might "corrupt" the ideal, or pure, character of each group's original genius reintroduces its own quite dangerous essentialisms.[20] Of course, as I note in Chapter 2, some of these tendencies are reiterated in deterministic assumptions about culture that continued to shape early twentieth-century American anthropology. Ruth Benedict, for instance, in *Patterns of Culture*, was not immune to the seductions of the deterministic organicism that is implicit in Herder's *Reflections*. But cultural anthropologists have often insisted that one culture might learn something from the beliefs, habits, and customs of another. It is not without reason that early twentieth-century developments of social science were taken to be a source of optimism about the moral openness of human cultures. It was in this spirit of optimism that Margaret Mead made a conscious effort in *Coming of Age in Samoa* to suggest how another culture's attitude toward adolescence might be adapted to a new cultural context. But such efforts are antithetical to central principles of Herder's deterministic organicism, just as they are incompatible with the contemporary (and all too influential) analogues of those principles.

There is yet another important irony—indeed, an incoherence— bound up with efforts to treat cultures as the exclusive preserve of a single people: proponents of this view often go on to insist that the cultures they defend provide important lessons for, and valuable criticisms of, cultures which seem to have excluded them. Yet these stances cannot be coherently combined. The tendency to think otherwise has weakened the claims of some proponents of contemporary multiculturalism. But here we confront two contradictory strains in contemporary multiculturalism. The anthropologist Terence Turner helpfully describes these strains as "difference multiculturalism" and "critical multiculturalism" (Turner 1993). Difference multiculturalists, on his view, tend to assume that culture simply reduces to racial or ethnic identity. They simply assume, further, that essentialist understandings of notions such as "race" and "ethnicity" have some plausibility. Critical multiculturalists, in contrast, typically reject these assumptions, and instead have developed the idea that new and diverse cultural assumptions (because they are not inextricably linked to any essential group identity) can profitably challenge and revitalize existing cultural assumptions of complex societies. The aim of critical multiculturalism, Turner continues, is to create a more vital "common culture" for all the inhabitants of modern heterogeneous societies.

But as Turner also notes, one cannot consistently defend both critical and difference multiculturalism. Difference multiculturalists, in particular, often end up defending the isolationist notion of the "impenetrable other"—a notion that, as I have shown, ultimately undermines the claim that it is possible to understand diverse cultures at all. Those who would argue for a more constructive critical multiculturalism would do well to relinquish the contradictory, and potentially quite dangerous, assumptions of difference multiculturalism. Of course, the separatist tendencies of difference multiculturalism have tended to dominate public understanding of multiculturalism. Arthur Schlesinger speaks for many in forecasting the "disuniting" of those democratic societies in which the excesses of difference multiculturalism have been most vividly displayed (Schlesinger 1991). Yet even in debating difference multiculturalism, critics would do well to remember Victor Turner's insistence that no culture is ever a coherent whole, but is rather the "fall-out or debris" of past cultural influences. The openness of human social groups toward the future—indeed their very survival—is dependent on their ability not to suppress all internal conflicts, but sometimes to take those conflicts as an occasion to renegotiate a new, more inclusive cultural identity.

Critical multiculturalism has urgently revealed the need to renegotiate the collective cultural identities of the societies (principally Britain and the United States) in which it has emerged. This revelation has sometimes exposed the defenders of critical multiculturalism to vituperation from opponents who, often, simply seem unwilling to scrutinize their current self-conceptions. Yet debates about the influence of multiculturalism—especially in controversies about the Western Civilization courses once widely taught in American colleges and universities—have raised the problem of collective cultural identity in a particularly instructive way. For while they have sometimes degenerated into petty spats about the cultural contributions of "dead white European men," they have also exposed a particularly challenging fact: cultural identities are always in flux. Of course, American cultural identity may be unusually fluid. Historians of American higher education have suggested that the conception of American democratic culture embodied in the Western Civilization course is the product of a particular era, a time during which many Americans could be persuaded to view themselves as partners with European democracies "in a great Atlantic civilization, formed from a common history, challenged by a common enemy, and destined to a common future" (Allardyce 1982, 695). This self-conception would have been unfamiliar in mid-nineteenth-century America, and on the brink of a new century it has once again become unfamiliar. Changing patterns of immigration, global shifts in the centers of economic and technological power, and especially the gradual inclusion in official public life of previously excluded racial and ethnic minorities have combined to call central features of this collective self-conception into question. Yet instead of simply lamenting such changes, as many critics of multiculturalism are wont to do, societies challenged by the arguments of a *responsible* critical multiculturalism have an opportunity to forge new cultural identities.

Properly debated and scrutinized, these new identities—to adapt Arnold's famous phrase—might come to preserve *all* the best that has been thought and known, and not just a select portion of it.

It must also be recognized that shifts in American cultural identity have not been the solitary work of multiculturalists. Even American descendants of European immigrants who may be deeply suspicious of multiculturalism find it difficult to identify themselves as partners in "a great Atlantic civilization" with a common history. Midway through a semester-long introduction to ethics, just such a student demanded that I convince him that the history of Western moral philosophy—especially "that Aristotle stuff"—should mean anything to him. Those who share Bernard Williams's conviction that the culture of ancient Greece bears a special relation to "our" modern self-understanding would do well to reflect on the implications of this student's bewilderment. Like many of his peers, he in an important sense inhabits a different culture from that shared by those who imbibed the triumphalist history once taught in Western Civilization courses. These students share their contemporary culture's preference for technical knowledge that will make them more "competitive" in the future, and its consequent disregard for the importance of historical memory. Attempts to convince them of the enduring value of Aristotle (or Hobbes, or Kant, for that matter) cannot simply appeal to the notion that one is teaching them "their own" culture, or even important antecedents of their own culture. It is necessary to provide compelling reasons for them to *find* value in a culture that they no longer inhabit. Of course, on my account of moral language and inquiry, it is genuinely possible to reinterpret the moral thinking of the past so as to find lessons that help clarify vexing moral problems in the present. Yet it is necessary to recognize a student's bewilderment about the past as evidence of a kind of cultural disagreement, and to take seriously the multiculturalist's reminder that human social groups survive only if they are able to take such disagreements as occasions to seek a new, and more reflective, collective identity.

Critical multiculturalists have frequently been reviled for insisting that, at any point in time, the dominant understanding of "the best that has been thought and known" is partly the product of decidedly "political" considerations. Resistance to multiculturalism's alleged "politicizing" of education, moreover, has been the source of more general resistance to the constructive lessons of the position. Yet there is nothing subversive or anti-intellectual in the idea that any particular historical understanding is, at least in part, the gradual outcome of an intellectual system of "spoils." Philosophers in particular should consider Bruce Kuklick's compelling argument that contemporary conceptions of the history of modern philosophy have been powerfully shaped by the preoccupations of the contemporary "victors" in philosophy (Kuklick 1984). More generally, the place of specific figures, events, and cultural ties in any group's historical self-understanding will always reflect the dictum that to the victors belong the spoils. It is disingenuous to criticize multiculturalist proposals for educational reform simply because they make explicit the forces that implicitly shape cultural life.[21]

To be sure, proponents of multicultural reforms must resist the unjustified assumption that a "spoils system" need always be opposed to a "merit system." Jeffersonian notions of equality, for instance, are genuinely worthy of the place they have assumed in the American cultural identity. But critics of multiculturalism must resist the historical relativism implicit in efforts to silence moral criticism of figures such as Jefferson. As I have argued throughout, an adequate understanding of the relation between morality and culture shows that moral concepts cannot be confined within particular cultural and historical boundaries. Indeed, this is one of the beneficial lessons of a genuinely critical multiculturalism. A sufficiently rich account of moral inquiry and culture and the relation between them makes it clear why there is no reason to fear such lessons. For they help illuminate the very processes by which Jeffersonian ideals, among others, might continue to enrich contemporary moral debate—despite their origins in a culture, and an individual life, that failed to embody them fully.

EPILOGUE

I have argued that moral reflection is capable of transcending cultural and historical boundaries to enrich moral imagination in extraordinary ways. The richness and complexity of moral inquiry are reflected, as in the case of Jeffersonian notions of equality, in the continued possibilities for interpretation and reinterpretation of the ideas of one's predecessors. But the richness of moral reflection is also manifested in cross-cultural arguments. Thus, for instance, indigenous peoples—for whom the language of rights may be initially unfamiliar—sometimes find that the idea of rights to cultural survival helps to articulate morally relevant dimensions of their increasingly precarious predicament. All such efforts are intelligible, and indeed possible, because the community of moral inquirers extends—in principle, and sometimes in practice—to any human being capable of reflection and self-scrutiny.

That moral inquirers form such a community has special implications for a moral philosophy that genuinely seeks to contribute to everyday moral reflection. In particular, it means that moral philosophy can never be more than a participant in ongoing moral inquiry, and indeed that the best moral philosophy will constructively embrace the link between philosophical moral inquiry and non-philosophical reflection on the life worth living. Many contemporary philosophers persist in thinking that philosophy ought to make authoritative pronouncements about the possibilities for validating moral conceptions. But the most constructive way to acknowledge the link between moral philosophy and non-philosophical moral inquiry is to recognize that philosophy is an interpretive discipline, and that as an interpretive discipline moral philosophy is most plausibly aligned with other interpretive disciplines—including history, ethnography, and literary investigations of the moral imagination—and not with natural science.

Yet while philosophers can learn much from moral inquiry carried out in other interpretive disciplines—about the moral importance of culture and history, for instance, as well as the essential role of imagination in moral reasoning—none of these disciplines can provide a model of inquiry to which moral philosophy should conform. Moral philosophy is distinguished by several characteristics which no other discipline possesses to the same degree. Like philosophy in general, the discipline of moral philosophy produces familiarity with—and usually special commitment to—standards of reasonableness in argument. Study of the history of moral philosophy produces specialized knowledge of the strengths and weaknesses of a great variety of moral interpretations and a special appreciation of canons for scrutinizing new moral interpretations. In addition, great moral philosophers typically possess special abilities to generate richly imaginative reinterpretations of the structure of moral experience—reinterpretations that may or may not take the form of "systematic" moral theory. Taken together, imaginative reinterpretations produced by moral philosophers provide the reflective person the opportunity to contemplate a variety of possible ways of life shaped by different, even competing, moral conceptions. There is thus no need to look for a "successor" to moral philosophy in order to take moral disagreement seriously. Moral philosophy—of the right sort—can be an indispensable aid to understanding and adjudicating moral conflicts in the culturally heterogeneous moral world.

The model of philosophical moral inquiry most likely to succeed in these pursuits is the Socratic model which puts the connection between self-scrutiny and moral reflection at the center of the discipline. This model embodies a commitment to interpretation: it encourages the articulation and evaluation of unstated, and usually unreflective, moral convictions. The Socratic stance also constructively affirms the link between moral philosophy and everyday moral inquiry. This is not to endorse the Socratic doctrine that no one ever does wrong intentionally; on my view, it is typically an *affected* (not an involuntary) ignorance that shields moral convictions from reflection. But no moral philosophy contains the whole moral truth, any more than any one culture does. Further, Socrates' example of how to engage in moral inquiry is itself subject to interpretation and reinterpretation. For instance, Hume once argued that Socrates' refusal to escape from prison, as described in Plato's *Crito*, "builds a *tory* consequence of passive obedience, on a *whig* foundation of the original contract" (Hume [1777] 1964b, 460). Yet nearly two centuries later Martin Luther King, Jr., appealed to the

Socratic conception of moral inquiry to support an argument for non-violent civil disobedience.

Socratic engagement with the public life of the marketplace also provides a model of engagement with the world—in effect, of moral fieldwork—that contemporary moral philosophy needs to emulate more often. Although the growth of applied ethics has encouraged increased philosophical engagement with everyday life, theorists of applied ethics tend to concentrate on problems of medical ethics and political ethics which few people will be required to reflect upon on a daily basis. Further, some applied ethicists write as though difficult moral issues might be analogous to problems in science or even mathematics in having discrete "solutions" which, once reached, end discussion once and for all. This simplistic model of moral reasoning, as I have argued, ignores the complexity of moral conflict.

Contemporary moral philosophy that is not primarily concerned with applied ethics—even when it is not endlessly debating complex philosophical theses *about* morality—is even further removed from everyday moral inquiry. Most often it lacks appeal to a broader reflective audience because its central examples bear little relation to the problems that concern ordinary moral inquirers. The hypothetical examples discussed in most contemporary moral philosophy are usually too trivial or too outlandish to engage everyday moral concern, and philosophical attempts to discuss real moral problems tend to detach those problems from the social and historical contexts which constitute their moral complexity. In order to remedy these deficiencies, serious moral philosophy must undertake a more deliberate engagement with the preoccupations of everyday moral inquiry. But doing so requires more careful attention to the complexity of moral experience than most contemporary philosophers have deemed necessary.[1] Philosophical inquiry that proceeds on the assumptions defended here may not advance philosophical debate about the structure of plausible moral theories. Yet, as I have shown, there is often more to be learned from the engaged moral inquiry of "workmanlike" moral agents and inquirers than from the disengaged speculations of moral theorists and social scientists.[2] Moral philosophy intended to aid everyday moral inquiry must be a responsibly engaged and richly Socratic fieldwork in familiar places.

NOTES

INTRODUCTION

1. By moral inquiry, I simply mean that critical (sometimes unsystematic) reflection on the kind of life worth living that human experience consistently renders unavoidable.

2. A "culture," in the most general sense in which I use the word throughout this book, is the way of life of a social group, a complex phenomenon that consists of intricate, overlapping, and sometimes competing patterns of socially developed normative expectations about emotion, thought, and action. On occasion I use the word in an extended sense to encompass the shared assumptions of smaller social units—in this passage in the text, for instance, I discuss the culture of contemporary "Western" intellectuals. A variety of more specific definitions of "culture" have been offered by anthropologists. Helpful introductions to the richness and variety of these definitions are provided in Applebaum (1987); Kroeber and Kluckhohn (1963); and Stocking (1982).

3. See Harman (1975; 1977; 1984); and Wong (1984; 1986). I discuss their claims in Chapters 1 and 2.

4. R. B. Brandt's still influential examination of the methodology of anthropology is one notable exception. See Brandt (1959; 1967). Brandt's views, and his own attempt at a "descriptive ethics" of Hopi Indian culture, are discussed at length in Chapter 1.

5. Many of the most important contributions to the rationality and relativism debates are contained in Wilson (1970), Hollis and Lukes (1982), Krausz and Meiland (1982), and to some extent Krausz (1989). Disagreement about the nature of cultural difference continues to divide anthropologists. Gannath Obeyesekere (1992) and Marshall Sahlins (1995) have been engaged in a quite acrimonious debate about whether or not eighteenth-century Hawaiians conceived of Captain James Cook as a supernatural being. This debate has important similarities to an earlier conflict between the work of Margaret Mead (1928) on Samoan culture and Derek Freeman's criticism of that work (1983). I discuss the Mead-Freeman controversy at some length in Chapter 1. In a review of the current controversy, Clifford Geertz has argued that what really divides Obeyesekere and Sahlins—and a good portion of the profession of anthropology—is "their understanding of cultural difference: what it is, what produces it, what maintains it, and how deeply it goes. For Sahlins, it is substance; for Obeyesekere, it is surface" (Geertz 1995, 5). My claim, of course, is that the underlying issue is not an empirical matter; it is not as if merely by

amassing enough empirical data one suddenly discovers through observation the true nature of cultural difference.

6. Geertz discusses the central elements of his conception in Geertz (1973; 1983). For important critical discussion of Geertz's claims, see Walters (1980), Shankman (1984), Sperber (1985), and Martin (1993). Several essays in Rabinow and Sullivan (1979) discuss the more general debate about interpretive social science.

7. The growth of professionalism in American philosophy is discussed in Kuklick (1977). A somewhat narrower account of the related phenomenon in Britain—culminating in the work of Sidgwick—is contained in the first two chapters of MacKillop (1986). Helpful discussion of Moore and the Cambridge Apostles is provided in Levy (1979).

8. Sill others have sought to explain away any ground for criticizing Jefferson. Dumas Malone, for instance, insists that Jefferson's refusal to free all of his slaves during his lifetime should be understood as a manifestation of a "realistic and humane philosophy" (Malone 1962, 208–209).

1 · TAKING DISAGREEMENT SERIOUSLY

1. Harman's theory is particularly troubling in this regard. If morality truly were relative, what assurance could Harman have that the workings of certain kinds of moral judgments familiar in "our" moral language (such as the "moral ought" judgments he seeks to analyze) would tell us anything about the central moral concepts of human cultures generally? Surely moral relativity would be registered in the kinds of concepts in which any group's morality is expressed.

2. Brandt uses the term "fundamental disagreement" in a very similar fashion in his 1967 *Encyclopedia of Philosophy* article "Ethical Relativism." In Brandt's usage, to say that a disagreement is fundamental "means that it would not be removed even if there were perfect agreement about the properties of the thing being evaluated" (Brandt 1967, 75).

3. The most fundamental social scientific sense of the word *culture*—as the way of life of a given (usually human) social group—is neutral between competing understandings of the forms, practices, and beliefs that constitute a culture. But for a classic discussion of some of the varied sociological and anthropological senses in which a group's way of life can be understood, see Kroeber and Kluckhohn (1963). The anthropological texts excerpted or reprinted in Applebaum (1987) more fully discuss influential developments in competing understandings of culture—including Tylor's nineteenth-century evolutionism, Boas's historical particularism, the structuralism and functionalism of British social anthropology, psychological anthropology, cultural materialism, economic anthropology, Lévi-Strauss's

structuralism, cognitive anthropology, sociobiology, and symbolic and interpretive anthropology.

4. For a defense of the view that Harman's argument does not fundamentally rely on claims about cultural diversity, see Langenfus (1988–89).

5. Harman initially suggests in earlier writings that he is simply trying to develop his assumption that "the possession of rationality is not sufficient to provide a source for relevant reasons, that certain desires, goals, or intentions are also necessary" (Harman 1975, 9). This would suggest that what is really at issue in Harman's view of motivation is his dispute with those views (such as Kant's and Plato's) on which reason alone can be a source of motivation. As I show, Harman never explains why one needs to be a moral relativist in order to mount a genuine challenge to the idea that the possession of rationality is sufficient to provide relevant reasons.

6. Any plausible understanding of Hitler's motivations must refer, at least in part, to the widespread anti-Semitism on which the principles of Nazism were based. Harman might seek to treat Hitler's principles as relevant to a group morality in "the limiting case" of a group with only one member. But this would result in an implausible view of history. Hundreds of thousands of people (at least) chose to participate in the institutionalized cruelty and murder of the Nazi Holocaust, often because they shared many of the hatreds on which that cruelty and murder were based. For a rich philosophical account of how the massive social evil of the Holocaust could be perpetrated by "ordinary" people—as well as by those who, like Hitler, stand out as embodiments of evil—see Laurence Thomas, *Vessels of Evil: American Slavery and the Holocaust* (1993). For a somewhat different view of the central issues of moral motivation—especially in interpreting Milgram's famous experiment on "obedience to authority"—see Moody-Adams (1994a). I discuss related worries about moral motivation in more detail in Chapter 2.

7. The details of Harman's own thought experiment about a group of professional criminals named "Murder Incorporated" forcefully support my point. Harman's hypothetical "Murder Inc." is a society of professional criminals who raise their children to honor and respect no one but members of their own criminal society (Harman 1975, 5–6). Their practices clearly constitute a distinctive way of life—and hence a distinctive culture. Even further, recent developments in social science show that the concept of culture is flexible enough to accommodate Harman's thought experiments about Martians and other intelligent beings from outer space. Primatologists who study the social habits of chimpanzees and gorillas have challenged nineteenth-century orthodoxies about culture, insisting that some non-human beings might reasonably be considered to have cultures.

8. Sapir argued that the idea of the culture of a group and the concept of an individual culture are interdependent, since "a healthy national culture is

never a passively accepted heritage from the past, but implies the creative participation of members of the community." He later settled on the idea that each individual is always "a representative of at least one sub-culture" (Sapir 1949, 321; 515).

9. Similar claims about Martians, and hypothetical cannibals and criminals, figure in many of Harman's examples (1975; 1977; 1982).

10. Of course, some philosophers challenge the underlying presumption that weakness of the will is possible. The fact that Harman does not is naturally a function of his view of rationality.

11. This is, of course, what social scientists such as Stanley Milgram were trying to show. I discuss some of the difficulties with Milgram's claims about his results in Moody-Adams (1994a).

12. Arendt's notion of the banality of evil was an obvious—and, in my view, much misunderstood—attempt to do just that.

13. I refer to Harman's "Murder Incorporated" example (Harman 1975, 5–6), also discussed in note 7. What makes my suggestion seem plausible, as I mention in note 6, is that the choices at issue are intelligible only as part of a framework of massive social evil. Only on a fictionalized history would it make sense to suggest that Hitler's evil took place in a social vacuum. For a general discussion of the difficulties of Harman's use of "fictions" in his arguments for relativism, see Matilal (1989).

14. As Rabinow (1983) has noted, Herskovits's arguments, in *Man and His Works* and in influential essays first published in the 1950s and 1960s, contain the most complete expression of the relativism that dominated American cultural anthropology for much of the twentieth century. See also Renteln (1988) for a more recent attempt by an anthropologist to defend Herskovits's relativism against philosophical objections.

15. See, especially, George Stocking, *Race, Culture, and Evolution* (1968).

16. Thus I reject Rorty's claim, in "On Ethnocentrism," in *Objectivity, Relativism, and Truth* (1991, 204), that "some human communities are such monads, some not."

17. On the notion of "essentially contested concepts," see Gallie (1964).

18. I discuss this stance in greater detail in Chapter 3 and, especially, Chapter 5.

19. Wong also claims—like Hampshire—that morality has its source in conflict: "the point of morality" is "to regulate internal and interpersonal conflicts" (Wong 1986, 101–102).

20. Judith DeCew (1990) discusses the complexities of Hampshire's denial of relativism.

21. See Duncker (1939) and Wertheimer (1935). See also Solomon Asch, "The Fact of Culture and the Problem of Relativism" (1952, 364–384). It is worth noting that in discussing the Gestalt view in his 1959 *Ethical Theory*, Brandt rejects Duncker's claim. Yet in his 1967 *Encyclopedia of*

Philosophy article "Ethical Relativism," Brandt is more sympathetic to the Gestalt attack on relativism; indeed, in the bibliography to that article, he describes Asch's version of the Gestalt argument as an "excellent critique of the evidential basis for descriptive relativism" (Brandt 1967, 78).

22. See Asch (1952, 381). After extended discussion of Duncker's and Wertheimer's objections to the evidential basis for descriptive relativism (Asch 1952, 376–384) Asch concludes that these objections cannot "settle the extent to which values are invariant, but rather . . . suggest a way of thinking about their identities and differences" that amounts to an "alternative to the positions of absolutism and diversity" p. 376–384; (Asch 1952, 383).

23. For a vehement, if occasionally confused, attempt to defend Herskovits's view on similar grounds, see Renteln (1988, 60–61).

24. See Renteln (1988) for a criticism of Brandt's views from within anthropology. See also DeCew (1990), who—from within philosophy—simply accepts the truth of Brandt's claims without argument.

25. See also Brandt, *Hopi Ethics* ([1954] 1974, 231–215; 245–246; 373).

26. In an early review of *Hopi Ethics*, Hubert Alexander (1955) also notes the problems with Brandt's reliance on such appeals.

27. For discussion of some of the problematic features of the debate between Gilligan and Kohlberg, see Moody-Adams (1991b).

28. Brandt suggests here that a belief that animals are unconscious automata—or even that animals would be rewarded in an afterlife for suffering in this life—would have served the purpose.

29. This aspect of the doctrine of cultural integration is discussed in Archer (1988), Herbert (1991), and Kroeber and Kluckhohn (1963).

30. See also Schwartz (1983, 920).

31. In the introduction to *Coming of Age in Samoa*, Mead first notes that, at the time, there was "a paucity of women ethnologists," and that anthropological knowledge of girls was thus far more limited than that of boys. She explicitly contends that as a young woman she could obtain greater intimacy with adolescent girls than with adolescent boys (Mead [1928] 1961, 8–9). For further discussion of the possibility that different kinds of informants will yeild different kinds of data about a culture, see Scheper-Hughes (1984), and Weiner (1983). For an assessment of the Mead-Freeman controversy by an anthropologist who restudied the people and villages actually studied by Mead, see Holmes (1987).

32. See, in particular, Burton (1992) and Geertz (1988).

33. Geertz makes this claim in a conversation cited in Shweder and Levine (1984, 18–19).

34. Arens (1970, 7–9) notes that accusations of socially sanctioned cannibalism are one of the most common means of demonizing and dehumanizing another people. This point is worthy of special mention in light of my discussion in this chapter of Brandt's treatment of cannibalism. It is also

worth noting that Arens's argument in *The Man-Eating Myth* generated extraordinary controversy for its denial that there has ever been a documentable case of a society that practiced socially sanctioned ritualistic cannibalism. For some not very satisfactory attempts to respond to Arens's claims, see the essays in Brown and Tuzin (1983).

35. Cooper (1978) makes a similar claim. The relevant arguments from Davidson are contained in Davidson (1984).

36. Peter French makes a similar argument (French 1992, 102–110; esp. 104–106).

37. In his review of Sidgwick's *Elements of Politics* (Ritchie 1891–92).

2 · THE USE AND ABUSE OF HISTORY

1. Indeed, Benedict claims that such societies provide the best "laboratory of social forms" since their comparative isolation has given them centuries in which to elaborate "cultural themes that they have made their own" (Benedict 1934b, 17).

2. The main positions in the rationality and relativism debates are well represented in Wilson (1970) and Hollis and Lukes (1982).

3. Contemporary ethnographers and historians have finally begun to describe how initial contacts with Western societies drastically altered the ways in which traditional societies constructed their own histories. See, for instance, Marcus and Fischer (1986 97–98); also Rosaldo (1989).

4. I borrow the term "border crossings" from Gupta and Ferguson (1992).

5. James Clifford (1988)—despite an otherwise critical understanding of many of the fundamental assumptions of traditional cultural anthropology—defends the plausibility of the idea of culture on these very terms. But serious difficulties with the notion of culture are discussed in Said (1978) and Wolf (1982, 387–388).

6. Extensive discussion of these issues is contained in Victor Turner (1974) and Midgley (1991). Several of the essays in Turner and Bruner (1986) and Ashley (1990) are also helpful.

7. Victor Turner makes a similar claim in *Dramas, Fields, and Metaphors* (1974).

8. For a compelling argument that the set of rituals surrounding the processes of pregnancy and birth in American culture constitute the processes as rites of passage in Van Gennep's sense, see Davis-Floyd (1992).

9. See especially the projects described in Mead and Metreaux (1953).

10. See the writings of Ramos (1992) on contemporary attitudes toward the Yanomami people of Brazil and Venezuela. For detailed discussion of some quite genuine threats to the survival of the Yanomami, see Chagnon (1992). Important details of Chagnon's classic account of the Yanomami—

as the "Fierce People" (Chagnon 1968)—have been revised in his 1992 discussion of their "last days of Eden." (In a dispute internal to ethnographers who study this region, Chagnon prefers the name Yanomamo to Yanomami.)

11. See especially Burton (1992).

12. Evans-Pritchard's "Zande Kings and Princes" dates from 1957, and is published as part of the 1962 collection *Social Anthropology and Other Essays.*

13. The readiness to gloss over the effects of colonial rule is all the more striking in view of Evans-Pritchard's unexpectedly detailed account of the complicated cultural history of the Azande before the arrival of the British (see, e.g., Evans-Pritchard 1937, 14–18). But, as I indicate in the text, my aim is to provide a sympathetic reading of Evans-Pritchard. For more controversial discussions of the specifics of Evans-Pritchard's links to colonialism, see Burton (1992, 14–18; 39–40). On the more general issue of the links between British anthropology and colonialism, see Stauder (1993). For a still more general discussion of the question whether the apparent links between anthropology and colonialism undermine the former's claims to objectivity, see Maquet (1964).

14. See, for instance, Lear (1984).

15. There has been a loud chorus of criticism of Turnbull's work from within anthropology itself; see Beidelman (1973); Spencer (1973); Barth (1974); Heine (1985).

16. Heine (1985) most fully discusses the Ik's concerns about Turnbull's depiction of them.

17. Williams suggests, at one point, that there are some "exotic" traditional societies in the contemporary world where the position of anthropologists is analogous to that of "game-wardens" tending "endangered species" (Williams 1985, 165).

18. At one point Williams assumes—in his words "artificially"—the possibility of a "hypertraditional" society that is "maximally homogeneous and minimally given to general reflection" (Williams 1985, 142–148). But in discussing the relativism of distance, he often blurs the line between a philosopher's artifice and historical reality.

19. See Elkins (1976).

20. See, for instance, Henry Louis Gates (ed.), *The Classic Slave Narratives* (1987).

21. This debate appears in an exchange between Davis (1987) and Haskell (1987).

22. David Brion Davis briefly criticizes such claims (Davis 1966, 224–225). More recently, in an even more detailed comparative history, Patterson argues that there simply is not enough data about premodern slaveholding societies to license legitimate or informative comparisons concerning the cruelty of modern and premodern slave systems (Patterson, 1982 205–

208). In matters such as the use of violence against slaves; conditions of housing, diet, and health; or what most slaves in such societies actually thought and did about their condition, historians simply lack sufficient knowledge about the precise conditions of premodern slavery. As Patterson notes, the experience of slaves in the slave states of the United States will always be more vivid, simply because there is more data—including testimony of numerous former slaves (Patterson 1982, 206). Perhaps moral realists such as Sturgeon are misled by the very simple fact that there is more detailed knowledge of the conditions of U.S. slavery—especially more explicit testimony from slaves, as well as slave narratives.

23. See *Summa Theologica* 1, 6–8 (Aquinas 1927). I discuss this notion and its implications (in these contexts) for the theory of responsibility in Moody-Adams (1994a). Donagan (1977) makes somewhat different uses of the relevant passages from Aquinas, especially in chap. 4.

24. Mike Martin (1986, 6–7) raises a similar example to discuss the general problem of self-deception.

25. I discuss this phenomenon at greater length in Moody-Adams (1994a).

3 · MORALITY AND ITS DISCONTENTS

1. Nozick has described a conception of philosophy that he calls "coercive": on this conception, he claims, philosophical arguments are successful when they force someone to a belief, on pain of being described as irrational for failing to believe (Nozick 1981, 4–7). I have adapted Nozick's notion of coercive argument in philosophy to characterize a particularly influential way of thinking about rationality in general.

2. The decision in these cases is effectively non-deferrable, as Benjamin suggests, because in both cases remaining with the status quo (continuing treatment of the patient in the critical care unit, or allowing access to legal abortion) affirms one, rather than the other, stance in the disagreement.

3. For criticisms of the criminalization of "fetal abuse," see Paltrow (1989); Losco (1992); and Moody-Adams (1997).

4. On the importance of such debate to liberal democracies in particular, see Gutmann and Thompson (1990).

5. Stout (1988) makes a similar point about MacIntyre's view.

6. The quotation is from Barry Goldwater, during his 1964 campaign for the U.S. presidency.

7. Consider, in this regard, Mill's famous objection, in *Utilitarianism*, that nothing prevents a "rule of utter selfishness" from passing the test of the categorical imperative.

8. David Cooper makes this point against Sartre's understanding of the conflict (Cooper 1978).

9. Taylor 1976 has called this "strong evaluation."

10. I offer fuller discussion of some difficulties with Quine's claims about ethics in Moody-Adams (1990a).

11. Quine acknowledges that there are degrees of observationality, even in scientific theories. Yet he believes that a scientific theory, or a reasonably inclusive portion of a theory, always implies "observation sentences"—sentences for which there is firm agreement on the truth values among sincere and well-placed observers who speak the same language. Moreover, implicit in his claim about the methodological infirmity of ethics is the notion that no sentence implied by an ethical theory could be an observation sentence. See Quine (1981, 70–71) and Moody-Adams (1990a, 226–229).

12. Ken Winkler provided helpful discussion on this point.

13. See, for instance, Polanyi (1962) and Merton (1973).

14. A particularly helpful account of Hume's view is provided in Popkin (1977).

15. In the *Critique of Practical Reason* Kant chides a critic who argued that there was "no new principle" in the *Groundwork*, but only a "new formula." I show in greater detail in Chapter 4 that Kant does not think it the place of moral philosophy to introduce a new principle of morality, "as if the world had hitherto been ignorant of its duty or had been thoroughly wrong about it" (Kant [1788] 1956, 8n).

16. See Kilborn (1991). Interestingly, despite palpable evidence of their deliberate departure from local conventions about male and female roles, many of the women quoted in this article nonetheless refused to describe themselves as feminists. This suggests that the demonization of feminism, which I noted briefly in Chapter 1, is deeply embedded in contemporary public discourse.

4 · MORAL INQUIRY AND THE MORAL LIFE

1. Although I agree with Johnson's view about the role of imagination in moral reasoning, it remains unclear why he thinks that one needs cognitive science to discover this. One can recognize the centrality of metaphor and narrative to moral reasoning utterly independent of the research that Johnson cites. Further, what Johnson describes as "the prototype structure" of concepts, for instance, has been described by philosophers as diverse as Wittgenstein and H. L. A. Hart in helpful terms; consider Hart's notion of the "open texture" of concepts (Hart 1961), and Wittgenstein's notion of "family resemblance."

2. By the "structure of moral experience" I mean, more precisely, whatever it is about the world, and/or about the human capacity to experience the

world, by virtue of which human beings are able to care about the kind of life worth living (to care, that is, about morality). As I will suggest, the structure of moral experience is most likely a complex function of several phenomena, including some "transcultural" facts about fundamental human capacities, as well as cultural conventions and practices, along with various facts about the kind of world human beings must inhabit in order to survive.

3. I will argue, however, that attempts—in philosophy, psychology, or anthropology—to get beyond interpretations in order to provide a "pure" account of the structure of moral experience are implausible and ultimately unhelpful.

4. Thus, I reject Norman Daniels's claim (Daniels 1980b) that philosophical theories which draw on a connection between moral theory and anthropology are in some way suspect.

5. The quotation from Wittgenstein is taken from *Zettel* (Wittgenstein 1970).

6. Walzer may be confusing the methodology by which Rawls seeks to argue for the principles with the process of interpretation by which Rawls comes up with the content of the principles. Early on in *A Theory of Justice*, Rawls distinguishes between a concept and a conception of justice (Rawls 1971, 5–6). Some measure of agreement in conceptions of justice, he argues, is what "establishes the bonds of civic friendship"; a public conception of justice constitutes the "fundamental charter of a well-ordered human association" (Rawls 1971, 5). The two principles, their lexical ordering, and the specific interpretation of each part of the second principle are clearly *together* an interpretation—a "conception"—of the concept of justice. Justifying that interpretation is, of course, a separate matter.

7. Yet the claim itself is not as novel or as unfamiliar as critics such as Walzer have suggested. I have taught undergraduate philosophy students who can understand the difference principle only if they see it as a secular interpretation of the notion that good fortune is always attributable to the undeserved favor of God. For these students, the maximin reasoning in the original position becomes a secular interpretation of the maxim "There but for the grace of God go I."

8. Walzer briefly considers, and then summarily dismisses, the possibility that the difference principle might be the result of interpretation (Walzer 1987, 27). But Rawls *explicitly* claims to be engaged in an interpretive enterprise, in several places. In Section 40 of *A Theory of Justice*, for instance, he claims to provide a "Kantian interpretation" of the concept of justice. Further, the original position is described as a "procedural interpretation" of the Kantian conception of autonomy (Rawls 1971, 256). Anyone (including Daniels 1980b) who is unwilling to take seriously Rawls's references to the interpretive dimensions of the enterprise will surely misunderstand some of the most important features of Rawls's views.

9. See Gilligan (1982), but see also my criticisms of some of Gilligan's methods in Moody-Adams (1991b).

10. It is worth comparing Trilling's account of chap. 16 of *Huckleberry Finn* with, say, Jonathan Bennett's account in "The Conscience of Huckleberry Finn" (Bennett 1974, esp. 124–127), which overlooks the irony in Twain's account of Huck's attitude toward defenses of slavery. He thus misinterprets Twain's point about the nature of Huck's moral crisis.

11. See, for instance, *Sincerity and Authenticity* (Trilling 1972), which makes a compelling and richly textured case for a view that I go on to reject: the idea that there can be radical change in moral concepts.

12. On "edifying discourse," see Rorty (1979, 360–372).

13. A host of contemporary thinkers concerned to defend the "interpretive turn" in philosophy have begun to insist on the reasonableness of this view. Two helpful anthologies addressing the interpretive turn are Hiley, Bohman, and Shusterman (1991) and Mitchell and Rosen (1983).

14. Whether this knowledge is itself a piece of moral knowledge is, in my view, open to question. But, like Socrates, I think that it is certainly central to one's ability to use any moral knowledge one might possess.

15. Daniels discusses the implications of Rawls's method from different perspectives in three articles (Daniels 1979; 1980a; 1980b).

16. Daniels even thinks it possible to find "coherence constraints" relevant to the construction and contemplation of moral theories that function "very much like those in science" (Daniels 1979, 279).

17. Indeed, not long after the publication of *A Theory of Justice*, Rawls proclaimed the "independence" of moral theory from epistemology (Rawls 1974–75, 9).

18. Other expressions of moral realist confidence in common moral convictions, such as the view defended by Sturgeon, are more hedged. It is not entirely clear what it means to claim, as Sturgeon does, that "our ordinary methods" of moral judgment provide some "approximate" knowledge of moral truths (Sturgeon 1986, 116–117).

19. Moral conflicts, for instance, are conflicts not between some allegedly isolable moral entities or qualities, but between human beings who accept different interpretations of moral experience yet who are always capable of revising interpretations to accommodate some element of the moral claims previously rejected. Any such revision involves trying to fit a formerly rejected evaluation into one's current moral interpretation. But evaluations make sense *as* moral evaluations only insofar as they are part of some complex interpretation of moral experience—not as isolable entities or properties.

20. Contemporary moral realists offer claims about the real existence of isolable moral facts and properties in order to reject non-cognitivist accounts of moral language and moral argument. But the facts and properties described

on these views are also problematic. Some moral realisms, as I note in Chapter 2, propose treating moral facts and properties as "natural" facts and properties that might figure, for instance, in causal explanations of other natural phenomena. Thus, the wrongness of slavery was to be understood as a property of institutions, and New World slavery eventually caused people to "see" its wrongness because it simply became more cruel than ever before. But the persistence of slavery in the New World cannot plausibly be attributed to some failure to perceive a moral property of "wrongness." Slavery persisted because of a widespread willingness to affect ignorance of the suffering of enslaved human beings. Realist claims to the contrary distract moral attention from the attitudes and behavior of real human beings. Some versions of realism resist claims about the causal efficacy of facts and properties. But these views also detach moral language from meaningful contexts of inquiry and action. According to one such view, for instance, a kind person is one who "has a reliable sensitivity to a certain sort of requirement that situations impose on behavior" (McDowell 1989, 88). But surely a kind person is someone who regularly responds generously and openly to living beings and their needs and wants—not to properties of or "requirements" imposed by "situations."

21. On the Golden Rule, see Singer (1967).
22. See Frye (1982, xvii).

5 · MORALITY AND CULTURE THROUGH THICK AND THIN

1. As I argued in Chapter 1 on the fundamental sense of "culture"—as used in the social sciences—a group's implicit agreement to accept moral rules would obviously be a central element of culture. Thus, Harman's view is clearly committed to the claim that some kinds of moral judgments are not accessible, or even really intelligible, across cultures.
2. I follow Walzer (1987) in believing that Gramsci's notion of hegemony is best interpreted along these lines. I thus reject a series of familiar claims about history, morality, and the concept of hegemony defended, for instance, by T. J. Jackson Lears (1985).
3. The phrase "extra-moral" here includes a variety of phenomena from legal intervention and action to military struggles and even war.
4. Benjamin (1990) discusses the frequency of such problems in everyday life, and offers a helpful analysis of moral integrity that might allow those concerned about it to engage in more fruitful moral argument.
5. It is important that Williams appeals to a notion of moral confidence very different from that defended here. "Ethical confidence" for Williams means something like conviction in one's moral (he says "ethical") beliefs (Williams 1985, 170). He is concerned, for instance, with how people

might "come to possess a practical confidence that . . . will come from strength and not from the weakness of self-deception and dogmatism" (Williams 1985, 171). My conception of moral confidence, it should be clear, is far more robust than this.

6. Episodes of this sort are richly depicted in interviews included in the documentary *Eyes on the Prize: America's Civil Rights Years* (1986).

7. In a particularly powerful irony, the famous photographic image of the lone student stepping in front of the armored tanks was at one point exhibited by the Chinese government as evidence of the *restraint* of Chinese troops. On this version of the incident, the tank drivers could be seen as choosing not to harm someone who was trying to block the march of tanks called in to contain student violence (Goldberg 1991, 251).

8. Not everyone agrees on this interpretation, as Goldberg (1991, 251) notes. But disagreement about how to interpret this image does not show either the relativity or the subjectivity of morality, nor does it establish the truth of Rorty's ethnocentrism, nor does it show the plausibility of any emotivist accounts of moral judgments.

9. That moral faith may in some instances be inseparable from religious faith. I see no objection to this. Some who would disparage movements spurred on by considerations of religious faith seem to assume that religious faith will necessarily issue in moral smugness. But this assumption embodies an extremely simplistic view of the consequences of religious faith. Equally important, moral smugness can be rooted in the most secular of attitudes toward experience. There are any number of utilitarian moral thinkers, for instance, who claim not to understand how any rational person could not be a utilitarian!

10. The fragmentation of value is most likely a function of the structure of moral experience, attributable in part to facts about the complex ways in which human beings experience the world, and to facts about the varied kinds of "claims" that the world may make on human beings. The fragmentation of value means that there are several sources of moral value which cannot be given a complete and final hierarchical ordering.

11. France has been particularly active in this regard. In one particularly controversial case in January 1993, for instance, a French court sent a Gambian woman to jail on charges of "causing the wounding and mutilation of minors" for allowing a midwife to perform female circumcision on her two young daughters.

12. Most of the societies in which the practice continues are Muslim societies. But some sub-Saharan African societies in which female circumcision is practiced are not, or at least not primarily, Muslim countries. In many such societies the practice is often claimed to be rooted in other social traditions. Even in societies where efforts are made to link the practice to the

requirements of Islam, there is disagreement within those societies about whether the Koran in fact requires the practice.

13. Some of these rituals, it should be noted, have led to serious injury and death.

14. Whether the complex practices described as "female circumcision" actually fall into this category is an issue I shall not attempt to settle here. The reader will note that I have carefully avoided using the phrase "genital mutilation," which is sometimes used to characterize these practices.

15. Marglin (1990, 27; 14–15) claims to recognize the dangers inherent in such a stance, but he never offers any careful discussion of what it might mean to care about these dangers in real cases—for instance, when a woman pleads for her daughters to be protected from circumcision.

16. Taylor suggests, of course, that it may be possible to defend a more discriminating "ethics of authenticity" (Taylor 1991).

17. The difficulties with this assumption, especially with the concept of race, are too numerous to discuss here. For two anthologies that enumerate some of the most serious difficulties—and that direct the reader to some of the most important secondary sources on this issue—see Montagu (1964) and Harding (1993).

18. This belief gives rise, for instance, to the curious idea that it makes sense to ignore the linguistic and national differences between peoples who are inhabitants of, or are descended from inhabitants of, the countries of Asia and the Pacific Rim—as though there were a single phenomenon rightly described as "Asian culture." A different kind of example reveals that even greater absurdities may follow on this effort to link race and culture. During the late 1980s it was common for American music critics and social commentators to suggest that rap music (which originated in the urban culture of some young urban black Americans) somehow manifested qualities that were "essentially"—or, in one critic's words, "quintessentially"—black. One corollary of this stance was the outrageous claim that any black American who denied the link between rap music (that is, its performance and enjoyment) and race was "inauthentic"—not "really" black. The purveyors of such claims rarely ask why one of the largest audiences for rap music's most violent and misogynist manifestations is (still) composed largely of white suburban American teenage males.

19. A particularly useful discussion of this development is provided by George Stocking's writings on the history of anthropology (Stocking 1982).

20. This reading of the ambiguity of Herder's views is shared by many commentators, including Stocking (1982, 213–214) and to a certain extent Berlin (1976, 143–216).

21. Schlesinger's otherwise quite measured critique is marred by continual manifestations of this unfortunate tendency (Schlesinger 1992).

EPILOGUE

1. I have attempted this kind of inquiry, for instance, on the topic of surrogate motherhood (Moody-Adams 1991a), on the relation between race, class, and self-respect (Moody-Adams 1992–93), and on the question of whether an upbringing in a culture can ever constitute an excuse from responsibility (Moody-Adams 1994a).

2. This is the lesson that philosophers such as Michael Walzer (1983) and Philip Hallie (1979), and social thinkers such as Lionel Trilling (1970) and Robert Coles (1967; 1981; 1986), so richly teach.

WORKS CITED

Alexander, Hubert G. 1955. "Brandt on Hopi Ethics." *Review of Metaphysics* 9:106–111.

Allardyce, Gilbert. 1982. "The Rise and Fall of the Western Civilization Course." *American Historical Review* 87:695–725.

Amnesty International. 1973. *Report on Torture*. London: Duckworth.

Amnesty International. 1984. *Report on Torture in the Eighties*. London: Amnesty International.

Applebaum, Herbert, ed. 1987. *Perspectives in Cultural Anthropology*. Albany: State University of New York Press.

Aquinas. 1927. *Summa Theologica*. London: Burns Oates and Washbourne.

Archer, Margaret S. 1988. *Culture and Agency: The Place of Culture in Social Theory*. Cambridge: Cambridge University Press.

Ardener, Edwin. 1975. "Belief and the Problem of Women." In *Perceiving Women*. Edited by Shirley Ardener. New York: John Wiley and Sons.

Arens, W. 1970. *The Man-Eating Myth*. New York: Oxford University Press.

Asch, Solomon. 1952. *Social Psychology*. New York: Prentice-Hall.

Ashley, Kathleen, ed. 1990. *Victor Turner and the Construction of Cultural Criticism*. Bloomington: Indiana University Press.

Ashworth, John. 1987. "The Relationship between Capitalism and Humanitarianism." *American Historical Review* 92:813–828.

Ayer, A. J. [1946] 1971. *Language, Truth, and Logic*. 2d ed. Harmondsworth: Pelican Books.

——— 1984. *Freedom and Morality and Other Essays*. Oxford: Oxford University Press.

Baier, Annette. 1985. "Doing without Moral Theory." In *Postures of the Mind: Essays on Mind and Morals*. Minneapolis: University of Minnesota Press.

Barnes, Barry, and David Bloor. 1982. "Relativism, Rationalism, and the Sociology of Knowledge." In *Rationality and Relativism*. Edited by Martin Hollis and Steven Lukes. Cambridge, Mass.: MIT Press.

Barth, Frederick. 1974. "On Responsibility and Humanity: Calling a Colleague to Account." *Current Anthropology* 15:99–103.

Beidelman, T. O. 1973. "Review of *The Mountain People*." *Africa* 43:170–171.

Benedict, Ruth. 1934a. "Anthropology and the Abnormal." *Journal of General Psychology* 10:59–82.

——— 1934b. *Patterns of Culture*. Boston: Houghton Mifflin.

——— 1946. *The Chrysanthemum and the Sword*. Boston: Houghton Mifflin.

Benjamin, Martin. 1990. *Splitting the Difference.* Lawrence: University of Kansas Press.

Bennett, Jonathan. 1974. "The Conscience of Huckleberry Finn." *Philosophy* 49:122–134.

Bentham, Jeremy. 1983. *Deontology, together with a Table of the Springs of Action and the Article on Utilitarianism,* edited by Amnon Goldworth. Oxford: Clarendon Press.

Berlin, Isaiah. [1958] 1969. "Two Concepts of Liberty." In *Four Essays on Liberty.* New York: Oxford University Press.

———— 1976. *Vico and Herder: Two Studies in the History of Ideas.* London: Hogarth.

———— 1991. *The Crooked Timber of Humanity: Chapters in the History of Ideas.* New York: Knopf.

Bettelheim, Bruno. 1943. "Individual and Mass Behavior in Extreme Situations." *Journal of Abnormal Psychology* 38:417–452.

Bilimoria, Parasottama. 1991. "Indian Ethics." In *A Companion to Ethics.* Edited by Peter Singer. Oxford: Basil Blackwell.

Bloor, David. 1991. *Knowledge and Social Imagery.* 2d ed. Chicago: University of Chicago Press.

Bock, Philip K. 1983. "The Samoan Puberty Blues." *Journal of Anthropological Research* 39:336–340.

Brady, Ivan, ed. 1983. "Speaking in the Name of the Real: Freeman and Mead on Samoa: Symposium." *American Anthropologist* 85:908–947.

Brandt, Richard. 1959. *Ethical Theory.* Englewood Cliffs, N.J.: Prentice-Hall.

———— 1967. "Ethical Relativism." In *Encyclopedia of Philosophy.* Vol. 3. Edited by Paul Edwards. New York: Macmillan and Free Press.

———— [1954] 1974. *Hopi Ethics: A Theoretical Analysis.* Chicago: University of Chicago Press.

Brink, David O. 1986. "Externalist Moral Realism." *Southern Journal of Philosophy* Supp. 24:23–41.

———— 1989. *Moral Realism and the Foundation of Ethics.* Cambridge: Cambridge University Press.

Broad, C. D. [1930] 1979. *Five Types of Ethical Theory.* London: Routledge and Kegan Paul.

Brown, Paula, and Donald Tuzin, eds. 1983. *The Ethnography of Cannibalism.* Washington D.C.: Society for Psychological Anthropology.

Burton, John W. 1992. *An Introduction to Evans-Pritchard.* Fribourg, Switzerland: University Press.

Carrithers, Michael. 1992. *Why Humans Have Cultures: Explaining Anthropology and Diversity.* Oxford: Oxford University Press.

Cavell, Stanley. 1979. *The Claim of Reason.* New York: Oxford University Press.

Chagnon, Napoleon. 1968. *Yanomamo: The Fierce People.* New York: Holt, Rinehart and Winston.

———— 1992. *Yanomamo: The Last Days of Eden.* San Diego: Harcourt Brace Jovanovich.

Clarke, Stanley G., and Evan Simpson, eds. 1989. *Anti-Theory in Ethics and Moral Conservatism.* Albany: State University of New York Press.

Clifford, James. 1988. *The Predicament of Culture.* Cambridge, Mass.: Harvard University Press.

Clifford, James, and George E. Marcus, eds. 1986. *Writing Culture: The Poetics and Politics of Ethnography.* Berkeley: University of California Press.

Coles, Robert. 1967. *Children of Crisis.* Vol. 1. *A Study of Courage and Fear.* Boston: Atlantic–Little Brown.

———— 1981. "On the Nature of Character: Some Preliminary Field Notes," *Daedalus* 110:131–143.

———— 1986. *The Moral Life of Children.* Boston: Atlantic Monthly Press.

Cooper, David E. 1978. "Moral Relativism." In *Midwest Studies in Philosophy.* Vol. 3. *Studies in Ethical Theory.* Edited by Peter French, Theodore Uehling, and Howard Wettstein. Morris: University of Minnesota Press.

Daniels, Norman. 1979. "Wide Reflective Equilibrium and Theory Acceptance in Ethics." *Journal of Philosophy* 76:256–282.

———— 1980a. "Methods of Ethics and Linguistics." *Philosophical Studies* 37:21–36.

———— 1980b. "Reflective Equilibrium and Archimedean Points." *Canadian Journal of Philosophy* 10:83–103.

Davidson, Donald. [1974] 1984. "On the Very Idea of a Conceptual Scheme." Reprinted in *Inquiries into Truth and Interpretation.* Oxford: Clarendon Press.

Davis, David Brion. 1966. *The Problem of Slavery in Western Culture.* Ithaca, N.Y.: Cornell University Press.

———— 1984. *Slavery and Human Progress.* New York: Oxford University Press.

———— 1987. "Reflections on Abolitionism and Ideological Hegemony." *American Historical Review* 92:797–812.

Davis-Floyd, Robbie. 1992. *Birth as an American Rite of Passage.* Berkeley: University of California Press.

DeCew, Judith W. 1990. "Moral Conflicts and Ethical Relativism." *Ethics* 101:27–41.

Dewey, John. 1994. *The Moral Writings of John Dewey.* Revised Edition. Edited by James Gouinlock. Amherst, N.Y.: Prometheus Books.

Donagan, Alan. 1977. *The Theory of Morality.* Chicago: University of Chicago Press.

Douglass, Frederick. [1845] 1989. *Narrative of the Life of Frederick Douglass, An American Slave. Written by Himself.* New York: Anchor/Doubleday.

Dover, K. J. 1974. *Greek Popular Morality in the Time of Plato and Aristotle.* Oxford: Basil Blackwell.

Duncker, Karl. 1939. "Ethical Relativity? (An Inquiry into the Psychology of Ethics)." *Mind* 48:39–57.

Elkins, Stanley M. 1976. *Slavery: A Problem in American Institutional and Intellectual Life.* 3d ed. rev. Chicago: University of Chicago Press.

Evans-Pritchard, E. E. 1937. *Witchcraft, Oracles, and Magic among the Azande.* Oxford: Oxford University Press.

———— 1962. *Social Anthropology and Other Essays.* New York: Free Press.

———— 1966. "Foreword." In Lucien Lévy-Bruhl, *The "Soul" of the Primitive.* New York: Frederick A. Praeger.

———— [1940] 1969. *The Nuer.* New York: Oxford University Press.

———— 1971. *The Azande: History and Political Institutions.* Oxford: Oxford University Press.

Fabian, Johannes. 1983. *Time and the Other: How Anthropology Makes Its Object.* New York: Columbia University Press.

Feinberg, Joel. 1970. *Doing and Deserving: Essays in the Theory of Responsibility.* Princeton: Princeton University Press.

Feinberg, Richard. 1988. "Margaret Mead on Samoa: *Coming of Age* in Fact and Fiction." *American Anthropologist* 90:656–663.

Flanagan, Owen. 1982. "Quinean Ethics." *Ethics* 93:56–74.

Flanagan, Owen. 1988. "Pragmatism, Ethics, and Correspondence Truth: Response to Gibson and Quine." *Ethics* 98:541–549.

Frankena, William. 1973. *Ethics.* Englewood Cliffs, N.J.: Prentice-Hall.

Freeman, Derek. 1983. *Margaret Mead and Samoa: The Making and Unmaking of an Anthropological Myth.* Cambridge, Mass.: Harvard University Press.

French, Peter. 1992. *Responsibility Matters.* Lawrence: University of Kansas Press.

Frye, Northrop. 1982. *The Great Code.* New York: Harvest Press/Harcourt Brace Jovanovich.

Gallie, W. B. 1964. *Philosophy and the Historical Understanding.* New York: Schocken Books.

Gandhi, Mohandas K. [1927] 1957. *An Autobiography: The Story of My Experiments with Truth.* Boston: Beacon Press.

Gates, Henry Louis, ed. 1987. *The Classic Slave Narratives.* New York: New American Library.

Geertz, Clifford. 1973. *The Interpretation of Cultures.* New York: Basic Books.

———— 1983. *Local Knowledge: Further Essays in Interpretive Anthropology.* New York: Basic Books.

———— 1984. "Anti Anti-Relativism." *American Anthropologist* 86:263–278.

———— 1986. "The Uses of Diversity." In *The Tanner Lectures on Human Values*. Vol. 7. Edited by S. McMurrin. Cambridge: Cambridge University Press.

———— 1988. *Works and Lives: The Anthropologist as Author*. Stanford: Stanford University Press.

———— 1995. "Culture Wars," *New York Review of Books*. November 30, 1995: 4–6.

Gewirth, Alan. 1978. *Reason and Morality*. Chicago: University of Chicago Press.

Gilligan, Carol. 1982. *In a Different Voice*. Cambridge, Mass.: Harvard University Press.

Goffman, Erving. 1961. *Asylums*. New York: Doubleday.

Goldberg, Vicki. 1991. *The Power of Photography: How Photographs Changed Our Lives*. New York: Abbeville Press.

Greenfield, Jeanette. 1989. *The Return of Cultural Treasures*. Cambridge: Cambridge University Press.

Gupta, Akhil, and James Ferguson. 1992. "Beyond 'Culture': Space, Identity, and the Politics of Difference." *Cultural Anthropology* 7:6–23.

Gutmann, Amy, and Dennis Thompson. 1990. "Moral Conflict and Political Consensus." *Ethics* 101:64–88.

Haan, Norma, Robert N. Bellah, Paul Rabinow, and William M. Sullivan, eds. 1983. *Social Science as Moral Inquiry*. New York: Columbia University Press.

Hallie, Philip. 1979. *Lest Innocent Blood Be Shed*. New York: Harper and Row.

Hampshire, Stuart. 1983. *Morality and Conflict*. Cambridge, Mass.: Harvard University Press.

Harding, Sandra, ed. 1993. *The "Racial" Economy of Science*. Bloomington: Indiana University Press.

Hare, R. M. 1963. *Freedom and Reason*. Oxford: Oxford University Press.

———— 1967. "Philosophical Discoveries." In *The Linguistic Turn*. Edited by Richard Rorty. Chicago: University of Chicago Press.

———— 1981. *Moral Thinking*. Oxford: Clarendon Press.

———— 1991. "Universal Prescriptivism." In *A Companion to Ethics*. Edited by Peter Singer. Oxford: Basil Blackwell.

Harman, Gilbert. 1975. "Moral Relativism Defended." *Philosophical Review* 84:3–22.

———— 1977. *The Nature of Morality*. New York: Oxford University Press.

———— 1978a. "Relativistic Ethics: Morality as Politics." In *Midwest Studies in Philosophy*. Vol. 3. *Studies in Ethical Theory*. Edited by Peter French, Theodore Uhling, and Howard Wettstein. Morris: University of Minnesota Press. 109–121.

—— 1978b. "What is Moral Relativism?" In *Values and Morals.* Edited by A. I. Goldman and Jaegwon Kim. Dordrecht, Holland: D. Reidel.

—— 1982. "Metaphysical Realism and Moral Relativism: Reflections on Hilary Putnam's *Reason, Truth, and History.*" *Journal of Philosophy* 79:568–575.

—— [1984]. 1989. "Is There a Single True Morality?" Reprinted in *Relativism: Interpretation and Confrontation.* Edited by Michael Krausz. Notre Dame: University of Notre Dame Press.

Hart, H. L. A. 1961. *The Concept of Law.* Oxford: Clarendon Press.

Haskell, Thomas. 1985a. "Capitalism and the Origins of the Humanitarian Sensibility, Part I." *American Historical Review* 90:339–362.

—— 1985b. "Capitalism and the Origins of the Humanitarian Sensibility, Part II." *American Historical Review* 90:547–567.

—— 1987. "Convention and Hegemonic Interest in the Debate over Slavery: A Reply to Davis and Ashworth." *American Historical Review* 92:829–879.

Heider, Karl G. 1988. "The Rashomon Effect: Where Ethnographers Disagree." *American Anthropologist* 90:73–81.

Heine, Bernd. 1985. "The Mountain People: Some Notes on the Ik of Northeastern Uganda." *Africa* 55(1):3–16.

Held, Virginia. 1982. "The Political 'Testing' of Moral Theories." *Midwest Studies in Philosophy.* Vol. 7. *Social and Political Philosophy.* Edited by Peter French, Theodore Uehling, and Howard Wettstein. Minneapolis: University of Minnesota Press.

Herbert, Christoper. 1991. *Culture and Anomie: Ethnographic Imagination in the Nineteenth Century.* Chicago: University of Chicago Press.

Herder, J. G. [1784–1791]. 1968. *Reflections on the Phiosophy of the History of Mankind.* Translated by Frank E. Manuel. Chicago: University of Chicago Press.

Herskovits, Melville. 1964. *Man and His Works: The Science of Cultural Anthropology.* New York: Alfred A. Knopf.

—— 1972. *Cultural Relativism: Perspectives in Cultural Pluralism.* Edited by Frances Herskovits. New York: Random House.

Hiley, David. 1988. *Philosophy in Question: Essays on a Pyrrhonian Theme.* Chicago: University of Chicago Press.

Hiley, David, James F. Bohman, and Richard Shusterman, eds. 1991. *The Interpretive Turn: Philosophy, Science, Culture.* Ithaca, N.Y.: Cornell University Press.

Hollis, Martin, and Steven Lukes, eds. 1982. *Rationality and Relativism.* Cambridge, Mass.: MIT Press.

Holmes, Lowell. 1987. *Quest for the Real Samoa. The Mead/ Freeman Controversy and Beyond.* South Hadley, Mass.: Bergin and Garvey.

Hume, David. [1777] 1964a. "Of National Characters." In *Essays Moral, Political, and Literary*. edited by T. H. Green and T. H. Grose. Darmstadt: Scientia Verlag Allen.

———— [1777] 1964b. "Of the Original Contract" In *Essays Moral, Political, and Literary*. edited by T. H. Green and T. H. Grose. Darmstadt: Scientia Verlag Allen.

———— [1739] 1978. *A Treatise of Human Nature*, edited by L. A. Selby-Bigge, revised by P. H. Nidditch. Oxford: Clarendon Press.

Jacobs, Harriet A. [1861] 1987. *Incidents in the Life of a Slave Girl: Written by Herself*, edited by Jean Fagan Yellin. Cambridge, Mass.: Harvard University Press.

James, William. [1891] 1974. "The Moral Philosopher and the Moral Life." In *Essays in Pragmatism*. New York: Hafner Press.

Johnson, Mark. 1993. *Moral Imagination: Implications of Cognitive Science for Ethics*. Chicago: University of Chicago Press.

Jonsen, Albert, and Stephen Toulmin. 1988. *The Abuse of Casuistry: A History of Moral Reasoning*. Berkeley: University of California Press.

Kant, I. [1788] 1956. *Critique of Practical Reason*. Translated by L. W. Beck. Indianapolis: Bobbs-Merrill.

———— [1785] 1964. *Groundwork of the Metaphysic of Morals*. Translated by H. J. Paton. New York: Harper and Row.

Kilborn, Peter. 1991. "In Appalachia, from Homemaker to Wage Earner." *New York Times*. July 7, p. 1.

King, Martin Luther. [1963] 1964. "Letter From Birmingham Jail." In *Why We Can't Wait*. New York: New American Library.

Kluckhohn, Clyde. 1962. *Culture and Behavior: Collected Essays*, edited by Richard Kluckhohn. New York: Free Press of Glencoe.

———— [1944] 1963. *Mirror for Man: A Survey of Human Behavior and Social Attitudes*. New York: Fawcett Publishing.

Krausz, Michael, ed. 1989. *Relativism: Interpretation and Confrontation*. Notre Dame: University of Notre Dame Press.

Krausz, Michael, and Jack W. Meiland, eds. 1982. *Relativism: Cognitive and Moral*. Notre Dame: University of Notre Dame Press.

Kraybill, Donald. 1989. *The Riddle of Amish Culture*. Baltimore: Johns Hopkins University Press.

Kraybill, Donald, ed. 1993. *The Amish and the State*. Baltimore: Johns Hopkins University Press.

Kroeber, A. L., and Clyde Kluckhohn. [1952] 1963. *Culture: A Critical Review of Concepts and Definitions*. New York: Vintage Books.

Kuhn, T. S. 1970. *The Structure of Scientific Revolutions*. 2d ed. Chicago: University of Chicago Press.

———— 1977. "Objectivity, Value Judgment, and Theory Choice." In *The Essential Tension*, Chicago: University of Chicago Press.

Kuklick, Bruce. 1977. *The Rise of American Philosophy*. New Haven: Yale University Press.

———— 1984. "Seven Thinkers and How They Grew: Descartes, Spinoza, Leibniz; Locke, Berkeley, Hume; Kant." In *Philosophy in History*. Edited by R. Rorty, J. B. Schneewind, and Quentin Skinner. Cambridge: Cambridge University Press.

Kuper, Adam. 1983. *Anthropology and Anthropologists: The Modern British School*. London: Routledge and Kegan Paul.

Ladd, John. 1957. *The Structure of a Moral Code*. Cambridge, Mass.: Harvard University Press.

———— 1985. "The Issue of Relativism." In *Ethical Relativism*. Edited by John Ladd. Lanham, Md.: University Press of America.

Langenfus, William L. 1988–89. "A Problem for Harman's Moral Relativism." *Philosophy Research Archives* 14:121–136.

Larmore, Charles. 1987. *Patterns of Moral Complexity*. Cambridge: Cambridge University Press.

Lear, Jonathan. 1984. "Moral Objectivity." In *Objectivity and Cultural Divergence*. Edited by S. C. Brown. Cambridge: Cambridge University Press.

Lears, T. J. Jackson. 1985. "The Concept of Cultural Hegemony: Problems and Possibilities." *American Historical Review* 90:567–593.

Levy, Paul. 1979. *G. E. Moore and the Cambridge Apostles*. New York: Holt, Rinehart and Winston.

Lévy-Bruhl, Lucien. 1923. *Primitive Mentality*. Translated by Lilian A. Clare. New York: Macmillan.

———— [1927] 1966. *The "Soul" of the Primitive*. Translated by Lilian A. Clare, foreword by E. E. Evans-Pritchard. New York: Frederick A. Praeger.

Losco, Joseph. 1992. "Fetal Rights and Feminism." In *Feminist Jurisprudence*. Edited by Leslie Friedman Goldstein. Lanham, Md.: Rowman and Littlefield.

Louden, Robert B. 1992. *Morality and Moral Theory*. New York: Oxford University Press.

Lowie, Robert H. 1933. "Primitive Skeptics." *American Mercury* 29:320–323.

Lukes, Steven. 1991. *Moral Conflict and Politics*. Oxford: Clarendon Press.

MacIntyre, Alasdair. 1981. *After Virtue*. Notre Dame: University of Notre Dame Press.

———— 1988. *Whose Justice? Which Rationality?* Notre Dame: University of Notre Dame Press.

Mackie, J. L. 1977. *Ethics: Inventing Right and Wrong*. Harmondsworth: Penguin Books.

MacKillop, I. D. 1986. *The British Ethical Societies*. Cambridge: Cambridge University Press.

Malone, Douglas. 1962. *Jefferson and the Ordeal of Liberty*. Boston: Little, Brown.

Maquet, Jacques. 1964. "Objectivity in Anthropology." *Current Anthropology* 5:47–55.

Marcus, George E., ed. 1992. *Rereading Cultural Anthropology*. Durham, N.C.: Duke University Press.

Marcus, George E., and Michael M. J. Fischer. 1986. *Anthropology as Cultural Critique*. Chicago: University of Chicago Press.

Marglin, Stephen A. 1990. "Towards the Decolonization of the Mind." In *Dominating Knowledge: Development, Culture, and Resistance*. Edited by Fréderique Marglin and Stephen A. Marglin. Oxford: Clarendon Press.

Martin, Michael. 1993. "Geertz and the Interpretive Approach in Anthropology." *Synthèse* 976:269–286.

Martin, Mike W. 1986. *Self-Deception and Morality*. Lawrence: University of Kansas Press.

Matilal, Bimal Krishna. 1989. "Ethical Relativism and Confrontation of Cultures." In *Relativism: Interpretation and Confrontation*. Edited by Michael E. Krausz. Notre Dame: University of Notre Dame Press.

Matson, Wallace I. and Adam Leite. 1991. "Socrates' Critique of Cognitivism." *Philosophy* 66:145–167.

McCarthy, Thomas. 1989. "Contra Relativism: A Thought-Experiment." In *Relativism: Interpretation and Confrontation*. Edited by Michael E. Kransz. Notre Dame: University of Notre Dame Press.

——— 1992. "Doing the Right Thing in Cultural Representation." *Ethics* 102:635–649.

McDowell, John. 1989. "Virtue and Reason." In *Anti-Theory inEthics and Moral Conservatism*. Edited by Stanley Clarke and Evan Simpson. Albany: State University of New York Press.

Mead, Margaret. [1928] 1961. *Coming of Age in Samoa*. New York: William Morrow.

Mead, Margaret, and Rhoda Metreaux, eds. 1953. *The Study of Culture at a Distance*. Chicago: University of Chicago Press.

Merton, Robert K. 1973. *The Sociology of Science: Theoretical and Empirical Investigations*. Edited by Norman W. Storer. Chicago: University of Chicago Press.

Midgley, Mary. 1981. *Heart and Mind; The Varieties of Moral Experience*. New York: St. Martin's Press.

——— 1991. *Can't We Make Moral Judgments?* New York: St. Martin's Press.

Mill, J. S. [1859] 1978. *On Liberty*. Indianapolis: Hackett.

——— [1859] 1979. *Utilitarianism*. Indianapolis: Hackett.

Mitchell, Solace, and Michael Rosen, eds. 1983. *The Need for Interpretation: Contemporary Conceptions of the Philosophers's Task*. London: Athlone Press.

Montagu, Ashley, ed. 1964. *The Concept of Race*. New York: Free Press.

Montaigne, Michel de. 1958. *The Complete Essays of Montaigne.* Translated by Donald M. Frame. Stanford: Stanford University Press.

Moody-Adams, Michele M. 1990a. "On the Alleged Methodological Infirmity of Ethics." *American Philosophical Quarterly* 27:225–235.

———— 1990b. "On the Old Saw That Character Is Destiny." In *Identity, Character, and Morality.* Edited by Owen Flanagan and Amelie O. Rorty. Cambridge, Mass.: MIT Press.

———— 1991a. "On Surrogacy: Morality, Markets, and Motherhood." *Public Affairs Quarterly* 5:175–192.

———— 1991b. "Gender and the Complexity of Moral Voices." In *Feminist Ethics.* Edited by Claudia Card. Lawrence: University of Kansas Press.

———— 1992–93. "Race, Class, and the Social Construction of Self-Respect." *Philosophical Forum* 24:251–266.

———— 1994a. "Culture, Responsibility, and Affected Ignorance." *Ethics* 104:291–309.

———— 1994b. "Theory, Practice, and the Contingency of Rorty's Irony." *Journal of Social Philosophy* 25: 207–225.

———— 1997. "The Social Construction and Reconstruction of Care." In *Sex, Preference, and Family.* Edited by David M. Estlung and Martha C. Nussbaum. New York: Oxford University Press.

Moore, John H. 1974. "The Culture Concept as Ideology." *American Ethnologist* 1:537–549.

Morris, Aldon C. 1984. *The Origins of the Civil Rights Movement.* New York: Free Press.

Murray, Stephen O. 1990. "Problematic Aspects of Freeman's Account of Boasian Culture." *Current Anthropology* 31:401–407.

Nagel, Thomas. 1979. "The Fragmentation of Value." In *Mortal Questions.* Cambridge: Cambridge University Press.

———— 1987. "Moral Conflict and Political Legitimacy." *Philosophy and Public Affairs* 16:215–240.

National Academy of Sciences. 1989. *On Being a Scientist.* Washington, D.C.: National Academy Press.

Nietzsche, Friedrich. 1967. *The Birth of Tragedy.* Translated by Walter Kaufmann. New York: Random House.

Noble, Cheryl. [1979] 1989. "Normative Ethical Theories." In *Anti-Theory in Ethics and Moral Conservatism.* Edited by Stanley Clarke and Evan Simpson. Albany: State University of New York Press.

Nozick, Robert. 1974. *Anarchy, State, and Utopia.* New York: Basic Books.

———— 1981. *Philosophical Explanations.* Cambridge, Mass.: Harvard University Press.

Obeyesekere, Gananath. 1992. *The Apotheosis of Captain Cook: European Mythmaking in the Pacific.* Princeton: Princeton University Press.

Orwell, George. 1950. "Reflections on Gandhi." In *Shooting an Elephant and Other Essays*. New York: Harcourt, Brace and Company.

Paltrow, Lynn. 1989. " 'Fetal Abuse': Should We Recognize It as a Crime? No." *American Bar Association Journal* 75 (August):39.

Patterson, Orlando. 1982. *Slavery and Social Death*. Cambridge, Mass.: Harvard University Press.

Plato. 1956. *Euthyphro, Apology, Crito*. Translated by F. J. Church. Indianapolis: Library of Liberal Arts/Bobbs-Merrill.

Polanyi, Michael. 1962. *Personal Knowledge: Towards a Post-Critical Philosophy*. Chicago: University of Chicago Press.

Popkin, Richard. 1977. "Hume's Racism." *Philosophical Forum* 9:211–226.

Pratt, Mary Louise. 1986. "Fieldwork in Common Places." In *Writing Culture: The Poetics and Politics of Ethnography*. Edited by James Clifford and George E. Marcus. Berkeley: University of California Press.

Putnam, Hilary. 1981. *Reason, Truth, and History*. Cambridge: Cambridge University Press.

———— 1983. "Why Reason Can't Be Naturalized." In *Philosophical Papers*. Vol. 3. *Realism and Reason*. Cambridge: Cambridge University Press.

———— 1987. *The Many Faces of Realism*. La Salle, Ill.: Open Court Publishing.

———— 1990. *Realism with a Human Face*. Cambridge, Mass.: Harvard University Press.

Quine, W. V. O. 1981. *Theories and Things*. Cambridge, Mass.: Harvard University Press.

———— 1986. "Reply to Morton White." In *The Philosophy of W. V. O. Quine*, edited by L. E. Hahn and P. A. Schilpp. La Salle, Ill.: Open Court Publishing.

Quine, W. V. O., and Ullian, J. S. 1978. *The Web of Belief*. 2d ed. New York: Random House.

Rabinow, Paul. 1983. "Humanism as Nihilism: The Bracketing of Truth and Seriousness in American Cultural Inquiry." In *Social Science as Moral Inquiry*. Edited by Norma Haan, Robert N. Bellah, Paul Rabinow, and William Sullivan. New York: Columbia University Press.

Rabinow, Paul, and William Sullivan, eds. 1979. *Interpretive Social Science: A Reader*. Berkeley: University of California Press.

Ramos, Alcida. 1992. "Reflections on the Yanomami: Ethnographic Images and the Pursuit of the Exotic." In *Rereading Cultural Anthropology*. Edited by George Marcus. Durham, N.C.: Duke University Press.

Rawls, John. 1971. *A Theory of Justice*. Cambridge, Mass.: Harvard University Press.

———— 1974–75. "The Independence of Moral Theory." *Proceedings of the American Philosophical Association* 47:5–22.

———— 1980. "Kantian Constructivism in Moral Theory." *Journal of Philosophy* 72:515–572.

———— 1985. "Justice as Fairness: Political Not Metaphysical." *Philosophy and Public Affairs* 14:223–251.

———— 1994. *Political Liberalism.* New York: Columbia University Press.

Raz, Joseph. 1994. "Multiculturalism: A Liberal Perspective." *Dissent.* Winter: 67–79.

Renteln, Alison D. 1988. "Relativism and the Search for Human Rights." *American Anthropologist* 90:56–72.

Ritchie, D. G. 1891–92. "Review of *The Elements of Politics* by Henry Sidgwick." *International Journal of Ethics* 2:254–257.

Rorty, Richard. 1979. *Philosophy and the Mirrow of Nature.* Princeton: Princeton University Press.

———— 1982a. "Contemporary Philosophy of Mind." *Synthèse* 83:323–348.

———— 1982b. *Consequences of Pragmatism.* Minneapolis: University of Minnesota Press.

———— 1989. *Contingency, Irony, and Solidarity.* Cambridge: Cambridge University Press.

———— 1990. "Truth and Freedom: A Reply to Thomas McCarthy." *Critical Inquiry* 16:633–643.

———— 1991a. *Philosophical Papers.* Vol. 1. *Objectivity, Relativism, and Truth.* Cambridge: Cambridge University Press.

———— 1991b. "Feminism and Pragmatism." *Michigan Quarterly Review* 30:231–266.

Rosaldo, Renato. 1989. *Culture and Truth.* Boston: Beacon Press.

Ryle, Gilbert. 1971. *Collected Papers.* Vol. 1. *Critical Essays.* Vol 2. *Collected Essays, 1929–1968.* London: Hutchinson.

Sahlins, Marshall. 1995. *How "Natives" Think: About Captain Cook, For Example.* Chicago: University of Chicago Press.

Said, Edward. 1978. *Orientalism.* New York: Random House.

Sapir, Edward. [1949] 1985. *Selected Writings in Language, Culture, and Personality,* Edited by David G. Mandelbaum. Berkeley: University of California Press.

Sartre, Jean-Paul. 1965. *Essays in Existentialism,* edited, with a foreword, by Wade Baskin. Secaucus, N.J.: Citadel Press.

Scarry, Elaine. 1985. *The Body in Pain.* New York: Oxford University Press.

Scheper-Hughes, Nancy. 1984. "The Margaret Mead Controversy: Culture, Biology, and Anthropological Inquiry." *Human Organization* 43:85–93.

Schlesinger, Arthur M. 1992. *The Disuniting of America: Reflections on a Multicultural Society.* New York: W. W. Norton.

Schwartz, Theodore. 1983. "Anthropology: A Quaint Science." *American Anthropologist* 85:919–929.

Shankman, Paul. 1984. "The Thick and the Thin: On the Interpretive Theoretical Program of Clifford Geertz." *Current Anthropology* 25:261–279.

Shklar, Judith. 1984. *Ordinary Vices.* Cambridge, Mass.: Harvard University Press.

Shore, Brad. 1983. "Paradox Regained: Freeman's *Margaret Mead and Samoa.*" *American Anthropologist* 85:935–944.

Shweder, Richard A. 1991. *Thinking through Cultures.* Cambridge, Mass.: Harvard University Press.

Shweder, Richard A., and Robert A. Levine, eds. 1984. *Culture Theory: Essays on Mind, Self, and Emotion.* Cambridge: Cambridge University Press.

Sidgwick, Henry. 1895. "The Philosophy of Common Sense." *Mind* 1:145–158.

Singer, Marcus G. 1967. "The Golden Rule." In *The Encyclopedia of Philosophy.* Vol. 3. Edited by Paul Edwards. New York: Macmillan and The Free Press.

Singer, Peter, ed. 1991. *A Companion to Ethics.* Oxford: Basil Blackwell.

Slote, Michael. 1982. "Is Virtue Possible?" In *The Virtues.* Edited by Robert Kruschwitz and Robert Roberts. Belmont Calif.: Wadsworth Press.

Spencer, Paul. 1973. "Review of Colin M. Turnbull, *The Mountain People.*" *Man* 8:651–652.

Sperber, Dan. 1985. *On Anthropological Knowledge.* Cambridge: Cambridge University Press.

Spiro, Melford E. 1982. *Oedipus in the Trobriands.* Chicago: University of Chicago Press.

Stauder, Jack. 1993. "The 'Relevance' of Anthropology to Colonialism and Imperialism." In *The "Racial" Economy of Science.* Edited by Sandra Harding. Bloomington: Indiana University Press.

Stevenson, C. L. 1944. *Ethics and Language.* New Haven: Yale University Press.

Stewart, Robert M., and Lynn L. Thomas. 1991. "Recent Work on Ethical Relativism." *American Philosophical Quarterly* 28:85–100.

Stocker, Michael. 1990. *Plural and Conflicting Values.* Oxford: Oxford University Press.

Stocking, George W. [1968] 1982. *Race, Culture, and Evolution: Essays in the History of Anthropology.* Chicago: University of Chicago Press.

Stout, Jeffrey. 1988. *Ethics after Babel: The Languages of Morals and Their Discontents.* Boston: Beacon Press.

Sturgeon, Nicholas. [1985]. 1988. "Moral Explanations" In Geoffrey Sayre-McCord. *Essays in Moral Realism.* Edited by Ithaca, N.Y.: Cornell University Press.

——— 1986. "What Difference Does It Make Whether Moral Realism Is True?" *Southern Journal of Philosophy* 24 (Supplement):115–141.

Taylor, Charles. 1976. "Responsibility for Self." In *The Identities of Persons.* Edited by Amelie O. Rorty. Berkeley: University of California Press.

—— 1991. *The Ethics of Authenticity.* Cambridge, Mass.: Harvard University Press.

—— 1992. *Multiculturalism and "The Politics of Recognition."* Edited by Amy Gutmann. Princeton: Princeton University Press.

Thomas, Laurence Mordekhai. 1993. *Vessels of Evil: American Slavery and the Holocaust.* Philadelphia: Temple University Press.

Trilling, Lionel. [1950] 1970. "Huckleberry Finn." In *The Liberal Imagination: Essays in Literature and Society.* Harmondsworth: Penguin Books.

—— 1972. *Sincerity and Authenticity.* Cambridge, Mass.: Harvard University Press.

Turnbull, Colin. 1973. *The Mountain People.* London: Picador.

Turner, Terence. 1993. "Anthropology and Multiculturalism: What Is Anthropology That Multiculturalists Should Be Mindful of It?" *Cultural Anthropology* 8:411–429.

Turner, Victor. 1969. *The Ritual Process.* Ithaca, N.Y.: Cornell University Press.

—— 1974. *Dramas, Fields, and Metaphors: Symbolic Action in Human Society.* Ithaca, N.Y.: Cornell University Press.

Turner, Victor, and Edward M. Bruner, eds. 1986. *The Anthropology of Experience.* Urbana: University of Illinois Press.

Tylor, E. B. [1871] 1958. *Primitive Culture.* New York: Harper Press.

Van Gennep, Arnold. [1908] 1960. *The Rites of Passage.* Translated by Monika Vizedon and Gabrielle L. Caffee. Chicago: University of Chicago Press.

Vansina, Jan. 1985. *Oral Tradition as History.* Madison: University of Wisconsin Press.

Varley, H. Paul. 1970. *Samurai.* New York: Delacorte Press.

Vlastos, Gregory. 1991. *Socrates: Ironist and Moral Philosopher.* Ithaca, N.Y.: Cornell University Press.

Walters, Ronald. C. 1980. "Signs of the Times: Clifford Geertz and Historians." *Social Research* 47:537–556.

Walzer, Michael. 1981. "Philosophy and Democracy." *Political Theory* 9:379–399.

—— 1983. *Spheres of Justice.* New York: Basic Books.

—— 1987. *Interpretation and Social Criticism.* Cambridge, Mass.: Harvard University Press.

—— 1989. "A Critique of Philosophical Conversation." *Philosophical Forum* 21:182–196.

—— 1994. *Thick and Thin: Moral Argument at Home and Abroad.* Notre Dame: University of Notre Dame Press.

Warnock, Mary. 1978. *Ethics since 1900*. Oxford: Oxford University Press.

Weber, Max. 1946. "Science as a Vocation." In *From Max Weber: Essays in Sociology*. Translated and edited by H. H. Gerth and C. Wright Mills. Oxford: Oxford University Press.

Weiner, Annette B. 1976. *Women of Value, Men of Renown: New Perspectives in Trobriand Exchange*. Austin: University of Texas Press.

——— 1983. "Ethnographic Determinism: Samoa and the Margaret Mead Controversy." *American Anthropologist* 85:909–919.

Wertheimer, Max. 1935. "Some Problems in the Theory of Ethics." *Social Research* 2:353–367.

Williams, Bernard. [1974] 1981. "The Truth in Relativism." In *Moral Luck*. Cambridge: Cambridge University Press.

——— 1985. *Ethics and the Limits of Philosophy*. Cambridge, Mass.: Harvard University Press.

——— 1993. *Shame and Necessity*. Berkeley: University of California Press.

Wilson, Bryan, ed. 1970. *Rationality*. New York: Harper and Row.

Wilson, Douglas. 1992. "Thomas Jefferson and the Character Issue." *Atlantic Monthly* November: 57–50.

Winch, Peter. 1972. "Understanding a Primitive Society." In *Ethics and Action*. London: Routledge and Kegan Paul.

Wittgenstein, Ludwig. 1970. *Zettel*. Translated by G. E. M. Anscombe. Berkeley: University of California Press.

——— 1978. *Philosophical Investigations*. Translated by G. E. M. Anscombe. Oxford: Basil Blackwell.

——— 1979. *On Certainty*. Translated by Denis Paul and G. E. M. Anscombe. Oxford: Basil Blackwell.

Wolf, Eric. 1982. *Europe and the People without History*. Berkeley: University of California Press.

——— 1994. "Perilous Ideas: Race, Culture, People." *Current Anthropology* 35:1–12.

Wolf, Susan L. 1992. "Two Levels of Pluralism." *Ethics* 102:785–798.

Wong, David. 1984. *Moral Relativity*. Berkeley: University of California Press.

——— 1986. "On Moral Realism without Foundations." *Southern Journal of Philosophy* 24 (Supp.): 95–113.

——— 1992. "Coping with Moral Conflict and Ambiguity." *Ethics* 102:763–784.

INDEX

Abortion, 9, 36, 107, 113–114, 118, 119, 120–121, 144, 146–147, 148, 183, 195, 197, 205

Adjudication, and moral conflict, 143–145

Affected ignorance, 101–103, 105, 108, 169

Agency, conditions of, 4, 21, 82–83, 123, 129. *See also* Motivation

Animal cruelty, 39–44, 54

Anthropology: assumptions and methods of, 3–4, 5, 8–9, 14, 21, 22, 29–31, 36–39, 41–59, 63–68, 71–80, 157, 159, 217; and the "ethnographic present," 31, 74; and relativism, 4–7, 13–15, 23–25, 29–30, 37–38, 56–59

Anti-theory arguments, 160–169

Aquinas, Thomas, 101

Archer, Margaret, 51

Ardener, Edwin, 47

Arendt, Hannah, 228n12

Arens, W., 54, 229n34

Aristotle, 87, 103, 220

Arnold, Matthew, 220

Asch, Solomon, 34–35, 96, 229n22

Ashworth, John, 97

Austen, Jane, 160

Authenticity, 214–216

Ayer, A. J., 1, 6, 113–114, 116, 119, 136, 141, 149

Baier, Annette, 161, 162, 164, 172

Barnes, Barry, 76

Benedict, Ruth, 2, 4, 5, 24, 37, 45, 47, 62–63, 68, 70, 71–72, 74, 82, 89, 217

Benjamin, Martin, 112–113, 120, 142, 236n4

Bennett, Jonathan, 235n10

Bentham, Jeremy, 106, 154, 167

Berlin, Isaiah, 9, 108, 121–124, 128, 161, 174, 202, 203, 238n20

Bettelheim, Bruno, 84

Bloor, David, 5, 75, 76

Boas, Franz, 24, 37, 217

Brandt, R. B., 15, 30, 31, 34, 36, 37–44, 46, 54–55, 80, 153, 226n2, 228n21

Brink, David, 33, 137, 150, 174–175

Broad, C. D., 137–138, 173

Cannibalism, 18, 37–38, 54–55, 229n34

Capital punishment, 147

Carnap, Rudolf, 115

Carrithers, Michael, 54

Casuistry, 127

Categorical Imperative, 150–151, 170, 235n15

Cavell, Stanley, 110, 111

Chagnon, Napoleon, 230n10, 231n10

Civil disobedience, 31, 199–200, 224

Clifford, James, 67, 230n10

Clinical medicine, compared with moral inquiry, 127, 183

Colonialism, 24, 66, 67, 75–78, 79, 210

Communitarianism, 83. *See also* MacIntyre, A.; Walzer, M.

Compromise, 120–121

Convergence, 108, 174, 180, 182–183, 195–196

Cooper, David, 55, 230n35, 232n8

Cultural determinism, 21, 48, 62, 95, 217–218

Culture: authoritative voices in, 31–32, 43–44, 78–79, 91, 193, 214; definitions of, 15, 157, 226n3, 227n7; and identity, 82–84, 215, 216; individuation of, 21, 62, 63–68, 79–80, 82, 151; integration of beliefs and practices in, 21, 41–47, 51–54, 62, 63, 68, 151; internal complexity of, 69–71, 81–85, 206; internal skepticism toward, 49–51, 60, 70–71; moral weight of, 6, 7, 222; respect for, 24–25, 52, 53, 56–60, 73–74, 77–78, 100–101, 193, 207–214, 217

Daniels, Norman, 170–171, 172, 234n4, 235n15

Davidson, Donald, 55, 230n35

Davis, David Brion, 98, 159, 231n21

DeCew, Judith, 228n20, 229n24

Descriptive morality: Brandt's *Hopi Ethics* as example of, 37–43; Gestalt accounts of, 34–37; limits of, 56–60; non-empirical commitments of, 16, 30–34

Dewey, John, 5, 90, 172

Disagreement. *See* Fundamental disagreement; Incommensurability; Relativism

Douglass, Frederick, 93

Dover, K. J., 101

Duncker, Karl, 34–37, 141, 146, 228n21

Elkins, Stanley, 84

Emotivism, 1, 6, 9, 113–119, 121, 131, 196, 199

Enculturation, 21, 23, 36, 56, 82–83, 217

Enlightenment: and counter-Enlightenment on culture, 217; idea of equality, 88, 96

Ethnocentrism, 23, 25–28, 57

Evans-Pritchard, E. E., 2, 4, 5, 38, 45–46, 50–52, 63–66, 68, 70, 71, 72–79, 190

Exoticism, 34, 64–65, 73–74, 213–214

Fabian, Johannes, 73

Feinberg, Joel, 128

Female circumcision, 33, 193, 207, 208, 213, 214, 237n12, 238nn13,14

Feminism, 90, 209, 213–214

Fischer, Michael M. J., 74, 80

Flanagan, Owen, 131–132, 138

Forgiveness, 102–103, 185

Foucault, Michel, 84

Frankena, William, 15, 34

Freeman, Derek, 48–49, 225n5

French, Peter, 230n36

Fundamental disagreement: belief in as basis of moral skepticism, 126–130; Berlin on, 121–124; Brandt on, 37–43; defined, 32, 226n1; difficulties with the idea of, 108, 109–114; distinguished from serious disagreement, 9, 108, 116, 144; emotivists on, 114–116; Gestalt criticism of belief in, 34–37; MacIntyre on, 117–121; philosophical consensus on, 32–34, 107–114; Wong on, 116

Gallie, W. B., 30

Gandhi, M., 191, 192, 200

Geertz, Clifford, 5, 11, 13, 22, 23, 26, 53, 83, 107, 157–158, 159, 160, 168, 225nn5,6

Gestalt theory, 34–37, 58, 96

Gewirth, Alan, 176–177

Gilligan, Carol, 42, 158

Goffman, Erving, 84

Golden rule: and abortion, 118; across cultures, 183; and humanitarianism, 97; Mill's interpretation of, 154

Hampshire, Stuart, 32–33, 34, 109, 124

Harding, Sandra, 238n17

Hare, R. M., 149

Harman, Gilbert, 3, 13–14, 18–22, 38, 105, 107, 150, 189, 226n1, 227n7, 228n13

Hart, H. L. A., 127, 128

Haskell, Thomas, 96–99, 159

Hegel, G. W. F., 90, 92

Heider, Karl, 47

Heine, Bernd, 231n16

Heine, Heinrik, 122

Held, Virginia, 131

Herbert, Christopher, 45

Herder, J. G., 5, 45, 217, 218

Herodotus, 2, 64

Herskovits, Melville, 4, 22–25, 29, 32, 36, 37, 47, 56–59, 82, 212, 228n14

History: and ethnography, 71–80; Evans-Pritchard on, 73–79; of the Holocaust, 20, 21, 84, 227n6, 228n13; and interconnection of cultures, 8, 66–68; as interpretive discipline, 222; and moral change, 92, 96, 105–107;

and moral criticism, 85–105; and multiculturalism, 61–62, 219–221; Rorty on, 26, 89–90, 92–93; Williams on, 80–81, 99, 100. *See also* Haskell, T.; Patterson, O.; Relativism: historical form of; Slavery

Hitler, in arguments for relativism, 18, 19, 20, 200, 227n6

Hobbes, Thomas, 201, 220

Hollis, Martin, 225n5

Huckleberry Finn, 69, 160, 165, 235n10

Hume, David, 104–105, 137, 154, 161, 164–165, 175, 182, 223

Imagination, and moral argument, 106, 147–148, 184–185, 204–205, 222

Immigration, 112, 206, 207, 210–211, 219

Incommensurability, 14, 33, 38, 52, 119–120, 128–130

Interpretation: and moral action, 187; and moral argument, 106, 147–151, 187, 197–198; and moral philosophy, 10, 152–157, 159–171, 176–177, 189, 222; requirements of, 55–56; and thick description, 157–159, 191, 192

Jacobs, Harriet, 93

James, William, 11, 29, 128, 153, 161, 193, 194

Jefferson, Thomas, 8, 61, 192, 221, 226n8

Johnson, Mark, 147, 233n1

Jonsen, Albert, 127

Justice, theories of, 133, 141–142, 170–172

Justification, 170–173, 175–177, 194

Kant, Immanuel, 90, 105–106, 124, 126, 138, 140, 150–151, 167, 170, 217, 220

King, M. L., 99, 191, 223

Kluckhohn, Clyde, 67, 225n2

Kohlberg, Lawrence, 42

Krausz, Michael, 225n5

Kroeber, A. L., 67, 225n2

Kuhn, Thomas, 132, 133, 134–135

Kuklick, Bruce, 221, 226n7

Ladd, John, 16, 30–31, 37, 55, 153

Larmore, Charles, 107–108

Lear, Jonathan, 63

Levy-Bruhl, Lucien, 52

Liminality, 69–70, 85

Locke, John, 96, 137, 175

Lowie, Robert, 50

Lukes, Steven, 225n5

McCarthy, Thomas, 47, 74

McDowell, John, 236n20

MacIntyre, Alasdair, 3, 107, 108, 117–121, 153

Mackie, J. L., 16, 37

Malinowski, Bronislaw, 47, 72, 77

Malone, Douglas, 226n8

Mandeville, Bernard, 97

Marcus, George, 74, 80

Matilal, B. K., 38

Mead, G. H., 5

Mead, Margaret, 4, 24, 48–49, 72, 217

Meiland, Jack, 225n5

Merton, Robert, 134

Midgley, Mary, 17, 66, 67, 81–82

Milgram, Stanley, 20, 228n11

Mill, John Stuart, 106, 112, 154–155, 204

Montagu, Ashley, 238n17

Montaigne, Michel de, 13

Moral absolutism, 22, 28

Moral confidence, 23, 197–200

Moral criticism: culturally external, 86–90, 96–98, 100–103, 193, 208–214; culturally internal, 84–85, 92–95, 100, 102, 190, 191–192, 209, 214

Moral education: and language, 18, 61, 100; and rules, 163–164

Moral inquiry: compared with science, 130–145, 180–183; and cultural conflict, 207–214; in and across cultures, 188–194; defined, 148, 225n1; engaged with public life, 223–224; as interpretation, 55–56, 128–130, 146–160; and moral

Moral inquiry *(continued)*
confidence, 197–198; and moral maturity, 123–136; non-violent protest as,
199–200; and objectivity, 177–186;
and openness toward future, 196–197;
in private disagreements, 110–113,
123–130; in public controversies,
120–121; and requirements of in
moral judgment, 127–130
Moral isolationism: criticisms of,
205–214; defined, 17
Moral knowledge, 168, 175, 185, 193,
235n14
Moral language: and affected ignorance,
102, 106; and cultural conflict, 80–81,
88, 89–90, 93, 96, 100, 106, 220; and
moral disagreement, 117–121; thick
and thin interpretations of, 189–192
Moral realism, 8, 33, 98, 137, 149–150,
174–175, 236n20
Moral philosophy: authority of, 10–12,
91–92, 106, 153–154, 162–168,
170–177, 184–185, 223–224; as
interpretation, 10, 148–157, 159–171,
176–177, 189, 222; limitations of,
135–136, 137–138
Moral Progress, 8, 62, 90–91, 92, 96,
105, 106, 137–138, 174, 191
Moral reasoning: and adjudication,
144–145; and complexity of
experience, 177–178, 184–185,
224–225; limits of
decision-procedures in, 127–130,
147–148, 175, 176; as self-reflective
ethnography, 128–129, 157–160; and
unshakeable convictions, 124–125
Motivation: and action-guidingness of
morality, 104–105; and moral
backsliding, 20, 104–105; and reasons
for action, 13, 14, 18–19, 20, 21,
227nn5,6; and weakness of the will,
42, 223
Multiculturalism, 6, 7, 61–62, 218–221

Nagel, Thomas, 202
Nietzsche, Friedrich, 125

Noble, Cheryl, 161, 165, 167–168,
172–175
Noncomparability. *See*
Incommensurability
Nozick, Robert, 110, 133, 141, 232n1

Obeyesekere, Gananath, 225n5
Objectivity: and human aspirations,
179–186; in moral inquiry, 1–3,
10–11, 16, 18, 40, 178, 198–203
Orwell, George, 200

Pain, expression of, 93–95
Parricide, 35–36, 54
Patterson, Orlando, 92, 231n22
Plato, 99, 109, 136, 139, 149, 199, 223
Pluralism, 3, 9, 108, 121–125, 128, 146,
161, 174, 202–208, 210–213
Polanyi, Michael, 134
Political liberty, and moral conflict, 26,
27–28, 108, 112, 121–124, 133,
141–142, 155, 203, 209, 213
Polygamy, 55–60
Pratt, Mary Louise, 74
Property: cultural treasures as, 6, 7, 162;
conceptions of in moral education,
164; philosophical conceptions of,
162–163; as "theft," 131
Putnam, Hilary, 74, 136, 144

Quine, W. V. O., 1, 3, 29, 130–131,
133, 138, 181, 182

Rabinow, Paul, 216, 228n14
Race, and racism, 137, 174, 175, 191,
193, 199, 216–217, 219, 238n18,
239n1
Radcliffe-Brown, A. R., 77
Rashomon Effect: in anthropology, 47,
48; in moral philosophy, 153–154,
173–174
Rationality: coercive conception of,
110–112, 177, 180, 199; general
concerns about, 1, 3, 5, 107, 109; of
moral inquiry, 1, 2, 109, 130–145,
181–185, 188, 193, 196–204; and

relativism debate, 4, 225n5. *See also* Relativism: as claim about rationality

Rawls, John, 124, 133, 140, 141–142, 152, 155–156, 170–172

Raz, Joseph, 210

Reflectiveness, 52–53, 57–58, 59–60, 208–209

Regret, 126, 185

Relativism: as account of moral language, 189–190, 196; as attempted neutrality, 207–213; as claim about rationality, 5, 22, 76; cognitive form of, 5, 76; descriptive cultural form of, 7, 15, 18, 20–23, 29–46, 55–59, 146; as explanation of behavior, 13, 14, 19–21, 65, 100–106, 227n6; as general claim about morality, 2, 3, 7, 13–15, 38, 55, 56, 198; historical form of, 8, 61–69, 71–82, 85–96, 99, 103–104; individualistic form of, 17–18; meta-ethical form of, 9, 16–21, 24, 32, 56, 62, 107, 116; normative ethical form of, 17

Religious belief: and abortion, 119; and cultural conflict, 54, 65, 205, 213; embodied in action, 187, 237n9; and liberal pluralism, 123, 124–125; in moral education, 163; no obstacle to cross-cultural interpretation, 191, 192, 237n12; philosophical interpretations of, 106, 151, 154–155, 234n7; philosophical suspicion of, 137–138, 174, 190, 237n9

Republic, 25

Rights: in abortion debates, 117, 119–120; in cultural property and cultural survival claims, 6–7, 162, 222; in disputes about welfare, 162

Rorty, Richard, 2, 10, 12, 25–28, 82, 86, 88–90, 92–95, 98–99, 100, 103, 105, 161, 164, 172, 188, 200–201

Ryle, Gilbert, 11, 157, 160

Sahlins, Marshall, 225n5

Sapir, Edward, 19, 46–47, 227n8, 228n8

Sartre, Jean Paul, 125, 128, 129

Scarry, Elaine, 95

Scheper-Hughes, Nancy, 32, 47, 48, 49

Schlesinger, Arthur, 218, 238n21

Schumpeter, Joseph, 123

Science: aspirations of, 179–180; broadly compared with moral inquiry, 140–144, 180–183; constraints on theory-choice in, 131–133; denigration of ethics in comparison with, 130–132, 179–182; research communities in, 134–135; as standard of rationality, 2, 5, 9, 13

Self-understanding: defined, 138–139; and moral conflict, 128–130; and moral inquiry, 138–143, 148–149, 185–186; social and cultural dimensions of, 11, 82–84, 172, 216, 220–221, 222

Shklar, Judith, 27

Shweder, Richard, 13, 14, 24, 52, 64

Sidgwick, Henry, 59, 91, 226n7

Singer, Peter, 174

Slavery: ancient, 86–88, 92, 96, 100–101, 104–105, 159; comparative history of, 231n22, 236n20; New World, 8, 84, 92, 96–99, 106, 137–138, 159, 174–175, 191

Slote, Michael, 86–87, 88, 89, 100, 103, 104, 105

Socrates, 99, 109, 121, 125, 136, 138, 145, 199, 223

Sperber, Dan, 45

Spiro, Melford, 47

Stevenson, C. L., 1, 114–116, 119, 131, 142, 197, 199

Stocker, Michael, 126

Stocking, George, 216, 217, 225n2, 238nn19,20

Stout, Jeffrey, 158

Sturgeon, Nicholas, 98, 99, 104, 150, 235n18

Taylor, Charles, 129, 130, 211, 213, 215, 233n9

Thick Description: defined, 156–160; of moral inquiry and practices, 11, 189–195, 220–221

Thomas, Laurence M., 227n6

Tolerance: and critical pluralism, 202–203, 211–214; as liberal value, 27–28, 122–124; and normative ethical relativism, 17; and prudence, 24–25

Toulmin, Stephen, 127

Trilling, Lionel, 160, 165, 215, 235nn10,11

Turnbull, Colin, 79–80, 231n15

Turner, Terence, 206, 216, 217, 218

Turner, Victor, 54, 69–71, 195, 206, 219

Tylor, E. B., 24

Utilitarianism, 105–106, 154, 156. *See also* Bentham, J.; Mill, J. S.

Van Gennep, Arnold, 69, 230n8

Walzer, Michael, 10, 11, 99, 106, 147, 148, 151–159, 160, 161, 163, 165, 170, 172, 190, 191, 197, 234nn6,7,8, 236n2

Warnock, Mary, 23, 24

Weber, Max, 125

Weiner, Annette, 47, 49

Wertheimer, Max, 34

Williams, Bernard, 2, 8, 10, 14, 52–53, 61, 64, 80–81, 86, 87–89, 92, 96, 99–100, 103–105, 160, 161, 179–180, 188, 189–190, 198, 208, 220, 236n5

Wilson, Bryan, 78, 225n5

Winch, Peter, 5, 38–39, 52, 53, 54, 57–58, 65, 208

Witchcraft, 38, 39, 50–52, 65, 75–76

Wittgenstein, Ludwig, 63, 94, 143, 153

Wolf, Eric, 216

Wolf, Susan, 183, 207

Women: as cultural informants, 47, 49, 68, 229n31; as cultural and political dissidents, 70–71, 207–209, 213–214; and development economics, 206–207; disagreement about roles of, 110–111, 146–147, 210; and historical relativism, 90; as "internal outsiders," 68–69; and polygamy, 58; as possibly distinct moral voice, 158–159

Wong, David, 3, 5, 14, 32, 75, 81, 116, 150, 228n19

ACN7919